LIVES,
WORKS
&
TRANSFORMATIONS

Other Books by Robert Kirsch

FICTION:
Do Not Go Gentle, a novella
In the Wrong Rain
Madeleine Austrian
The Wars of Pardon

Under the pseudonym Robert Dundee:
The Restless Lovers
Pandora's Box
Inferno

Under the pseudonym Robert Bancroft:
Knight of the Scimitar
The Castilian Rose

NON-FICTION:
West of the West: Witnesses to the California Experience, 1542-1906
(with William S. Murphy)

LIVES,
WORKS
&
TRANSFORMATIONS

A Quarter Century of
Book Reviews and Essays
by ROBERT KIRSCH

Linda Rolens, editor

CAPRA PRESS / 1978 / Santa Barbara

With grateful acknowledgement to the
Los Angeles Times where these columns
first appeared.

Library of Congress Cataloging in Publication Data
Kirsch, Robert R., 1922-
    Lives, works & transformations.

    I. Title
PS3561.I75L5   028.1   78-18767
ISBN 0-88496-085-4

CAPRA PRESS
631 State Street
Santa Barbara, California 93101

Contents

Editor's Preface / vii
Introduction: "Some Thoughts on Being Collected" / ix

LIVES

W. Jackson Bate, *Samuel Johnson* / 3
Romano Guardini, *The Death of Socrates* / 7
Michael Grant, *St. Paul* / 9
John C. Beaglehole, *The Life of Captain James Cook*
Robert Lacey, *Sir Walter Ralegh* / 13
Edgar H. Cohen, *Mademoiselle Libertine: A Portrait of Ninon de Lenclos* / 19
Michael Davis, *William Blake: A New Kind of Man* / 22
Bettina Knapp and Myra Chipman, *That Was Yvette: The Biography of the Great
    Diseuse* / 26
Maurice Goudeket, *Close to Colette* / 28
Audrey Hodes, *Martin Buber: An Intimate Portrait* / 30
W. A. Swanbert, *Dreiser* / 34
Andrew Turnbull, *Thomas Wolfe* / 38
Andrew Sinclair, *Dylan Thomas: No Man More Magical* / 42
Lawrance Thompson, *Robert Frost: The Years of Triumph* / 46
Hannah Tillich, *From Time To Time* / 51
John Leggett, *Ross and Tom: Two American Tragedies* / 53
Carlos Baker, *Ernest Hemingway: A Life Story* / 58

WORKS

Somerset Maugham, *The Summing Up* / 65
Henry Miller, *Henry Miller's Book of Friends: A Tribute to Friends of Long Ago* / 67
Harry Golden, *Only in America* / 69
Donald M. Frame, trans., *The Complete Essays of Montaigne* / 71
Why a Dearth of Novels Reviewed? / 72
Ross Macdonald, *The Underground Man* / 74

Philip Durham, *Down These Mean Streets a Man Must Go* / 77

David Madden, ed., *Tough Guy Writers of the Thirties* / 80

Arthur Bremer, *An Assassin's Diary: Arthur H. Bremer* / 81

Harry Mc Pherson, *A Political Education*
John Osborne, *The Third Year of the Nixon Watch*
Carl J. Burckhardt, *Richelieu and His Age* / 84

Edward Bliss, ed., *In Search of Light: The Broadcasts of Edward R. Murrow* / 90

William White, ed., *By-Line: Ernest Hemingway, Selected Articles and Dispatches of Four Decades* / 92

Allen Churchill, *The Literary Decade* / 95

Carl Bode, ed., *The Young Mencken: The Best of His Work* / 100

Edmund Wilson, *A Window on Russia: For the Use of Foreign Readers*
   To The Finland Station: A Study in the Writing and Acting of History / 103

Vernon Hall, Jr., *A Short History of Literary Criticism* /108

Roland Barthes, *Mythologies; Critical Essays* / 110

Herman Hesse, *My Belief: Essays of Life and Art* / 112

Joyce Carol Oates, *The Edge of Impossibility: Tragic Forms in Literature* / 114

Ernest Raymond, *Gentle Greaves*
Joyce Carol Oates, *Marriages and Infidelities, Short Stories* / 116

Gunther Stuhlmann, ed., *The Diary of Anaïs Nin, 1931-1934* / 122

Philip K. Jason, ed., *Anaïs Nin Reader* / 126

&

On the Eve of a Sabbatical / 131

The Function of the Paperback / 133

Wilson Mizener, *The Sense of Life in the Modern Novel*
Marcus Klein, *After Alienation*
Frederick J. Hoffman, *The Mortal No: Death and the Modern Imagination* / 133

Anthony West, *Principles and Persuasions* / 138

Norman Mailer, *Advertisements for Myself* / 140

Donald Barthelme, *City Life* / 141

Lawrence Sterne, *Tristram Shandy* / 143

John O'Hara, *Assembly* / 144

Rupert Hart-Davis, ed., *The Letters of Oscar Wilde* / 146

Carolyn G. Heilbrun, *Toward a Recognition of Androgeny* / 150

Helen Gurley Brown, *Sex and the Single Girl* / 152

Elizabeth Taylor, *Elizabeth Taylor: An Informal Memoir* / 154

Errol Flynn, *My Wicked, Wicked Ways* / 156

Harold Gilliam, *The San Francisco Experience* / 158

John Lennon, *John Lennon in His Own Write* / 160

Paris Students Topple Ivory Tower / 163
Florida Scott-Maxwell, *The Measure of My Days* / 168

TRANSFORMATIONS

Isaiah Berlin, *Vico and Herder: Two Studies in the History of Ideas* / 173
Lewis Mumford, *The Myth of the Machine: The Pentagon of Power* / 177
Jacques Barzun, *Science: The Glorious Entertainment* / 181
Ben H. Bagdikian, *The Information Machines: Their Impact on Men
        and the Media* / 185
Donald F. Theall, *The Medium is the Rear View Mirror* / 190
David Daiches, *A Study of Literature: For Readers and Critics* / 192
Jaques Barzun, *Of Human Freedom* / 195
Alexander Solzhenitsyn, *For the Good of the Cause* / 198
John Wain, *A House For the Truth* / 201
Alec Craigs, *Suppressed Books: A History of the Conception of Literary Obscenity* / 203
Henry Miller, *Tropic of Capricorn* / 207
Frank Barron, *Creativity and Psychological Health* / 211
Leon Surmelian, *Techniques of Fiction Writing: Measure and Madness* / 214
Catherine Drinker Bowen, *Biography: The Craft and the Calling* / 217
Orville Prescott, ed., *History as Literature* / 221
C. V. Wedgewood, *The Sense of the Past: Thirteen Studies in the Theory and Practice of
        History* / 223
Page Smith, *The Historian and History* / 225
Rudolf Arnheim, *Visual Thinking* / 227
E. M. Cioran, *The Short History of Decay* / 229

Editor's Preface

When I started work on this book, stacks of scrapbooks containing more than seven and a half million words confronted me—sufficient material for one hundred books this size. As I read the daily columns of the last quarter century, and Robert Kirsch has not missed a day, I was staggered by his strenuous routine of reading several books and then writing a perceptive column six days each week.

The task of assembling a coherent manuscript was further compounded by Kirsch's ranging eclecticism: he considers everything in print fair game for review. In the course of a week he might review a biography, a book on Chinese cooking, a murder mystery, a first novel, a travel book and a collection of critical essays.

There was nothing to do but plunge, so plunge I did. After weeks of reading and rereading, patterns began to surface; areas of prolonged interest and deep concern emerged. Through continued reading and winnowing these interests became the basis for the sections entitled *Lives, Works & Transformations*. In *Lives* are the people who helped forge the world as we know it; *Works* offers insight into books which sparked his imagination; *Transformations* examines the ideas and forces that have shaped our times.

Not until the manuscript was well on the way to taking final form did Kirsch and I sit down to talk about the book. He was very helpful, recalling favorite and important columns and suggesting refienments in the progression of the pieces. When we finished, there was still a gap: some of the liveliest and most interesting columns could not be placed into any of the sections. So we created the *&* section as a gallery for Kirsch at his miscellaneous best.

Most of the pieces are presented here as they originally were printed. Sometimes they were trimmed by the make-up editor. A few columns were edited to afford space for other favorites, but on the whole they stand as they appeared two, ten or twenty years ago. I think you will find, as I do, that their freshness and acuity of insight stand well the test of time.

The process of compiling this book was an education in itself. I was allowed a close, encapsulated look at one man's vision of life and literature over the last quarter century. In the course of three months reading I saw schools of thought, national passions and pastimes, and generations of writers come and go.

I have also had a close look at the journalistic life of Robert Kirsch. I not only watched books change, I saw Kirsch change. A good part of a critic's job is to be responsive: his work is deeply tied to the times he inhabits. 1964 was a particularly significant year for books and Kirsch. Important books were being published regularly and issues such as censorship were in the fore. Kirsch caught both books and issues red-hot and put them in their proper cultural context with remarkable insight.

Before starting work on this book I had little idea what kind of man could flourish as a daily book reviewer. By the time we sat down to discuss the manuscript, I had come to respect and understand a good deal about Robert Kirsch. In the course of my reading I saw him become more mellow with himself and the world, learn to become generous in his reviewing. Not that he gives anything away, but because he acts from principles of pleasure and critical appreciation rather than from a defensive position, he is able to teach us to recognize the value in a work. He knows the debunking review is the easiest to write and its value lies only in the points it scores for the critic, not in what it gives to the reader. Kirsch serves as a readers' advocate, he is one of the few left who believe in and speak to an intelligent reading public.

In many of the pieces, what seems at first casual is often Kirsch's remarkable ease with himself and his beliefs. Perhaps the most important gift he has for us is his example of a man, unencumbered by dogma, living out a morality which opens possibilities rather than closing them off.

Genuinely eclectic, Kirsch is bound by no school of thought. Certainly he has had his teachers and holds his strong beliefs, but he is able to take value, pleasure and information from diverse sources. Bodies of information are pieces of the world and he seeks the world as actively as many critics shun it. Because Robert Kirsch does not demand that life come to him according to some prescribed formula, it does come to him whole and often in surprising shapes.

—LINDA ROLENS

Some Thoughts on Being Collected

"I would love to be the poet laureate of Coney Island. I would feel enormous satisfaction in being regarded as the voice of the average American," Thornton Wilder once said. I understand what he means. I was born and brought up in Coney Island. Perhaps I am the ultimate literary critic of that bizarre, roiling, surreal place, a symbol of pleasure, a symbol of mass escape.

I left Coney Island a long time ago, but Coney Island has not left me. Beyond the summer resort, which provided us with work and adventure, there was the Coney Island of other seasons, spring and autumn along the beaches or the bayside, fishing, walking, playing, fighting. Then winter with the garish rides and concessions closed, ruins reincarnated every season. Our town wasn't only the tawdry strip of Surf Avenue with Luna Park and Steeplechase (those simpler Disneylands we used to prefer to visit over the locked gates and fences, down the vast wooden slides in those silences), it was an extension of Europe and Africa. Along Mermaid Avenue, you heard the voices of the Shtetl, people arguing literature or politics in a marvelous Yiddish, on street corners or in cafes over glasses of tea, cigarets burning their fingers. Neptune Avenue was Italy, houses decorated by masons and tile-setters, ladies in black, men in their suits and caps, straight out of Sicily or Naples. Surf Avenue was Ireland, lace curtains, pale nuns collecting for charity, police captains and their families, politicians and their clubs. In the basement of Jewish tenements and brownstones lived the blacks, a mysterious minority, in some alliance with the Jews. In this Balkan place I learned to live, to read, to realize that the border between the illusory and the real was not so defined as we might believe.

Not everything I am came from that place, but so much of what I am, when I ran away at seventeen, hitch-hiked to California, went to school, became a small-town reporter in Merced, enlisted in the service, came out to study literature, became a professor, goes back to those formative days. My early fiction is all centered there. In fact, when I reflect on these matters what else is Los Angeles than a Coney Island of the Southwest?

I learned to read in Coney Island, picking out the words of comic strips before I ever went to school. I don't remember a time when I couldn't read. Much as I liked the solitary joy of reading in the attic of my grandmother's bungalow, I did it mostly on rainy days or snowy ones. At that time, boys who read were considered sissies or even too neurotic or introspective. Textbooks were an exception, but whoever wanted to read *them?* Often then when I wanted to stay home and read, I also wanted to get out to the beach and swim, or play touch football, or flirt with and chase the girls under the boardwalk. There are all kinds of pleasures and reading is only one of them. What enhances reading is that it is an extension, a vicarious experience potentially of all life.

I am still torn between a life of reading and one of action. I have tried to make a virtue of that ambivalence. I spend a lot of time living abroad or traveling. I say it gives me distance and detachment, keeps me from the circus of publicity and exploitation the book business has become in America, gives me the experience against which the judgment of books may be validated, allows me the intense focus necessary for reading under pressure and writing under the daily guillotine of the deadline.

"A critic," I once wrote, "must never bury himself behind a fortress of books, for in order to judge their worth or wisdom it is necessary to examine the sources of that wisdom in nature, experience and humanity." That's true. Even more true is that I have a police reporter's appetite for being where things are happening. I was a police reporter for seven years while I studied at UCLA. Out in the world, I have sometimes received a bit more experience, and a bit less wisdom than I have bargained for: beaten up by a burly CRS trooper in Paris during the 1968 *manifestations*. In Ibiza, in 1972, trapped between the warring factions of the Hughes empire while trying to find out the truth of the Clifford

Irving book; observing as an expert witness a travesty of justice in a trumped-up obscenity trial in Grand Rapids in 1963; watching the repression of writers and reporters in Prague after the Dubcek regime was ended by Russian tanks.

I will leave that for an autobiography. Sometimes my life has been more interesting than books I have had to review. What I have found in twenty-five years of reviewing I can only express tentatively. If I had to put it into a Chinese fortune cookie, I'd choose three words. "Never say never." For example, I never believed that I would become a book reviewer. I had wanted to be a scientist, a chemist, before the war, drifted into the graduate study of English and American literature because I had spent the war on a succession of Navy ships reading those marvelous pocket-sized paperbacks they distributed to the forces. This helped me conquer the two great diseases of war: fear and boredom. When I went back to school, I wanted to know everything. I studied psychology, archeology, economics, political science, took courses everywhere until I had enough units for two bachelor's degrees. I was a generalist before I knew it.

When I began to teach at UCLA, it became apparent I could not support my family on the salary of an instructor. I had to go back to newspaper work to pay for my teaching habit. At 31, I was an instructor, a copy-reader, an occasionally published short-story writer. It was then, after the death of the great daily book reviewer, Joseph Henry Jackson, that I was given a chance at this job.

I am unembarrassed to confess that I love the work, still feel the Christmas-day tremor in opening a package of books, love the reading, wrestle each day with the writing which has never come easily for me though I have done a great deal of it, accommodated myself to the occasional sorceror's apprentice feeling as a good part of the thousands of non-books and maybe-books keep coming over transom and through windows. I have learned a great deal from this marvelous opportunity, indulged the broad range of my interests from true crime to biography, cookbooks to history, archeology to zoology. Sometimes I am astonished at the synchronicity of need and book. If I should want to know about Edward Lear's nonsense verse or holistic medicine, Russian history or archeology in China, the appropriate book seems to turn up in a day or two.

Perhaps most of all I have learned, or validated my feeling, that readers are usually the good and decent people. At least mine are. I delight in hearing from them though often what prompts the letter is an error or argument. They never allow me to make the slightest mistake—and are more hawk-eyed than any editor or proof-reader on typography. Their letters are often more interesting than the reviews I do for them. They trust me and I trust them. I have never written down to them nor they to me.

Indeed, the essence of my task is to serve the reader, the common reader, someone intelligent, discerning, active rather than passive, critical rather than apathetic. My goal is to evoke the book fairly, wherever possible in the author's own words. Reviewing is a form of superior cultural journalism. It can be more and sometimes is. But in reviewing and in literary criticism, as the British critic Graham Hough puts it, the first obligation is an accurate description of the work and its context. The review should be interesting and informative but not at the expense of the book, certainly not exploited for the reviewer's ego or reputation.

Part of the distance from the news and gossip of the book world, from literary politics, I try to achieve by living abroad or away from the publishing centers. Frankly, I write my reviews and essays as though there were no other publication in the country reviewing books. That way I can review worthy and deserving books which may not be promoted, hustled, exploited, either by publishers or authors, reviewers or media shows. Unlike many critics I do not look down at the marketplace of books, the circus atmosphere. The book business has become an extension of entertainment, of journalism, of inspiration and self-help. I applaud this. My notion is that whatever motivates a person to read a book, at whatever level, is a good thing for reading and writing in the long run.

American readers are not a monolith, not a convenient statistical artifact. They are a varied and variegated collection, always in the process of testing taste, and occasionally improving it. Culture grows out of *kitsch* and well as *belles lettres*. We are a nation born of the notion of perfectibility; the idea still operates.

These years have been exciting ones for any observer of popular culture. The dominant factor in the past quarter century has been the rise of television as a part of the communication environment in which we live. No other era has been so totally exposed to a medium of entertainment and information. It has wrought changes in awareness and perception, in mores and behavior. There were those who said the book and indeed print media in general were doomed. The death sentence was premature. The paperback revolution paralleled the age of television. A mass readership developed while the tube was supposed to have made passive spectators out of all of us.

Though the journalistic age seems to accelerate communication, history still moves to another tempo. We may live by headlines but we survive through seeking wisdom and significance. There is a law of conservation of media and artifacts. When a new medium appears, competes with the old, it is a mistake to write it off. I can give you many examples. When radio began broadcasting music, free, many people thought the age of records and record players was over. But when you listen to the radio, you must hear what someone chooses for you. The record player gives you choice and convenience. It was thought that movies would wreck the American theater when the nickelodeon made film a mass industry. That was the moment when American drama went from Boucicault and Belasco to O'Neill and Anderson. Books haven't been made obsolete by the computer or television, or movies, or nay other competitive medium. They offer active rather than passive experience, an opportunity for imagination to enter an alliance with that of the writer.

I believe in books. I don't worship them uncritically. Books are a microcosm of the world. I believe in the essential good sense and insight of the general reader. Indeed, it is the *consensus gentium* which Aristotle saw as the most accurate and reliable validation of the endurance and worth of a work, that it could move people over generations of time.

There are those, particularly art critics, who mock people who say, "I know what I like." It is the kind of thoughtless deprecation which can take criticism away from important sources of knowledge about its function. To know what one likes may not be the ultimate sophistication in the experience of a book or a performance, but it is no small thing. I have known a lot of critics, some professors, and a good many graduate students who had forgotten that the whole enterprise of criticism is rooted in the physical and emotional response of pleasure or revulsion, boredom, irritation, distrust, or escape, happiness, laughter, tears.

I don't say this is the only measure, nor even the most accurate. But it is the initial response or close to it in approaching the performance. I try to suspend my judgment while reading the book. That can come later. The work itself deserves my full attention. Perhaps that subjective or impressionistic response can change. Yet, it is worth attending to. The critic should identify his private feelings; it is hiding them or masquerading in the guise of objectivity that gives the problem. That is why, years ago, I gave the spurious *we* up for the more direct *I*.

This sense or cluster of senses allows for development of tastes, for changes and maturations. It ought to be cultivated. I also believe that the unconscious mind can and does play important roles in the response to a reading experience.

One of the problems of daily book reviewing is that it is difficult to respond to the work, to get perspective on it under the daily guillotine of deadlines. When I first began to review I would finish the book and sit down to write the review. I found that I tended to overpraise or undervalue the book, to go to either/or extremes of response. I soon found that if I waited two to three weeks between the reading the book and the writing of the review, my understanding of the book was deeper, more of a dialogue, less passive. I read many books between the reading of the particular volume and reviewing, yet in the interim it seems as though a part of my mind keeps working on it. Sometimes ideas on the review would spring into my mind while I was doing other things. I'd make a note of it. This grace period is a boon.

One begins to develop a kind of trust, even some Emersonian idea of self-reliance. Book reviewing is not and cannot be a precise assessment. It is a rendering, perhaps, sometimes an informed judgment. The possibility of error, of bias remains. It can be minimized if the reviewer declares his interest. I regard this as the most important canon of ethics in this trade, the most often abused. The reviewer who assumes a magisterial or detached style when in fact he knows and hates or envies or admires the writer, maybe his best friend, his colleague, fellow alumnus, or even his brother-in-law, is a hypocrite and worse. Biases should be brought to the surface if the reviewer is aware of them. *And he ought to know himself.* I am aware that my distaste for talking animals, novels set in Florida, is irrational. But I do not let them go undeclared when they are relevant.

Not all of these ideas sprang full-blown from my forehead when I started twenty-five years ago. I had to unlearn a great deal of arrogance and narrowness which came from my literary education, to realize that most writing in most periods was time-bound in one way or another, that greatness was the rare commodity, that value could be found in entertainment, even in escape, and that in the end all writing had some value as evidence in social or intellectual history. I rediscovered too that not all wisdom was found in books; that literacy was only a part of the ways of knowing.

Soon enough I found that I had a lot to learn. When I started I thought I knew most everything; then I discovered everything wasn't enough. And anyway my wife knew more on her dullest day than I on my best. My children were born critics and have remained that way. When I loosened up, remembered that it was for someone like me I wrote, not necessarily for posterity (which could decide for itself), I began to see not only how I would survive as a book reviewer but how I might enjoy it.

Mostly I read books which give me pleasure, challenge me, satisfy my curiosity, allow me to escape the routine of daily life or illuminate some problem or entertain. Occasionally, I feel obliged to file a dissent on some overpraised (in my view) and overpromoted book, mainly to alert readers to wait for the paperback. I review paperbacks, pamphlets, works by small presses, anything in print which is available to the reader, even occasionally a best-seller. There are some 82,000 titles published in America each year now. I can review only a few hundred. I prefer to give my space to a deserving book for which it may be the only review.

I have not found the deadline altogether an enemy. It is there, immutable, inflexible, gives me closure when I might work forever to get it right. Better than perfection, for me, is balance, a kind of wholeness, something which melds intuition, rational analysis, common sense, compassion, emotional response. I have learned from people like Edmund Wilson and Joseph Wood Krutch and, of course, the greatest journalistic reviewer of them all, George Bernard Shaw. I owe other debts to family and friends, to colleagues and students, whose willingness to accept the eccentricities imposed by my work and sometimes my temperament, have made my work less arduous, my wandering life possible.

In the end, the pieces must speak for themselves. I have sought the most pleasant circumstances I could for this work. "Give me books, fruit, French wine and a little music out of doors, played by somebody I do not know," Keats wrote his sister Fanny in 1819. I wish you the reading of these pieces in your favorite places and situations. I have always tried to do that for myself: an attic room on rainy days in London, the green and leafy Jardin du Luxembourg in summer, Malibu or Santa Barbara beaches in spring or autumn. In the end, is all of it an attempt to recapture Coney Island and the lesson I learned there: "Live, read, grow, be a *mensch.*"?

R. K.
Santa Barbara, Calif.
March 1, 1978

LIVES

"Universal truths discussed here; the meaning of death, the meaning of life, the nature of the good life, of piety, the central question of justice."
—R. K.

W. JACKSON BATE

Samuel Johnson

"The biographical part of literature," Dr. Johnson told Boswell, "is what I love most." It gives us, he said, "what comes near to us, what we can turn to use." Boswell's biography of Johnson brought him near to us, too near perhaps, for he emerged to readers of succeeding generations as a virtuoso conversationalist, a witty, magisterial eccentric who talked so forcibly that on one occasion, when he said to Boswell, "We had good talk," the Scot replied, "Yes, Sir, you tossed and gored several persons."

That was a part of Johnson, for whom clubbable talk was something that fought off depression and gave him excitement and interest. He was the very gladiator of speech, doing his best to triumph "on every occasion and in every company," as his friend Edmond Malone, the Shakespearean scholar, put it, "to impart whatever he knew in the most forcible language he could put it in." Oliver Goldsmith said more aptly: "When his pistol misses fire, he knocks you down with the butt end of it."

Yet, that was not all of Johnson and there have been some attempts to rescue Johnson from Boswell, to see him as he was in the 18th century, how he dominated the intellectual literary life of his time, to perceive him in the light of his own writing—his *Dictionary* (of which Carlyle said, "Had Johnson left nothing but his *Dictionary*, one might have traced there a great intellect, a genuine man."), his edition of Shakespeare, his brilliant *Lives of the English Poets*, his journalism, his criticism.

What Prof. Bate has done (and he performed a similar accomplishment in his biographies of Keats and Coleridge) is to restore the whole Johnson, the very human, very admirable man behind the monument. Johnson's fame, which Boswell took for granted (indeed, with his publicist's heart, his desire to be near the

3

celebrated, Boswell sought Johnson as a subject and friend), is here explained, his work assessed and given its due.

Even more important, we see the character which informed the intellect of the awesome Johnson, we find a human being closer to our times in underlying temperament, in the challenges of success and fulfillment, of overcoming loneliness and melancholy. Bate's magnificent biography fills in the gaps of Johnson's inner life from his boyhood, as a half-blind, half-deaf, awkward youth, to his old age, where suffering an ordeal of dropsy, bronchitis, lung disease, all but abandoned by the woman he had deeply loved, he managed to keep through his immense courage a semblance of dignity. "I will be *conquered*," he said of his illnesses. "I will not capitulate."

It is a poignant story and an illuminating one. Johnson told Malone, speaking about the use of biography: "If nothing but the bright side of characters should be shown, we should sit down in despondency, and think it utterly impossible to imitate them in *anything*. The sacred writers related the vicious as well as the virtuous actions of men; which had this moral effect, that it kept mankind from *despair*.

Despair was the demon in his life. "Despair is criminal," he wrote. He was not alone in such a condition, and many will in our time recognize his anxieties, his ambitions to succeed, his divided self, his inner wars, his fears of insanity, as familiar. Bate captures his honesty, his eloquence, his practicality (perhaps his most engaging trait), his range of experience, his moral sincerity. Courage is not only grace under pressure, it is also the direct confrontation of that pressure. Bate's use of the ancient Greek epigram about Plato is equally apt about Johnson: "In whatever direction we go, we meet him on his way back."

It is in the early and late years Bate finds his best evidence of the inner Johnson. This balances against the caricature of the celebrated talker. We get a closer look at the Lichfield youth, son of a bookseller unlucky or a bit improvident. Johnson's mother, who gave birth at a late age for the period, put him out to a wet nurse, where he suffered an eye infection which was followed by a tubercular infection of the lymph gland, then called scrofula or the "King's Evil." It spread to the optic and auditory nerves, leaving him almost blind in the left eye, deaf in the left ear, with a scarred face. In notes he wrote many years later, he remembered his aunt telling him bluntly when he was young that "she would not have picked such a poor creature up in the street."

He compensated for the embarrassment and the physical limitations of illness by driving himself, by self-demand. One of the traits which helped Johnson deal with the assorted difficulties of his life was his willingness to take complete personal responsibility for himself. He blamed no one, tried to manage his life, looking always for distractions.

Johnson talked much about "management" of the mind, about diverting "distressing thoughts," not fighting them. Boswell, as we know now from the journals, suffered his own anxieties and depressions and had both literary and personal reasons to encourage Johnson to enlarge on these therapeutic devices. "All good-humour and compliance is acquired," he said. And again, years later, "A man's being in good or bad humour depends on his will."

Johnson was an amateur psychologist. Boswell asks: Couldn't one "think . . . down" distressing thoughts? "To attempt to *think them down* is madness," Johnson replied. "They have to be deflected or displaced. Let him take a course of chemistry, or a course of rope dancing." He himself tried chemical experiments in the late hours of the night when he could not sleep, tried "knotting," a kind of knitting or macrame, tried to learn the flute, couldn't, but managed a bit of gardening and regretted not learning to play cards. Despite his handicaps, he was strong and athletic, astonished a bathing attendant at the beach by his swimming, could jump over fences at an advanced age, loved walking.

Conversation was the great diversion. When he was older and more mellow, he tried to resist the temptation to "talk for victory," thought he never really quite succeeded. "That is the happiest conversation, where there is no competition, no vanity, but a calm quiet interchange of sentiments." It didn't much matter that he preached without practicing. People enjoyed his performance; he had become a character, even a myth. He organized his clubs in taverns around Soho, loved the talk, the late hours, the conviviality. His own home was depressing after his much older wife died. There was a brief period when Henry and Hester Thrale befriended him, when he was in love with Hester, that he felt happy.

But most of all, the clubs distracted him.

There is a touching anecdote when toward the end of his life in 1784 he brought some of the surviving members of the old Ivy Lane Club to the Queen's Arms. At 10 PM the old codgers left to go to bed. Johnson, prepared for an all-night session, "with a sigh that seemed to come from his heart," went to retire "to solitude and cheerless meditation."

He destroyed many of his papers before his death and this was a great loss. But so many of his friends left memoirs of him, including the fickle Hester (indeed, particularly Hester, to whom Johnson confided a great deal about his personal feelings and early life), that Bate is able to reconstruct the youthful years persuasively.

Though his father was in financial trouble and the family was impoverished, Johnson had some experience of a wealthier and more cultivated society. His cousin, Cornelius Ford, befriended him, filled him with stories of the literary life in London, inspired in him a desire to be part of what Johnson would always call "the living world, . . . a faithful mirror of manners and life."

Johnson made his way to that world, through Oxford, where he did not finish. Some called him a "gay and frolicksome fellow" but with his characteristic honesty, he said: " . . . I was mad and violent. It was bitterness they took for frolick. I was miserably poor, and thought to fight my way by literature and by my wit." His fees were in arrears. He was brilliant. His tutor said Johnson was "the best Scholar he ever knew to come to Oxford."

There was to be breakdown and despair, perhaps even, one witness says, contemplation of suicide before he found his way to London. He had married, become a schoolteacher, had written a drama called "Irene," went off to London with a stagestruck student named David Garrick, each to seek his fortune and his future.

By his close and sympathetic reading of Johnson's writing from his earliest to his last pieces, Bate has brought the work and life into meaningful counterpoint. He can bring from a single line in the last issue of *The Idler* a vibration, an echo of experience: "There are few things not purely evil of which we can say, without some emotion of uneasiness, *this is the last* . . . The secret horror of the last is inseparable from a thinking being."

His Johnson is a man who will never give up. At 70 he is ready to reform his life, "to begin a new life." He will not allow his illness to make him, as so many people are made, a scoundrel and a burden to others. If he seemed a bully at times in conversation, he was remembered for his kindness and sensitivity by many of his friends. In the end, he stayed with the living world. "Retreat from the world is flight rather than conquest," he said at the end, "and in those who have any power of benefiting others, may be considered as a kind of *moral suicide.*"

He did not opt for suicide of any kind, lived to the last, died with dignity. "Life is very short and very uncertain; let us spend it as well as we can."

Love dwelt in rocky places, he once said. He sought it and he gave it, in his own way. When he died, his friend William Hamilton said: "He has made a chasm, which . . . nothing can fill up . . . Johnson is dead—Let us go to the next best; There is nobody . . ."

January 8, 1978

ROMANO GUARDINO

The Death of Socrates

In his examination of the four Platonic dialogues dealing with the trial and death of Socrates, the noted Catholic scholar Romano Guardini has accomplished not merely an exegesis on the text but something more: a quality of witness to the events themselves and the nature and the ideas of the man who has become the very emblem of western philosophy.

Thus, in *The Death of Socrates* the reader is given the dramatic text—the Euthyphro, where Socrates, already under indictment, has a street-corner conversation, foreshadowing the issues of his trial; Apology, the trial itself, where Socrates defends his life and his ways before the high court of Athens; Crito, in which toward the end of his imprisonment, Socrates resists the well-meant advice of his friend to take flight; and finally, Phaedo, the scene of his last hours before drinking the hemlock. And we are given much more. The interpretation and commentary of Guardino matches the mood and the intent of the work: quiet, profound, seeking understanding.

It is as though Guardino has composed a musical score, taken the role of modest narrator and given us access to one of the profound and illuminating tragedies of western literature. This is his primary concern: "a real contact with the figure of Socrates."

Most commentators attempt to place Socrates and Plato in historical context, to order and restate the ideas and issues. Guardino's concern is that we, ourselves, come close to the universal truths discussed here: the meaning of death, the meaning of life, the nature of the good life, of piety, the central question of justice. The connection between our own lives and that of Socrates is palpable and immediate.

This notion of contact is central to any understanding of Socrates. For Socrates is not only a philosopher with a set of ideas and a method of questioning and irony, he is a man who lives his philosophy. We may in our fragmented age be able to separate what we think and the way we live. Socrates is incapable of this. It is the source both of his greatness and his doom.

Such a man's worth is not often clearly seen by his contemporaries. He is certainly not easy to have around; he asks embarrassing questions; he refuses to take the easy way; his skin is less important to him than the pursuit of the truth. Yet, he symbolizes the essence of personal, individual responsibility.

In this reading of the trial and death of Socrates the force is unspent. What is at issue is not the contention of good and evil—Socrates' accusers and his judges are not without certain qualities which he himself praises, indeed Socrates is at this trial both prosecutor and defendant—but the contention of one level of good against another. If there are evil and selfish men involved, it is only because his judges represent a cross-section of humanity. The indictment on the corruption of youth and the worshipping of false gods is only the excuse. What is being hammered out here is the ultimate destiny of the responsible individual in terms of the comity of men.

For Socrates sees more clearly than any around him that it is his knowledge which places on him a more profound trial than that which takes place in the courtroom. And his trial continues in his prison cell. Characteristically, when he is told that talking will make it harder for the hemlock to take immediate effect, he shakes aside the advice. He is not interested in an easy death or a hard death. He is interested in the meaning of death.

And we may, at the end, embrace the words of Plato: "Such was the end, Echecrates, of our friend, a man, I think, who was the wisest and justest, the best man that I have ever known."

July 18, 1962

MICHAEL GRANT

St. Paul

He was a man of three worlds, this Paul, called by Michael Grant "one of the most perpetually significant men who have ever lived." Paul was born Saul, a Jew of Tarsus, a Jew of the Dispersion. Tarsus was a Greek city, free (self-governing and privileged) and a center of Hellenic culture which he knew and whose language he had mastered. And finally, his father had been granted Roman citizenship, either as a reward for services to the Romans or because he was a freed slave or prisoner of war.

These worlds, Jewish, Greek and Roman, gave him access to a trio of cultures and prepared him for the role of bringing the Gospel to the Gentiles, changing Christianity from a Jewish sect to a new religion. Indeed, at the end of this fascinating study Grant suggests that where it is possible to compare and contrast the teaching of Jesus with the interpretations of Paul, " . . . What the two men preached was quite different, and the Christianity we have today is largely Paul's creation."

Grant is a student of ancient history rather than a theologian, and he argues that to regard Paul as a figure solely of religious significance is too limiting. His effect on secular history, for better or worse, continues "to an extent beyond measurement."

He goes on, echoing Lord Birkenhead "Scarcely anyone has ever changed the course of history more than Paul. By means of his life and his Letters, he has left a greater imprint on the human race than almost any other man."

And unlike other epoch-making figures, who are trapped in the amber of the past, Paul's personality and words are influential today. Grant's summing up is a bit facile, suggesting that Paul is profoundly relevant to a vastly wider circle today because Christians, Jews, and those who profess no religion can find in him an exemplar of the universalist impulse, the urge to break down the barriers between one human being and another. He sees Paul's life and character, his intellect and single-mindedness as evidence of the possibility of revival and change.

Of Paul's endurance, fortitude and perseverance, of his faith, there is no doubt. And seen in a certain way, his fanaticism can appear as a symbol of total change, a break with tradition and commitment, a capacity to imagine a world totally transformed, yet there is as much of the commissar and the functionary in Paul.

He was bossy, aggressive, combative, righteous. Paul's apostasy, as it affected the Jews, enhanced anti-Semitism; his derogatory remarks about worldly, fleshly things, his notions about the devil, fed repression and superstition.

The value of the study lies less in the few pages of conclusions than in an exceptional job of restoration, going beneath the revision of Paul's portrait by the church fathers in the second century to find the living, credible missionary. For immediately after Paul's death, the churches he founded do not seem to have flourished. The Christian communites of the cities in which he worked gave their allegiance to the apostles of the Jewish Christian Church he had opposed.

Two circumstances, both after his death, brought Paul's writings and work back into notice. First the Jewish revolt of 66-73 AD brought the Jews of the Roman Empire into discredit, and the Gentile emphasis of Paul's mission was rehabilitated by the church.

Then, a powerful heresy in the 2nd century AD grew up around the figure of Marcion, who preached total rejection of the pre-Christian, Jewish portion of the Bible. The Marcionites raised Paul to startling heights and probably collected Paul's "Epistles," but by the time of Polycarp a new Paul emerged, the Paul of the "Acts," snatched away from the heretics, less bold, less radical, saying less about the flesh and the spirit, explaining away his rejection of Jewish Law, bracketing himself with Peter though they had been so at variance in their lives.

This transformation into respectability, this neutralization, says Grant, makes Paul a shadow of his real self. Grant believes that in the Letters, despite their enigmas, is the most reliable source of information about his life, personality, and ways of thinking. It is here we see him not as a plaster saint but as a human being—persuasive, zealous, dynamic, intellectual. In the Letters John Donne called "thunder and universal thunder, thunder that passes through all the world," we see a restless mind, eccentric, undisciplined, ambiguous, busy.

Grant sees Paul's expression as only externally Hellenic, his association with Rome tactical (he used his Roman citizenship only on occasions where he could escape punishment through it), his inward meaning and the structure of his thought Jewish.

It is this meld of Jewish thought and Greek expression that accounts for the complaints of obscurity in some of his passes. Yet these passages set a challenge which Grant says must be taken up to understand Paul.

For the blinding vision of Jesus, which came to Paul on the road to Damascus was not the only vision ("I shall go on to tell of visions and revelations granted by the Lord"). Only one aspect of Paul, it yet was crucial, for he insisted that the vision made him an apostle, a teacher, and a prophet. The Jewish Christians did not take to this well. The 12 Apostles were men who had known Christ in His lifetime. Paul reacted furiously against their rejections of his claim. He was an apostle, "not by human appointment or human commission, but by commission from Jesus Christ and from God the Father."

He was sin-haunted and aware of evil in the world. More than aware, he saw the world as a horrible place plunged in evil. He would not accept the Greek notion that sin came out of ignorance. "What I do is not what I want to do but what I detest . . . when I want to do the right, only the wrong is within my reach."

The acceptance of Christ was only the beginning. Paul saw in retrospect that the Old Testament was with hints, omens and prophecies addressed to him and to his contemporaries. He took all of it personally, not theoretically. His life was a drama in which, despite all the tedious and demanding calls of missionary work and follow-up, the demons and the powers of evil pursued him. They could give him, he said, sharp physical pain. But equally, on being saved, he felt that his suffering, like Christ's, was redemptive, that his travels were a martyrdom, "every day I die," an inspiration for asceticism and single-minded devotion.

But bright, driven, single-minded, restless, he overwhelmed those around him, those who listened and those who were ready to lynch him as a troublemaker. But this more credible Paul is not only a symbol of individual power in history, he is also a man who has become a model for militants of all kinds, certain of their truths, intolerant of those who disagree.

September 16, 1976.

JOHN C. BEAGLEHOLE

The Life of Captain James Cook

ROBERT LACEY

Sir Walter Ralegh

There are some famous men about whom we know too little, others about whom we may think we know almost too much. Of the former, Capt. James Cook, perhaps the greatest seaman and explorer in history, is surely one. Of the latter, Sir Walter Ralegh is with equal certainty another.

I am speaking, of course, of character and private qualities, for the actions and accomplishments leading to fame must inevitably be recorded. Cook's three epic voyages of discovery, beginning in 1768 and ending for him with his death at the hands of a band of Hawaiians in 1780, have been extensively documented, and there have been several popular biographies. Ralegh's life has been told and retold many more times.

It is not surprising that the long-awaited definitive biography, *The Life of Captain James Cook* by John C. Beaglehole, the foremost scholar on Pacific exploration and editor of *Cook's Journals* and the *Journals of Joseph Banks*, who accompanied Cook on his first voyage, should turn out to be a portrait in depth of this complex and remarkable sailor. Prof. Beaglehole labored for 20 years on the project, dying in 1971 as he was in the midst of revision of the work. His son has completed that revision and seen the massive (nearly 800 pages) book through the press.

What is surprising is that Robert Lacey's *Sir Walter Ralegh*, a work which deals with a man so extensively written about, should succeed in producing so rich and evocative a portrait of the man and his times. Each work, though the subjects contrast in temperament and traits and though the styles contrast in tempo and approach, offers engrossing reading.

Cook was a private man, though in these pages we see evidence of introspection and of his concern for reputation. He left his journals and accounts of his voyages, but in the way of the times and of the professional he undoubtedly was, he kept the personal to himself. His widow, who survived him by 41 years, methodically destroyed letters and papers of a private nature. "We may regret, though respect, her destructive passion," Beaglehole writes. Some letters did remain and they are presented in these pages.

Cook has had his panegyrists; most great men do. But it is difficult to gainsay them for they were mainly the men who sailed with him and knew him. They found him quick and sure of judgment, humane as a captain in an age not noted for such concern, a good companion, though shy and with a certain modesty. He was neither a romantic nor a mystic, though Beaglehole cites—and the narrative shows over and over again—evidence of a "controlled imagination that could think out a great voyage in terms of what was possible for his own competence."

He went out with masses of instructions, and carried them out with "that sort of honest obedience (that) had been bred into him, or came natural to him, perhaps because of an equally natural passion for completeness." But, equally, there was room for elasticity and interpretation. Discovery by its very nature is venture. To a young French naval officer who had written to congratulate him, he had replied that a man would never accomplish much in discovery who only stuck to his orders. He had his ambitions: in the Southern Hemisphere he wanted not merely to reach a higher latitude than any man before him, but to go as far as a man could go. But it was the activity rather than fame which goaded him. When the third voyage was proposed, "Capt. Cook was so fired with the contemplation and representation of the object, that he started up, and declared that he himself would undertake the direction of the enterprise." The important point was that Lord Sandwich, his patron, had called him to the discussion thinking that he would have to persuade the captain to go.

He was not a paragon, a remote and unreal figure, but a good man, an intelligent man, who earned his chance by his own efforts, rising from an apprentice seaman in a Whitby collier to become master of his own ship, learning to navigate, learning to command, going at a comparatively late age into the navy, winning recognition through his service in Canada in the war against the French. There were other good seamen, competent navigators. His qualities as a leader of men become crucial.

He must have known fear, exhaustion, nervousness, the loneliness of command. But his midshipman Trevenen saw him as others who served with him did: "The coolness and conciseness with which Capt. Cook passes over the relations of dangers, the bare recollection of which makes everyone else shudder with horror, is very remarkable." His poise and self-control were part of the art of seamanship, the art of the possible. Beaglehole resists sentimentalizing the man. He was a pragmatist. "The preservation of the health of seamen was for him an aspect at once of humanity and efficiency—and hence of navigation; for with all the instruments in the world, it is difficult for a commander to navigate with men dying of scurvy."

He found fresh food, vegetables, fruits, roots, tried the new on himself, "the coarsest and most ungrateful food." But he kept his men healthy. And he insisted on exercise ashore. Some observers felt he was too lenient, for he did not believe in overworking men: He instituted three watches instead of two. He insisted on cleanliness. He was firm but fair. When food was short, it was divided equally from ship's boy to captain. When his sailmaker needed room to work, he have up his great cabin. He punished rarely and unwillingly. His treatment of the natives was patient and temperate. Ironically, he had criticized Magellan for risking confrontation unnecessarily, thus losing his life. Cook did the same.

Again, he was not perfect, which may have won his men's loyalty and affection more than anything else. He was saddened by the effect exposure to Europeans had had upon the natives. But there was nothing he could do. He had a temper and in the third voyage he displayed rage and fatigue. But he also regretted it. He was a complex man, summed up in the words of a New Zealand chief quoting an ancient Maori saying: A true man is not hid among many.

To go back to Ralegh after Cook is not only to view a man different in temperament and style but to cross that invisible frontier between modern times and the Renaissance. We recognize Cook more clearly: the professional, the specialist, the self-made man. Ralegh is somehow more theatrical, a stage figure, bejeweled, his cloak spread before the queen, proud, arrogant, ambitious, almost mythic, certainly tragic, in his 'fall.

Lacey's biography encompasses and surpasses the legendary figure, poet, soldier, sailor, historian, patron of exploration, one model of Renaissance man. But there is something more about Ralegh (Lacey prefers this spelling used by the man himself and most of his contemporaries). It is not simply that adversity ground away the unpleasant parts of his character to leave him at the end a man who finds a truer triumph in his execution than in most of his life. He was a child of his time but he was also in certain ways a forerunner of the future. It is this duality, this double-Ralegh which is the great achievement of the biography.

In one aspect, he played the game and lost, "All men that are ruined, are ruined on the side of their natural propensities," Edmund Burke wrote, and the words are applicable to Ralegh. He had placed his faith in monarchs, had flattered and cajoled, had won place and wealth, only to find that world hollow and slippery. His fall had begun long before James I ordered him to the Tower for the third and, as it turned out, last time. He had known disgrace under Elizabeth as well, had even attempted suicide.

James did give him a final gift: " . . . Had King James let Walter Ralegh die quietly in his bed of old age, posterity would merely have recorded the passing of an ambitious, gifted and flawed personality," Lacey writes. "As it was, Walter Ralegh died an ambitious, gifted and flawed martyr, the symbol of an age superceded, an eternal parable of passing time, an immortal."

The final scene played out the elements of tragedy. Sir Henry Yelverton, the attorney general and prosecutor, was moved to declare: "Sir Walter Ralegh hath been a statesman and a man who in regards to his parts and quality is to be pitied. He hath been a star at which the world hath gazed. But stars may fall, nay, they must fall when they trouble the sphere wherein they abide."

He troubled the sphere. The great historian, G. M. Trevelyan, was to pronounce an epilog that touched upon the future: " . . . The ghost of Ralegh pursued the House of Stuart to the scaffold."

James was to be plagued the rest of his life by books, satires, songs and demonstrations in which the spirit of Ralegh was evident. His son, Charles, was to die by the executioner's ax for the same abuse of power his father had begun.

But if Ralegh died a martyr in 1618, he never lived as a saint. In this biography, he emerges credibly human. It is easier to portray him in the broad and simple strokes of myth, his pride, his worldliness, his courtliness, his dashing, handsome appearance. There were other sides to him, some rising to the challenge of circumstance, some buried deep in a character of paradox. He could be open and forthright; he also had an appetite for conspiracy and plot. He could see the truth of the world clearly; he could panic and lie. He had the sensitivity of a poet; he could be callous, brutal and cruel.

He began with little but his own intelligence and appearance. Son of a Devon squire, with pride of ancestry but little in property, a fierce Puritan, stubborn and arrogant, Walter shared his father's contempt for public pressure. He had some connections: the Grenvilles, the Gilberts. But he had to make his own way. First, he went to join the Huguenots in the French wars. He proved his courage but saw on both sides "barbarous murders, devastations and other calamities . . . begun and carried on by some few great men of ambitious and turbulent spirits, deluding the people with the cloak and mask only of religion, to gain their assistance to what they did more especially aim it."

The new skepticism did not prevent him from trying his own aim. As a veteran soldier returning to Oxford, he had small patience for study. His intellect drew him to question the forms of society. His first poem, a preface to Gascoigne's "Steel Glass," expressed this:

> *This glass of steel impartially doth show*
> *Abuses to all, to such as in it look,*
> *From prince to poor, from high estate to low.*

Yet, he chose to go whither the power was. First to Ireland, to make a name for himself as a soldier. Then to the court, where he set about, and succeeded, in winning the attention and admiration of an aging queen. He had a way with women—it was to bring him conquests of the heart and high position. He was knighted, made captain of the Queen's guard, received support for his expeditions to the New World. He introduced the potato to Ireland and England, and smoking tobacco.

But privately he remained rebellious, questioning, intellectually curious. The Queen adored him—but remained in control. In a court of sycophants, Ralegh was a flatterer too. That was transparent. But his downfall began when his heart asserted control over his head. He fell in love with the woman he was to marry—Elizabeth Throckmorton, one of the Queen's attendants. The queen committed him to the Tower. Ultimately freed, he went on an expedition to the Orinoco in search of gold. On his return, he fought the Spanish triumphantly at Cadiz and the Azores.

His restoration was brief. With the accession of James, Ralegh was charged with treason and committed to the Tower again, where he began his history of the world. James released him in 1616 to lead the ill-fated expedition for gold in Guiana. Ralegh ignored his orders and attacked the Spanish town of San Tomas. He returned to be tried and convicted of treason for the second time in 1618.

In close witness to the last few days of his life, Lacey relates, as he has throughout, the unheroic as well as the heroic. Ralegh began to disintegrate under the stress of trial and imprisonment. He seemed to give way, his old pride beaten down. He appeared before his judges unkempt and depressed, fighting desperately for a pardon. He had even feigned madness and illness. But once the death sentence was passed, that other Ralegh seemed to emerge. He faced his death with courage and eloquence, determined to die as he had sometimes lived. He seemed to relish, as an old actor might, the curtain scene.

He could even joke. As he left the Tower, someone gave him a cup of sack wine which he drank. Asked if it pleased him, he replied: "I will answer you as did the fellow who drank of St. Giles's bowl as he went to Tyburn: 'It is a good drink, if a man but tarry by it.'"

Men gathered about him for his final words, and his going became a potent event of rejection of the character, policy and reputation of James I. He no longer had to trim or flatter or cajole. He spoke out of his heart and strangely the support of the public for which he had so long had contempt seem to rise toward him, an irony as well as a portent of new times.

The ax man did not pronounce the old words: "Behold the head of a traitor." Instead, a voice out of the crowd gave an epitaph: "We have not another such head to be cut off."

March 31, 1974

EDGAR H. COHEN

Mademoiselle Libertine: A Portrait of Ninon de Lenclos

I have need neither of fortune nor of mask.
–Ninon de Lenclos

I can see why today's feminists might be loath to accept Ninon de Lenclos, the fascinating 17th-century Frenchwoman who inspired such disparate figures as Voltaire and Simone de Beauvoir to adulation.

On the surface of her life, she is presented as little more than a plaything of men, known for her lovers, for her wit, for her friendship with the illustrious.

In this biography, we find the portrait of a remarkable human being, who confronted the world of double standards, the domination of men over women, and contrived by principle to triumph over it.

Reading of her long and intriguing life—she was over 80 when she died in 1705—we begin to understand why she had been celebrated by so many great writers—and a corps of others, not so great. And why Simone de Beauvoir saw in her a kindred spirit:

"The Frenchwoman whose independence seems to me the most like a man is perhaps Ninon de Lenclos . . . paradoxically, those women who exploit their femininity to the limit create for themselves a situation almost equivalent to that of a man . . . Not only do they make their own living like men, but they exist in a circle almost exclusively masculine; free in behavior and conversation, they can attain . . . to the rarest intellectual liberty. The most distinguished are often surrounded by writers and artists who are bored by 'good' women."

It is through these writers and artists that Cohen is able to bring Ninon alive. Only a few of her own writings survive, enough to prove that poetry was not her forte. Her letters, except for 30 or so, have not survived. But her influence was enormous. St. Evremonde, the classic gentleman of 17th-century France and the dominant influence in her life, wrote letters which are a primary source. Voltaire wrote about her. La Fontaine was helped by her.

If she became a symbol of love, the key to her emancipation lies in her capacity for friendship. Durability in friendship is not less rare than durability in love. Love was intimately tied to the contention between man and woman. They could be equal only in friendship.

The excitement of her affairs—she is reputed (though this probably a legend) to have been offered a fortune, 150,000 *livres* to become the mistress of Cardinal Richelieu, and to have rejected, saying that the sum was too much from a lover and too little from one she did not love—makes interesting reading. She was physically attractive, as adept as a geisha in the art of entertaining men. But, it was not her capacity for lovemaking which made her memorable.

This had to do with the independence, bitterly won, with which she was to approach friendship. She was not proof against the desires of the flesh, but she did not want to be the toy of men. Rather, she wished to come to them on their own terms.

The measure of her striving for independence lies in two decisions. First, she refused to marry. It was part of her fight against the double standard. She had witnessed the marriage of her own parents and other matches around her. Men could commit adultery with impunity. Women who had the same needs and desires, in her view, could not. She had nothing against promiscuity; what disturbed her was the deception and hypocrisy involved.

Second, she reserved the right to be free in all aspects of her life, religious, intellectual, social. When Cohen calls her a libertine, he is employing the oldest sense of the word, having to do with liberty. Ninon not only believed in free love; she believed in free thought. In her, Cohen finds a figure bridging the spirit of the Renaissance and the quest of the Enlightenment.

What did she seek out of life? That condition normally allowed only to men: to be an *homme honete,* which means more than the literal honest man. It suggests the life of quality, grace, poise and independence. It was to this she aspired.

The test was not in love but in friendship. Only in friendship with its implication of true equality, could a woman achieve that condition. In her life, she brought it to apotheosis.

It was a measure of her own traits that even rejected lovers became her close friends. None of this came easily. She was punished, sent to convents, criticized. She faced the burden of all women, aging, uncertain security, the disapproval of some. But in the end, she won regard, not only from men, but from women. La Bruyere paid her the ultimate compliment: "In her one finds all the merits of both sexes."

March 12, 1971

MICHAEL DAVIS

William Blake: A New Kind of Man

I have been near the Gates of Death & have returned very weak & an Old Man feeble & tottering, but not in Spirit & Life, not in The Real Man, the Imagination which Liveth for Ever. In that I am stronger & stronger as this Foolish body decays.
—William Blake at 70, in a letter April 12, 1827

Those who tried to explain William Blake almost always missed the point. Many could appreciate his pictures and poems for they rarely failed to move and excite, sometimes in awesome ways. Some called him peculiar, others thought him mad; some believed his talent that of a primitive, others thought him pitiable for he did not seem to fit the usual categories.

He was an artist, craftsman, poet, visionary, who "felt through all this fleshly dress Bright shoots of everlastingness," expressed his ecstasies and transports in works so vivid and language so extraordinary that he confused his explicators.

In Michael Davis, Blake has a biographer who allows Blake's life and works, for they are inseparable, to come to the reader untrammeled by the myths which have been embroidered round the man. "It is not surprising that tales about the oddities of this visionary artist, daring thinker, honest and outspoken man, should have been distorted and multiplied." But he adds emphatically and persuasively, "Blake, the whimsical lunatic, never existed."

But Blake, the rebel youngster who was taught to read at home ("Thank God, I never was sent to school/To be Flog'd into following the Style of a Fool"), the boy who roamed the fields and bathed naked in the ponds in unspoiled country not far from his Soho home, the child who was thrashed for seeing a tree full of angels on Peckham Rye, did exist.

He doesn't seem so strange to us these days. Indeed, he would be completely at home with those who have turned back to working with their hands, who feel a kinship with nature both spiritual and physical, who seek freedom to express themselves. For that period, at the dawn of the romantic age whose liberating spirit his own work expressed in a marriage of pictures and poems, Blake, more than Coleridge, Wordsworth or Southey, was a new kind of man.

Coleridge, who was lent a copy of Blake's *Songs of Innocence and of Experience,* saw in these "poems with very wild and interesting pictures, the work of a man of genius . . . a mystic, *emphatically.*" He wrote: "You perhaps smile at *my* calling another poet a mystic; but verily I am in the very mire of commonplace common sense compared with Mr. Blake."

The visions of his childhood were never lost for Blake but it is unfair to portray him as he was seen for many years as a menial laborer, uneducated and unaware of traditional art. His passion was drawing; he visited art collections and dealer's salesrooms as a boy. At 14, he had begun to collect prints—including works of Dürer, Raphael, Martin Heemskirk. Langford, the auctioneer, called Blake his "little connoisseur." He wanted to be apprenticed to a painter but his father could not afford the high premium, told him that paying it would deprive his brothers and sister of their due.

Instead he was apprenticed to James Basire, official engraver to the Society of Antiquaries and to the Royal Society. Painstaking and industrious, he was a good apprentice, became and remained all his life a master craftsman and a passionate workman. Basire encouraged him to go out and draw. He worked at Westminster Abbey, had a vision there of Christ and the Apostles, scoffed at the notion that a vision was "a cloudy vapor." Rather, he later said, it was "infinitely more perfect and more minutely organized than anything seen by his mortal eye."

At 16 he was official artist at the brief opening of the tomb of Edward I and he sketched the royal corpse and the regalia. He had read deeply in Shakespeare, Milton, the Bible, the mystics Jacob Boehme, Swedenborg, read and admired Wickelman's *Reflections on the Painting and Sculpture of the Greeks,* criticized Burke, Locke and Bacon for mocking "Inspiration & Vision . . . then & now . . . & I hope always . . . my Element, my Eternal dwelling place . . ."

A rather different Blake emerges in these pages. At 21, he was one of two dozen new students accepted by the Royal Academy in 1779. By the next year he exhibited at the academy's show. He made friends who would stand by him for years despite his touchy, fiery, sensitive nature. "I never made friends but by spiritual gifts, By severe contentions of Friendship & the burning fire of thought." But he did not do well under authority. George Michael Moser, the chief teacher, tried to discourage him from studying old drawings, asked him to examine finished paintings. "How I did secretly Rage! I also spoke my Mind . . . I said to Moser. 'These things that you call Finish'd are not Even Begun . . . The Man who does not know The Beginning never can know the End of Art.'"

It is not surprising that Blake, a revolutionary at heart, participated in the Gordon riots, helped to pull down Newgate prison. But he was never a dour and somber fanatic. He was by nature merry and convivial, a man of levels and complexities, open and natural. He married for love and sex. "In a wife I would desire/ what in whores is always found—/the lineaments of Gratified desire." That wasn't all, and Catherine Blake became a devoted wife, who partook of vision, became his assistant printer, helped color his prints. They had no children. His works, richly illustrated in color and black and white in this book, became "infants emanating from him."

Davis takes us through the years of Blake's life, his experimental color printing, his commercial work and his imaginative work, his personal life and the universe of new myths he composed in his prophetic books shows the influences on him, the transmutations of these ideas into his own. "I must Create a System or be enslav'd by another Man's./I will not Reason & Compare: my business is to Create."

He appealed to children of all ages, still does, to the innocent of heart, to those who are free, to those who can laugh. Yet, as those who love Blake know, he cannot be dismissed as a simple writer. In "Jerusalem," in "Milton," in "Songs of Experience," there are intricate and echoing levels of revelation. And in his aphorisms, some designed to parody Swedenborg, in whose work he had become disillusioned, was another aspect of his genius, one which combined well his penchant for print and picture. "The road of excess leads to the palace of wisdom." "Energy is Eternal Delight." "The cistern contains: the fountain overflows." "The tygers of wrath are wiser than the horses of instruction." "Damn braces: Bless relaxes."

He wanted to shock. His manner was open, he spoke to the point. But some of the stories—such as the one about the Blakes sitting naked in their summer house when his patron Thomas Butts called—may show his independence of mind as eccentricity. "Come in!" said Blake, "It's only Adam and Eve, you know!" Davis calls the story dubious, says "the pair might have been testing with their nude bodies, postures for use in Blake's designs." It is a rare instance of Davis being overwhelmed by the rationalizing impulse.

After some prosperity, Blake came upon difficult times. There was war and a banking crash; his prophetic books were not selling. Even the "mere drudgery of business," work as an engraver, did not come to him. His patrons helped and it is a measure of Blake's innate grace that when he wrote to Butts, he said: " . . . Having passed now near 20 years in ups & downs, I am used to them . . . Fortune . . . Alone is the Governor of Worldly Riches, & when it is Fit She will call on me; till then I wait with Patience in hopes that She is busied among my Friends."

He didn't give up. He continued writing and painting. "Designing & Poetry," as he called it, continued to "converse with my friends in Eternity, See Visions, Dream Dreams & prophecy & speak Parables unobserv'd . . ." He moved to the country and then back, was tried for assaulting some soldiers and uttering seditious sentiments, perhaps entrapped as a radical, but easily acquitted. He exhibited again at the Academy, met some acceptance and some scorn, took on his old antagonist Joshua Reynolds with his characteristic fire, wrote a friend: "I certainly do thank God that I am not like Reynolds!"

He persevered to the end, found friends and disciples among the young, lived creatively to the last. Blake hated generalizations, loved the detail and specifics of experience. In this excellent biography we see him in such close gravure as he, master craftsman, would appreciate. Of his works and pictures, well, they are as bright and compelling as they always were for those whose imagination resonates to his. Even Sir Thomas Lawrence, who became president of the Royal Academy in 1820, admired some of Blake's works enough to buy them. Of such establishment artists, Blake would say: "They pity me, but 'tis they are the just objects of pity; I possess my visions of peace. They have bartered their birthright for a mess of pottage."

The middle ground was never a place for Blake.

July 24, 1977

Bettina Knapp *and* Myra Chipman

That Was Yvette: The Biography of the Great Diseuse

"An artist," Yvette Guilbert once said, "is an exaggerated human being."

Her life, which spanned an exaggerated era between the end of the 19th century and the middle of the 20th, could have made a novel—and did. She knew success and failure, the love of crowds and the eclipse of popularity, became a legend among legendary characters.

Born Emma Guilbert (it was Maupassant who suggested the name Yvette when she began her career on the stage), she could have been a Zola character. Her father was marked for failure in Paris. He abandoned her and her mother. This brought the two of them together in an alliance against a hostile and arduous world.

Tall and thin as a whip, Yvette was strikingly out of style in an era which valued the buxom and the over-adorned. Poverty had not broken her spirit; rather, it had produced an almost frightening ambition and a love of money approaching avarice. She had vigor and self confidence. She needed it. Against the reality of the slum and the drudgery of modeling and selling dresses, she saw the other Paris: glittering, urbane, wealthy, decadent. An impresario promised her 20,000 francs a year if she would learn to be a circus rider. Her mother would not hear of it. But the theater offered an escape.

But she was untrained, ugly even. What she had was intelligence and, as one man put it, "the virtue of courage," though he conceded that virtue in show business "has never been as handy as a couple of vices."

There were other qualities: style and a certain air; a feeling for poetry and the *chanson*; a modest voice and the gift to use it above its natural limitations. She went on the stage and the path to stardom was long. Someone suggested the *cafes-concerts*, that particularly French form somewhere between vaudeville and the music-hall. Her debut in the provinces was disastrous. Audiences greeted her either with stony silence or with raucous shouts about her lack of equipment.

But she was wiser than her critics. She read the audience needs as few had. She developed an anti-style. Where most singers were large and loud; she was thin and quiet. Where most were raw and obvious, she found the subtle and the deeply moving. She dipped into an older French tradition and combined it with a sort of new *Comedie Humaine*. She designed herself, emphasizing all the qualities which were criticized. She was pale; she made herself even paler with rice powder; her hair was dull, she made it a rich henna; lacquered her lips a geranium red to bring out the whiteness of her teeth; shaded her eyes with a brown caught from candleflame on a porcelain saucer. The famed Lautrec caricature was more photographic than we realize.

For one who sang of love, there was, for a long time, no real love. When it came, she hardly knew it at first, this woman who gave so great an impression of experience. He was a German Jewish scientist named Max Schiller, whose loyalty and admiration contrasted with the shallowness and sophistication of those, from princes to poets, who threw themselves at her.

Much of her story involves the great and the near-great of those decades: Gounod, Eleonora Duse, Hammerstein, Sarah Bernhart, Freud and the Prince of Wales, Isadora Duncan and Pierre Loti.

Even if Yvette Guilbert were nothing more than a singer, a

personality, the progenitor of a style, her story would be worth telling. But, as we see from this sensitive and well written account, she was something far more complicated. She had a capacity for growth, for self-education. "Other women are just as clever as I am, but if I make up my mind that I will do a thing, I always do it. I try, and try, and try, until I succeed."

Barely educated, she became something of a scholar, contributed to the field of French musicology in her research; self-trained as an artist, she founded a school in which all the arts were unified; barely capable of love, she brought herself to return the love of her husband. This is no simple story but a complex and many-faceted portrait.

February 18, 1965

Maurice Goudeket

Close to Colette

"I was 15 or 16 years old when I discovered Colette, and received from the first reading of her a delicious shock. With the incredible pride and fanciful notions of that age, I said to my parents: 'I am going to marry that woman. She is the only one who will be able to understand me.' "

Maurice Goudeket went on to marry Colette, the woman of his adolescent dreams. He was her third and last husband, nearly 20 years her junior. By all common sense it should have been a difficult if not impossible match. It turned out to be a marriage of incredible tenderness and devotion.

"I am not priding myself, on that as though it were a prophecy," Goudeket continues. "Out of the countless desires we formulate, if one or other of them bears fruit, we call it premonition."

Premonition or not, their first meeting in 1925 when she was 52 and he was 35 was the beginning of a 30-year marriage. Until her death in 1955, "It was hand in hand that we made the long journey together . . . every moment was a moment of fulfillment and silent happiness."

Close to Colette, Goudeket's memoir of that remarkable woman with the sea-colored eyes, with the instincts of a Burgundian peasant and the soul of an artist, is one of the most tender and devoted documents I have ever read. It is not biography in the strictest sense; it is a journey through a soul.

He saw her for the first time in the house of a friend: "Her head . . . under its crown of disheveled hair," looking "like a large cat stretching herself," "that bronze voice of hers, rolling its Burgundian r's."

"But," he writes, "I could not take my eyes off that most individual profile of hers, with the eyes set so expressively in the shadow of a lock of ash-blond hair, the nose rather long at its end, the wide cheekbones, the thin bow of the mouth and the pointed chin. [She] shot me a look blue as night, ironical and quizzical but with an indefinable nostalgia, too. Something countrified and healthy emanated from her."

Goudeket in this memoir proves himself a writer as perceptive and skillful as Colette herself.

She was a complex individual with a facade which could keep people at their distance, especially after her books began to build her reputation as one of the best literary talents of France.

But Goudeket saw her beneath this facade. She had that inexpressible gift of the writer, that second sight which enables the vision beneath the surface of people and events. But in her personal life she retained the elements of her basic personality. She loved the simple things and the ordinary people who were the characters of her books.

"Her kindness to ordinary people," Goudeket says, "arose from the fact that she did not regard them as ordinary."

She loved to keep her house as spotless as a typical housewife. She knew the secrets of cooking and preserves and winemaking. She loved the natural life of the woods and could almost commune with animals. In her hotel rooms she scattered crumbs to feed the mice.

Passion and emotion embarrassed her. She did not yearn for the

Bohemian life. As much as she loved and needed Goudeket, she did not break down when he was arrested by the Germans in 1941. She touched him affectionately and said, "Off you go!" but she must have died inside as he left.

Perhaps the best which might be said of this unusual volume is that in depth of feeling and human understanding it is equal to any novel that Colette ever wrote.

May 31, 1957

AUBREY HODES

Martin Buber: An Intimate Portrait

Martin Buber was, above all, the philosopher of meeting, of dialog, of conversations deep enough to include silences. In 1919, he wrote, "You shall not withhold yourself. You, imprisoned in the shells in which society, state, church, school, economy, public opinion and your own pride have stuck you, indirect one among indirect ones, break through your shells, become direct; man, have contact with men!"

It is therefore seemly and appropriate that Aubrey Hodes' *Martin Buber: An Intimate Portrait* should be cast in the form of meetings and dialog, that, more than conventional biography, more than a critical assessment of Buber's ideas, it conveys the reality of the living man. Like those Hasidic tales Buber was fond of recounting, in which wisdom came out of situation and encounter, Hodes' memoir touches us deeply.

Hodes came to Buber the way troubled men came to the wonder rabbis, seeking solace and guidance, receiving not platitudes but linkage with the hidden significance of pain and tragedy and mystery in human existence. "All real living is meeting," Buber once said and in this book we see clearly and insistently what he meant.

The sense of that contact and encounter is to be found in one of Buber's favorite stories by the Yiddish writer, Isaac Loeb Peretz. Each Day of Atonement, the rabbi of a small town disappears from the synagogue for a few hours. One of his followers suspects he is secretly meeting with the Almighty and follows him.

He observes the rabbi don coarse peasant clothes, watches him go to the cottage of an invalid woman. Here he cleans her room, prepares her food and minsters to her in her illness. The disciple goes back to the synagogue, where he is asked, "Did the rabbi ascend to heaven?" The follower reflects for a moment, replies: "If not higher."

It is this Buber we find in these pages. True, there are quotations from his books, an effort to interpret the vast concerns of the poet-philosopher, the record of conversations, but in the end, the story is cast in the I-Thou of Buber's encompassing metaphor. Hodes, in 1953, in Israel, underwent a terrifying ordeal of personal difficulty, a spiritual ferment, somehow related to the mental illness of a close, beloved relative whom he visited twice a week in painful pilgrimage.

He felt drawn to Buber, then to him a half-legendary presence. He read the works of Buber, which, ironically he found austere and forbidding. Words on paper could not substitute for encounter. Then in one of Buber's books, *The Way of Man*, he read a quotation from the Baal-Shem Tov, the founder of Hasidism:

"No encounter with a being or thing in the course of our life lacks a hidden significance . . . The highest culture of the soul remains basically arid and barren unless, day by day, waters of life pour forth into the soul from those little encounters to which we give their due."

He called Buber on the telephone. The philosopher, surprisingly, told him to come immediately. It was the beginning of a dozen years of meetings which form the living pulse of this book. What Hodes did not know then was Buber's view of responsibility. He had once had a visit from an unknown young man. Their conversation had been casually attentive and open. But the young man had been in despair, and Buber reproached himself later, for not having guessed "the questions which he did not put." The young man "had come to me not casually but borne by destiny, not for a chat but for a decision. He had come to me, he had come in this hour. What do we expect when we are in despair and yet go to a man? Surely a presence by means of which we are told that nevertheless there is meaning."

But that young man left Buber and shortly afterward took his own life. It was a turning point in his own life, Buber told Hodes. "He came to consult me in the hour of his deepest need. He came to ask me whether he should choose life or death. I talked to him openly. I was sympathetic. I tried to answer his questions. But I answered only the questions he had asked me. And so I failed to see through to the man behind the questions."

Buber asked himself why he failed. The philosopher went on, "Because that morning before his visit, I had been filled with religious enthusiasm, a mystical ecstasy, in which I felt myself in tune with eternity and life beyond. Then this young man came to see me. It was an everyday event, an event of judgment. And it 'converted' me because it showed me that there could be no division between the life here and the life beyond."

The incident was central. "In the claim, I am claimed." Religion for Buber was not flight into another world, another state "but responding to the call that comes into your everyday life. Above all, listening to both the silent and the spoken voices when one man speaks to another, so that together they can remove the barrier between two human beings."

An impossible task, one might think, yet in striving toward it we find the central core of Buber's philosophy, his theology, his humanism, his effort to seek *rapprochement* between Jew and Arab in the Middle East, between Christian and Jew, his notions of history and education, of linguistics and ethics.

In a divided world, he spoke for unity and universality; in the babel of rhetoric, he sought to make acts as meaningful as words; in a God-centered universe, he remembered man. Hode's own experience, his test, came in the events of his own life, in moments which before meeting Buber, he might have slid by. These become the counterpoint to Buber's teaching.

And the teaching was never indoctrination, never "gift-wrapped grace," facile solutions. In a felicitous phrase, Hodes says, "He spoke to my condition, as the Quakers say. . . ." Like many of us, Hodes' love for humanity was too diffuse, too counter within an encounter, but in realization, image-ridden, too intellectualized.

Buber's contribution was to point up the encounter within an encounter, but in realization, opening yourself to I-Thou. His favorite illustration was the Hasidic legend about Rabbi Zusya, who said shortly before his death: "In the world to come I shall not be asked: 'Why were you not Moses?' I shall be asked: 'Why were you not Zusya?'"

Self-realization is the foundation of personal responsibility. If you transform yourself, you have transformed that part of the world which surrounds you. No scapegoating, no projection. In *The Way of Man*, Buber writes: "The origin of all conflict between me and my fellowmen is that I do not say what I mean and that I do not do what I say. For this confuses and poisons, again and again in increasing measure the situation between myself and the other man."

The subtle difference in expression must be noted. Too often, the statement is couched in terms of other people, or conditions. For Buber, the conflict starts within one, in one's own soul. The luxury of rationalization is not permitted. As Rabbi Bunam said, "When a man has made peace with himself, he will be able to make peace with the whole world."

It is no wonder that the golden age of Hasidism appealed to him. Its wisdom, its joy in nature, its love of common humanity in us all, but above all its practical sense of responsibility turned to the seeker. Its answers are inevitably in the form of questions turned on the questioner, with compassion, with empathy, with what the Hasidism of many years ago called *hesed*, the Hebrew word for loving-kindness.

But it was not alone in this sect he saw it. Erudite and transcending, he thrilled to the recognition of dialog and conciliation in other religions and cultures. In Israel, he was often a controversial figure, always the conscience which would break through narrow national boundaries. "Being true to the being in which and before which I am placed" expressed his activist, committed, world-affirming mysticism.

Buber's death brought grief to those who knew him and to those beyond his individual impact who had been moved by his books. And even here, the responsibility was left with the survivors. Hodes' book is part of that continuation of the reverberation of his spirit.

One day before his death, he spoke to Hodes about the need to devote one's entire personality to the struggle for truth. He searched for a word, came up with one derived from "kol," the Hebrew word for all. "Allness. Man in his allness. Tell me, is there is such a word in English? If not, there should be."

It is the word, Hodes concludes, which best describes the nature of the man, an allness transcending artificial boundaries, which raised human identities out of the mass. "Make the crowd no longer a crowd," he wrote, and he lived by these words.

July 18, 1971

W. A. SWANBERG

Dreiser

"Oh, many kinds of death are necessary," Dreiser had written in *Moods*. And many kinds of life make up a man. It is important in Dreiser's life for no simple profile was possible. He could be abrupt, wrong-headed, mendacious, suspicious, bigoted, self-indulgent, and cruel—and he was at various stages. But he could be attractive, kind, brave, compassionate, brilliant, intuitive and innocent. And he was these things at times.

"The dichotomous Dreiser," Swanberg calls him, "—on one plane a selfish, bullying, unreasonable, capricious, deceitful, evil old man—was in his other incarnation more than ever the awe-stricken contemplator of the creative force that made him what he helplessly was, a part of all nature in its infinite glory and sorrow."

This must be kept in mind as we read the story of his life. Those who tend toward the instant moral judgment of a man will have a field day with this book. Those who are willing to leave the judgment of men to the angels will emerge with that enhanced understanding of the human condition- which is, in the end, the most important message Dreiser, the writer, had to give his contemporaries and those who followed him.

For the best and the worst in him, as in the region and period which shaped him, were inextricably linked. He indulged an obsessive lechery privately while criticising license in others. He was driven by an abstract altruism and concern for social conditions while at the same time capable of the most thoughtless and heedless cruelty to those closest to him. He hungered for faith and answers while his own eyes were purblind to the ultimate implications of this impulse. He became a dupe for the Communists who played on his inadequacies.

Those who loved him, who saw in him the core of worth which stamped him out of the ordinary—men like Mencken, the publisher Liveright—were recipients of unbelievably raw treatment. His treatment of the women who loved him was that of the spoiled egocentric child. He exploited all of them.

When, out of their desire to help him, his friends tried to get him to recognize his faults, he dropped them. Mencken wrote of him (after displaying patience and tact for years): "I have no animosity to him, but he has become too tragic to be borne. Seeing him would be like visiting an old friend who has gone insane. . . ."

He lacked moderation, a balancing quality. Grinding poverty made him aggressive and ambitious, suspicious of chicanery in others, perhaps a projection of his own motives. His own family experience introduced him to the the matter which would one day be transmuted into *Sister Carrie* and *Jennie Gerhardt*. The realities of life he experienced were far more sordid than anything he wrote. One of the important points which Swanberg makes is Dreiser's experience with John S. Sumner and the infamous New York Society for the Suppression of Vice which resulted in the banning of *The Genius*. It compelled him to waste time and energy, diverted and distracted his attention, pointed up the immaturity and sheer cowardice of many in the American literary community.

It drove Dreiser farther and farther away from his audience and his work. It was to be years before he recovered enough to write his best work, *An American Tragedy*. He fought that battle with characteristic courage and folly. The two were inseparable. But the battle itself was to be won for the benefit of others.

To Dreiser, it was proof of what Swanberg calls Dreiser's Law: "Beliefs held by the multitude, the bourgeois and their leaders, are likely to be wrong, per se." The notion suggests an Ibsenish idea current around the turn of the century. In Dreiser's own life, it represented one pole of thought. Characteristically, he would use it to rationalize unconventional behavior and nonconformism. But it blinded him to the strongest factors of his own genius. His sensitivity, his observation, his keen sense of social justice required a free and open encounter with experience.

His best work emerged from this. His worst traits came from the irony that some of the values he most despised were an integral part of his own character. He is neither the first nor the last American writer to be caught in this love-hate tension.

In this sense, his life becomes a real American tragedy. He was a man at war with himself, without realizing that both sides of that encounter were contained within him. His responses then became extreme. He lacked either the capacity or the temperament or both to gain some kind of intellectual perspective on life. His responses were visceral and emotional, always exaggerated, always extreme, always torn between the wild horses of fundamental guilt and those of fundamental skepticism.

The victim, of course, of such a struggle is the man himself. He was prey to the senses, demolished by the aftermath; quick to accept ready-made answers, equally quick to project them to absolutes whatever the absurdity of the position. He embraced Hitler and Stalin with fervor and blindness.

He could not see that there was any contradiction between his latent anti-Semitism and his friendship for individual Jews. He could not see any contradiction between his stated beliefs about the integrity of the artist, and his use of women to correct and revise his writing, his immodest efforts to promote a Nobel Prize for himself, his occasional borrowing from other writers, his lack of responsibility about facts. He told the story (which turns out to be untrue) about the alleged suppression of *Sister Carrie* by Doubleday so many times that he became convinced of its truth.

In the light of all this, and much more, can anything emerge from the contemplation of Dreiser's life? Anything but an exercise in biography? Swanberg does not attempt to wrap up and explain the complexities and the inconsistencies. His task is to present the man and his world—". . . Dreiser the liar who demanded truth in the world; the hater who called for love; the money-grubber who denounced capital; the glorifier of the proletariat who held the mass in contempt; the relentless promoter of sexual intrigues, the love cheat who asked for a high moral order and 'more spiritual character'; the ego so vast that it exempted only himself from his own standards; the boy who never really reached maturity and yet who exuded at times a charm and sympathy that is warmly remembered to this day."

His friends and enemies attempted it. But their assessments could only provide part of the answer.

The reader will be tempted to try. His answer may not be more complete than that given by Dreiser's contemporaries. Drieser himself could not answer it. Indeed, he tried all his life and only obscured the situation. Yet, it was a question worthy of him at his best.

A few things emerged for me. One, which may seem curiously inadequate, was that he lacked humor. Not only in his writing but in his life. Laughter is the ultimate perspective. It redeemed Twain. It may yet redeem the regiments of humorless writers who have followed Dreiser. From this defect of the comic vision comes another flaw. Hypocrisy. It was, I think, in the end Dreiser's tragic flaw. He could find it in others, never in himself. Most of all, there was missing, for whatever reason, the quality of rational and intellectual perception which is the balance wheel of the human being. There was, for the greater part of his life, a contempt for the accumulated wisdom of the past. We have produced in America many such primitives. Dreiser was one of them. A self-educated man may have a fool for a teacher. Dreiser did.

May 2, 1965

ANDREW TURNBULL

Thomas Wolfe

Thomas Wolfe after death, as in life, was the kind of writer and man whose breadth and wildness intimidated most critics and biographers. Yet, there were a few in his lifetime and afterward who saw him as he was and gave of themselves a matching gift to his. Maxwell Perkins, of course, was one. Aline Bernstein rode out their stormy love to be another.

The source of genius is too complex to reveal its wellsprings easily. But surely there was an element of what can only be called luck involved. This does not vitiate nor cheapen talent, drive; it doesn't guarantee happiness. Whatever the cycles of his reputation, Wolfe remains an original in American literature. Flaws and all, he has a claim to be regarded as one of a handful of American novelists who deserved to be called great.

The Wolfe penchant for this fortunate connection is nowhere better shown than in the superb biography *Thomas Wolfe* by Andrew Turnbull. The novelist had been dead five years when Turnbull, serving the U.S. Navy aboard a destroyer on convoy duty, picked up a copy of *You Can't Go Home Again*, was compelled by the story to read the other Wolfe novels.

The luck involved was this: Turnbull is the first biographer of Wolfe who was not challenged to match Wolfe's intoxicating style; he does not equate the autobiographical novels in an algebraic relationship with the realities of Wolfe's life. He is neither in competition, nor is he overwhelmed. Given complete access by the Wolfe family to the unpublished papers, interviewing several hundred people, combining his clear analytical talents with a felicitous style, he has given us the other side of the novels.

In an appendix he speaks of Max Perkins and Aline Bernstein as "those twin engines that got Wolfe's heavy plane off the ground." He is the third engine. And beyond that he is the one who gives us the design of the man.

After Wolfe's death, one of editor Perkins' colleagues at Scribners said to Perkins: "You and Aline made Tom." "No," said

Perkins, "Tom had the wit to find us." Perhaps. But in the case of Turnbull, it was good luck.

So many surprising things emerge in this biography that it may be said it is the first biography to comprehend the whole of Wolfe when, as it should be, the volume is read in conjunction with the novels. Properly, it is not a substitute for the novels but rather a complement. The Gant self-portrait has the distortions of fiction and imagination. Unquestionably there are elements of it which are based on the roiling life and character of Wolfe. But that was his face for the reader of novels to see. There is another face behind the mask. It is the latter which is revealed in this book.

What the reader of the biography gets is not only the life and times of a demonic, driven, word-intoxicated writer but a dual angle of vision, a sense of how life is transmuted into fiction. This does not solve the mystery of creativity but it enables us to witness it in process. We can compare the actual figures and events with the characters and situations caught on paper. We have in this book a lens bringing into focus the light out of its penumbra.

I spoke of surprises. Wolfe's mother, Julia, and his father, W. O., his brothers and sisters, his teachers (including the noted George Pierce Baker) are presented in perspective. They are *not* exactly the characters they were molded to be in Wolfe's novels. Again allowing for Wolfe's genius, his career as a writer, his life as a human being, his travels and his education all had an effect, became the context in which that genius bloomed.

Born in Asheville, N. C., the youngest son of a mismatched couple, the tensions of his childhood and youth were there—but never so clear as the fiction would make them. His father, a stonecutter, given to declaiming Shakespeare and to occasional drunken sprees, was in contrast to his hard-headed, money-conscious mother. This was no ordinary family. His first admirer, Mrs. Margaret Roberts (who was electrified by a "ratty-looking" theme submitted to her teacher husband by an 11-year-old Tom Wolfe), bears out Tom's description of his family as possessing "a mad, original, disturbing quality which they did not suspect."

The Wolfes," she said, "are not common people—but eccentricity plus. Perhaps the bit of unusualness in each flowered in Tom."

She was a wise mentor to the boy who read omnivorously, this "beanpole sprite of a fencerail thinness, with absurdly long legs," whose "glance was that of a trapped animal begging for release, who will tear your hand if you free him." She corrected his compositions: "Pegasus has to be controlled even though it must be by one who has no wings." His editor Perkins would have agreed.

Discontented, swinging between good humor and somber moods, "forever enlarging his scope and honing his awareness," Wolfe was an excellent student in those subjects he liked. And he was, despite his gawkiness and height, not the solitary he often described himself. He got along well—both at the University of North Carolina and at Harvard. It is not simply in retrospect that so many who knew him at the various stages of his life discerned the extraordinary in him.

That awareness and perception came early. Prof. W. S. Bernard drew Wolfe to Greek literature—the first of many surprises is Wolfe's appreciation of the Greek classical spirit, not as form, but as the penetration of the importance of life. "How right the Greeks were in seeing the world as 'object.' " The world of detail and the world as experience gave Wolfe his supple vocabulary. The unexpected death of a roommate sent him into a daze. He slept for the rest of the term in an armchair in the house of friends: "Why has he died? Where has he gone?" he kept asking.

Love, friendship, poverty, war, the land—all the experience he had or sought produced imaginative, reflective response. Books he read, not for dry detail but for their validation of life. They lived for him. In a Harvard campus restaurant, he could conjure up the spirit of Shakespeare and talk to him as though the great writer still lived. Madness? Perhaps. But that form which is imagination.

Prof. Frederick Koch, a zealous believer in folk theater, captured Wolfe and turned him to writing dramas and tragedies of the hill people. In one way this seemed a detour, for at North Carolina and Harvard, and beyond, Wolfe was to fling himself against the challenge of a medium too narrow to contain the range of his interest. But even this was indispensable. All experiences worked, even those which resulted in failure. . . .

It was the creative side which won. Wolfe was too fond of life, of the excitement and adventure of living, to accept the goad and discipline of criticism. "Ultimately I came back to the same blind faith. That life in itself was very full, that what failed in it was our own apprehension. Is not this the true romantic feeling—not to desire to escape life, but to prevent life from escaping you?"

Yet, as always for the romantic, it was death which fascinated him. The death of his father in 1922 helped crystallize his own goals. "It's hard to see a big, strong man break down and lose his strength. They drink life in with great gulps and their experience of pleasure and pain is crowded and poignant." It brought to mind the kind of genius he admired in literature; speaking of Byron, and surprisingly of Kipling, he said one had to go behind the "de- clamatory" to "recognize the colossal and unquenchable energy which generates their work."

Wolfe goes on: "This is what I understand by 'genius' and though a man's work might be as full of flaws as a Swiss cheese it will somehow continue to endure if only it has fire when all the faultless little concoctions of the faultless little anemics have been buried."

The biography stands as a great accomplishment in the field which Thomas Wolfe chose for himself, the transmutation of life into words. Julia Wolfe once wrote her son about words: "Make them shine, Tom. You are a star and you must make your words shine like stars."

Another sort of writing is beautifully demonstrated here. The biographer's word must be honed and polished to reflect the luminosity of another. That is an art, also. Turnbull's words shine like stars on the quiet, smooth surface of water.

January 28, 1968

ANDREW SINCLAIR

Dylan Thomas: No Man More Magical

> *To hell with everything except the inner necessity for expression and the medium of expression, everything except the great need of forever striving after this mystery and meaning I moan about.*
> *—Dylan Thomas at 18*

When young, Dylan Thomas, the intense red-haired angel of the Augustus John portrait, was ready to conquer London and the world. Word-intoxicated, filled with innocence and bluster, he played a hundred roles, the loquacious poet anxious to impress, the pouting cherub, the doomed consumptive asking for sympathy, the bold drinker and smoker, the would-be lover.

His talent was recognized early. He was hailed as the new bard of Wales, a lyric poet of great attainment, with lines that rolled out like peals of an organ: "And death shall have no dominion. / No more may gulls cry at their ears / Or waves break loud on the seashores . . . " He would have been an adornment to any age. But he was a man of a particular period and setting, and his declaration of independence was to be tested by the demands of life and celebrity. He wanted freedom from the split of his origins, between Welsh tradition and English expression, between the fierce, proud, disappointed education of his father and the warm, simple, sociability of his chapel-worshipping mother, between his father's atheism and his mother's religion, between the demands of the flesh and the hell-fire puritanism which were deep in him.

He could not consign to hell the demands of life and the world. For that hell was within him. "Which is the world?" he had written. "Of our two sleepings, which / Shall fall awake when cures and their itch / Raise up this red-eyed earth?"

Like many a celebrity—for he was that in addition to being a poet—his life, fashioned into myth and legend, in the end came close to eclipsing his work: the outrageous Dylan, the pub-crawler, lady-killer, cult-darling, reshaped into a gargoyle, helped to die by admirers in America, paying the price of breaking the rules, somehow vindicating the fantasies of the puritans about artists. For their magic, they must pay with their lives. He lay in his coffin, his face fleshy and painted, wearing a loud suit, with a carnation in his buttonhole, a music hall caricature rather than a dead poet.

Andrew Sinclair's biography is less concerned with de-mythologizing the cult hero than with restoring a sense of life and perspective, with doing justice to the poet and his work. He concedes that there is evidence to support a variety of renderings. Sinclair's purpose is to evoke the living man and the timeless poet.

Thomas was both poet and performer, bard and actor. He was his own best witness, self-critical, unsparing, mocking, capable of expressing the most painful truths while doing his comic turns. And beyond this, he was a child of his broadcast times, of radio and film, of the magnification of stardom, reaching a new mass audience for poetry, intersecting with a rebellion against the traditional captors and guardians of the art. He took it out of arid closets and precious circles and restored it to an insistent life. He used "the machines of the world I tick in and revolve in," the microphone and the phonograph record, inspired new lyricists of rock and folk.

"Man himself is a work," Thomas said, and he tried as hard to create a public self as he did any of his poems, plays and stories. He succeeded only too well. But it is the writing and not the life, the poet rather than the cult figure, by which Thomas must ultimately be judged. There was something of the clown in Thomas—he loved to joke, to poke fun, not least at himself.

He could claim: "I am a painstaking, conscientious, and in-volved and devious craftsman in words, however unsuccessful the result so often appears and to whatever wrong uses I may apply my technical paraphernalia. I use everything and anything to make my poems work and move in directions I want them to: old tricks, new tricks, puns, portmanteau-words, paradox, allusion, paranomasia, paragram, catachresis, slang, assonantal rhyme, vowel rhyme, sprung rhythm. Every device there is in language is there to be used if you will. Poets have got to enjoy themselves sometimes, and the twisting and convolutions of words, the inventions of contrivances, are all part of the joy that is part of the painful, voluntary work."

There are, of course, those who will argue that such self-conscious, process-conscious testimony is suspect, a part of posturing which denies that poetic genuis can ever be anything but a total mystery. But to question that rational, conscious decisions of selection and craft play any role is to reject any evidence which challenges the myth, to send the act of criticism into a purely romantic realm. It is as much a mistake as its polar opposite, the assumption that everything in the creative process can be reduced to analytical and rational factors.

It is more likely a mixture as Thomas himself was: puritan and hedonist, wild spirit and seeker after financial security, torn between Wales and England, country and city, peace and excitement, private face and public mask.

Saying this no more sums up Thomas than any other poet or artist, but at least it eases the tiptoeing around the white lamb or sacrificial bull which worship has made of the man. Drink may have ruined him, but equally it did not produce his poetry. The reverse is true. It was life, domestic tribulation, troubles with the tax man, bills, debts, the soap-opera stress which made him, like many another alcoholic, turn to the bottle.

His poetry was his strength and his salvation. He dramatized it all; that was his nature. But he was a poet first. The social mask he put on to protect the inward poet was to prove fatal.

It is not as a defender of the man, "in his going as in his living . . . bled dry by interested strangers," that Sinclair calls into question the interpretations of Caitlin Thomas and John Malcolm Brinnin. He reminds us that some of the poet's best writing was done within the months before his death:

> . . . And this last blessing most,
> That the closer I move
> To death, one man through his sundered hulks,
> The louder the sun blooms
> And the tusked, ramshackling sea exults.

If the *enfant terrible* was living out the role of self-destroyer, there is a suggestion that as performer he became trapped in the performance. There is plenty of evidence of his own puritanical disapproval, "the dollar-mad nightingale" in pursuit of naked women, the "beer-cheapened hoddy-noddy" with "his sodden bounce, his mis-theatrical-demeanor, the boastful tuppence." Sinclair makes a case that Thomas did not want to die, and that "in his last agony there seems to have been nobody who could restrain or help him, and nobody to admit responsibility for not being able to do so."

The more important point is that, unlike many writers sacrificed on the altar of celebrity, unlike, say Fitzgerald, Thomas' life is not more interesting, not more eloquent than his work. Had he lived in a less-iconized time, had we known little or nothing of his experiences, as little as we know of Chaucer or Villon or even Shakespeare, the memorable lines would remain beyond any portrait.

The fact is that we do know what happened and Sinclair's great contribution is to connect the work and the man, his setting and his times, his vibrant readings on radio and in lecture hall, his attempts to restore the face-to-face contact between poet and listener, to take poems out of the closet, the dissection of classroom into an oral and aural experience. It brought him prominence and fame, and stardom ate away at him as much as it did to movie actors.

"Now I am no more no more," he wrote in *Lament*, "And a black reward for a roaring life / (Sighed the old ram rod, dying of strangers) . . ."

That he was a genius is beyond doubt. That his appetites, desires, aspirations and needs, however theatrically magnified, were not so different from others of his age is less apparent but no less surely true. The magic of talent elevated his words, made them potent and transcendent. But the fears and timidities, the shyness and insecurity were always there. Poetry and performance gave him a certain power and he took advantage of it. He paid a high price for what was given him, but in return left us poems of universal power:

To take to give is all, return what is
Hungrily given
Puffing the pounds of manna up through the dew to heaven,
The lovely gift of gab bangs back on a blind shaft . . .

He took all that life had offered him, not only the storied past, man as a metaphor, the hieroglyphic of nature, but also the challenge of his particular times:

In this our age the gunman and his moll,
The one-dimensional ghosts, love on a reel,
Strange to our solid eye,
And speak their midnight nothings as they swell;
When cameras shut they hurry to their hole . . .
This is the world: the lying likeness of
Our strips of stuff that tatter us as we move
Loving and being loth;
The dream that kicks the buried from their sack
And lets their trash be honored as the quick.
This is the world. Have faith.

November 16, 1975

LAWRANCE THOMPSON

Robert Frost: The Years of Triumph

In order to know where we are we must know opposites.
—Robert Frost, 1935

He was a handsome man and in his public image a charming one. For those who heard him reading his poems, or sat before him in the classrooms where he held forth on writing, Robert Frost seemed the apotheosis of the American poet: sprung from the soil, simple, casual, skeptical, deliberate, wise. He was to become the best-known and best-loved poet in 20th-century America, standing for the old virtues, the solid roots, the archetypal experiences of New England made universal by his art.

The truth about him was never so simple. When he returned at the age of 40 from England, where his first literary triumph sharpened his ever-present appetite for recognition, hardly anyone here knew anything about him. The American edition of *North of Boston* had just appeared and one reviewer asked in print, "Who is Robert Frost?"

It is this question which is answered in satisfying detail by his official biographer, Lawrance Thompson, in the second volume of what promises to be one of the best literary biographies of our time.

The image of "the plain New Hampshire farmer" is not a false one, it is simply not the whole truth. The man who wrote of contraries in "West-Running Brook" touched the theme many times:

> *It is this backward movement toward the source,*
> *Against the stream, that most of us see ourselves in,*
> *The tribute of the current to the source.*
> *It is from this in nature we are from.*
> *It is most us.*

Behind simplicity was complexity, behind the surface calm was chaos, behind the Spartan was the Athenian, behind the casualness was excitement and emotion. His early life in San Francisco where he witnessed domestic strife, where his father seemingly rejected the austere puritanism of New England, where he suffered slight and punishment, had made him vow to rise in triumph and vindication. Poetry was to be the means.

In public once, Frost said, "Don't trust me too far. I'm liable to tell you anything. Trust me on the poetry, but don't trust me on my life. Check up on me some."

This is precisely what Thompson has done. But, equally he has retained a critical perspective. With the materials he has gathered, the biographer could have stressed the fantasies and contradictions, the gossip (Frost himself loved to gossip which he found another means of triumphing over his enemies, never hesitating to alter the facts), the unappealing nether side of the man. Instead, he has tried to present "bursting unity of opposites" in balance and sympathy.

For when we come to the core, what man has not blurred the edges of his reality with fiction? And what man has not questioned the authenticity of his own identity?

Against the failures and disappointments which took him to early middle age, Frost's need to succeed not only persisted but grew stronger. In 1915 he began to receive the adulation he so desperately needed. In a literary sense, these were the years of triumph. But as so often happens, the dreams which come true can hardly satisfy needs so rooted in compulsion.

There is not much happiness in these pages. His marriage was stormy and punitive, though he loved his wife. His family was scourged by sickness. His teaching was marred by the jealousy of his colleagues. And the success of other poets was regarded by him as an affront. Much of his psychic energy went into keeping the mask of confidence on his face. Below was fear and jealousy. He envied Edwin Arlington Robinson when the latter was his serious competitor, felt relief when Robinson's reputation began to slip. He cultivated Amy Lowell, but slighted her just before her death and suffered the pangs of guilt for it. He took an "evil pleasure" in his triumph over Edna St. Vincent Millay when he was elected to the American Academy in 1930. Frost justified his attitude: "There can be only one heavyweight champion at a time."

Not very pleasant in a poet, this ferocious design. Yet, as we read this somber history of domestic tribulation, of anxiety, of honor that fails to assuage, of attack and bitterness, we begin to see something that almost any teacher of creative writing knows. Talent is one thing, essential, but not the driving demon of genius. It is a fact, unpleasant to contemplate, that very often talent must have this other muscle. It is no accident that Maupassant spoke of it in his advice to a young writer: "Be brutal." The brutality he referred to is precisely that which sends a boxer to the top. It works for the poet as well.

The tensions and turbulence of Frost's inner life, his fantasies of triumph and his fears of failure, became the engine of his genius. " . . . Oh, the agitated heart till someone really finds us out," is a cry, one of many, revealing the source. Frost once said, "And I suppose I am a brute . . ." and later, "A real artist delights in roughness for what he can do to it. He's the brute who can knock the corners off the marble block and drag the unbedded beauty out of bed."

This is not the whole explanation of Frost, obviously not. And it does not comport well with our own image of the poet, for we want to believe, with the romantics, in a poet hero, sensitive, wholly worthy, somehow too good for the Philistine world. It is an undeniable shock to see Frost gossiping about the adulteries of a village girl, target of angry outbursts by his wife and children, campaigning for his books, fertilizing the plant of his reputation, cultivating those who can help such as the influential critic Bernard DeVoto, suppressing his animosity against the powerful Ellery Sedgwick of *Atlantic Monthly*, trying to arrange favorable reviews. "I am become my own salesman," he said.

Out of these though another part of the man emerges. There is Yang and Yin in this complex personality. Love and hate are in him, meanness and charity, courage and fear. It is the measure of this biography that we begin to see him whole. For each trait has its contrary and opposite, helps him to penetrate and define life, urges him to the truth behind the myths and mysteries, " . . . trying to decide between God and the devil . . . between endless other things in pairs ordained to everlasting opposition."

When he sums up, "all in all it has been such a lucky and original life that I can't understand my ever being for a moment cross or difficult or dissatisfied or cast down," we know the irony for we have seen him as he really was. This is his myth-making as his sometime denial of his puritanism. In the end he was forced to concede his tie with puritanism, though he gave it his own interpretation: "And the thing New England gave most to America was the thing I am talking about: stubborn clinging to meaning— to purify words until they meant again what they should mean. Puritanism had that meaning entirely: a purifying of words and a renewal of words and a renewal of meaning. That's what brought the Puritans to America, and that's what kept them believing . . ."

Even here we have been alerted by the sum of experience in the biography to question. Suddenly, we are forced like the poet himself to read the ambiguities underneath. Strangely enough the life reminds us of Hawthorne's parables. Nothing is quite what it seems. But, the whole of the book does what every literary biography should. It illuminates the process of creation and sets the context of expression. Now the lines in "West-Running Brook" pierce our consciousness:

> *The black stream, catching on a sunken rock,*
> *Flung backward on itself in one white wave,*
> *And the white water rode the black forever . . .*
> *But, that rock of assertion is what is important.*

From Henri Bergson, Frost takes the notion of an *elan vital*, "some strange resistance in itself, / Not just a swerving, but a throwing back, / As if regret were in it and were sacred."

If meaning is all, then this biography serves Frost superbly. For it makes his meaning as a man more clear, and the meaning of art deeper. We know the source of his irony ("a kind of guardedness") and of his humor ("the most engaging cowardice"), the definition of his poetic thinking ("that attempt to say matter in terms of spirit and spirit in terms of matter"), and his belief that "a little thing touches a larger thing."

He was not the best of men nor the worst, but one whose human experience and weakness was somehow translated into a strength which echoed in ulterior meaning for most who read his work. "All that an artist needs," he once said, "is samples." In his life and temperament, he found enough of them.

September 13, 1970

HANNAH TILLICH

From Time to Time

Hannah Tillich, widow of theologian Paul Tillich, has written an agonizingly honest and deeply moving account of her life. Her husband, as she says, "was the event in my life," but do not assume that this work is a mere eulogy of the man. It is the unsparing story, on many levels, poetry, parable and detailed chronicle, of the struggle for an identity inside and outside of marriage.

The sensational aspects have already been reported in the encapsulated versions of news magazines. Paul Tillich was a man hungry for love. No one woman could satisfy him completely. His life was not only that of a thinker and writer, a philosopher ministering to the malaise of the time. It was also a search on less elevated levels for companionship, passion, adventure. Hannah knew of these matters from an early time, but this did not ease the torment.

It is a comment on the role of woman that our culture, committed to monogamy, tormented by the attractions of infidelity, places the greater burden on the wife. No matter how emancipated our talk, how free-ranging our view of open marriage, our leaning on divorce, the reality of a haunted past lingers. The banality—"it is the woman who pays"—is still true enough.

Yet, if this were merely a work of self-pity, a posthumous vindictiveness, it would not be so worthy of our attention. Hannah Tillich struggles not for a camouflaged dignity but for the much more difficult goal, to understand the significance of her life, and their life together, their separate identity. It is the knottiest problem of the relationship between the sexes, not only the question of double standards, but the essence of that most paradoxical human emotion, love.

It is not totally resolved in these pages. It is asking too much to hope for. The problem is raised honestly and forthrightly, with a minimum of self-indulgence. If love is in part selflessness, what portion of self remains to the lover, to the beloved? Is freedom within marriage possible? Or is marriage inevitably a process producing not two individuals but one creature, two-headed, four-handed, four-legged, unnatural?

If men and women were only intellectual beings, able to embrace a convincing ideology and live their lives according to it, this would be relatively simple. But men and women are too complex for this facile answer.

Indeed, the detailed narrative of the experience of Hannah and Paul Tillich is in itself the best evidence that there is too much more in the enterprise. The world with its upsets and demands, flights and punishments; children with their rights and presences; the past with its burdens of value and belief; places and settings, needs to earn a living, to express ideas. All are part.

If there was a fixation on the infidelities of Paulus (Hannah's name for him), the book would have its merits. It is more than this. The infidelities (the word itself is significant) cannot be ignored. But, in the end, they are also metaphors for other things. The love here is expressed in the acceptance of the man as a whole, complete with flaws and virtues.

She speaks of the house in which they lived in East Hampton, the house she had insisted they buy "for such a sordid reason, on my insistence. Our marriage had been broken into small pieces by the relentless assault of the many women—not only his sweetheart who functioned as his secretary and lived across the street from us in New York, but the émigré friends, newcomers, students, socialites, wives of friends. I had tried to get away. I had taken an extra course so I could teach in this country, to earn my own money. But how could I get away from a man whose life I had lived, whose children I had borne, whose thoughts I could guess, who was as close to me as my own heartbeat?"

She wanted the house for retreat from the see-saw of suffering and hate, the childish efforts to hide his affairs, from the letters and notes which were the constant reminders of the "demon" within him. Yet, it was the house which drew him back. Not only a residence but a symbol of something which went beyond the physical. There are other elements in relationship.

His death was release for her on one level. On a deeper level it forced her back to "try to come to an awareness of what I had lived," to learn to see herself as she was. She would go on living. This book is an expression of that search for significance and meaning, often confused, sometimes brilliant, always painfully honest.

November 21, 1973

JOHN LEGGETT

Ross and Tom: Two American Tragedies

The novelists Ross Lockridge Jr. and Thomas Heggen never met, though they knew of each other and shared some experiences. Both were talented young writers; both originated in the Midwest; they had the same publisher (Houghton Mifflin of Boston); both achieved wealth and fame with their first—and last—books, then found that success had dried out their will and capacity to write and brought depression in its wake.

Ross Lockridge Jr., shortly after the publication in 1948 of *Raintree County*, went into the garage of his new home, shut the door, started the engine of his new car and was later found dead. Tom Heggen, addicted to barbiturates and a heavy drinker, was found lifeless in his bath in 1949.

John Leggett, a novelist and contemporary of the two men, did not knew either of them personally. But he had a more than melancholy curiosity about them. "Ross, Tom and I grew up to the same music, worshiping the same idols, suffering from the same inhibitions.

"It was remarkably easy for me to slip into their adolescent skins. As an adult and writer, I could recognize in those highs of self-certainty, in those plunging lows of self-doubt, my own emotional weather. Finally, in each of their natures—one black, reckless; the other a marching band of virtues—I saw two halves of my own."

But if there are unities, there is no facile single theme, no easy solution. True, there are lessons to be drawn about the nature of success in America—the bitch goddess William Dean Howells wrote about; about celebrity, about the nature of the creative process, about the puritan impulse in American life, about publishing itself—that marriage of business and art, about perfectionism and recognition. No one who has had anything to do with the literary life in America—or, for that matter, with the pursuit of achievement in America—can fail to hear the relevant echoes. The book, quite apart from its fascinating narrative, its Rashomon quality of detection, has as much to say about the nature and quality of ourselves as about the two protagonists.

Despite the similarities in their backgrounds, the two men could scarcely have been less alike in their personalities. Lockridge was the all-American boy, "an oak of prudence and industry," handsome, reliable, confident. He married his hometown sweetheart, fathered four children, rarely drank and never smoked, remained faithful, worked passionately on his novel, believed in it, single-mindedly devoted himself to its promotion.

Heggen was the more obviously troubled. Though equally competitive, he disguised his ambition with a mischievous diffidence. If Lockridge pursued success, success chased Heggen. The latter's wartime marriage foundered quickly. A succession of unsatisfying affairs seemed to indicate an inability to love or be loved. Alcohol and pills blurred the frustration, added to the block. Though a tide of money came from *Mister Roberts* as novel and play, the latter work—written first in collaboration with Max Shulman, later with Josh Logan—sapped Heggen's feeling that he was his own man. Though he tried, he could not write independently again.

That "wondrous lovely storm that drove me," as Willa Cather wrote in *The Song of the Lark*, blew out for both men. Success not only did not bring happiness, it brought despair and depression. For Lockridge, certainly, and probably as well for Heggen, the very materials of his life and past were transmuted into fiction, took on an existence of their own, undermining—at least, in his own view—the propriety of private relationships made public and his own worthiness for success, which involved compromises or "sellouts" that produced unbearable guilt.

"In a very real sense, the writer writes in order to teach himself, to understand himself, to satisfy himself," Alfred Kazin has written. "The publishing of his ideas, though it brings gratifications, is a curious anticlimax."

It is not difficult to see why. Matter consciously or unconsciously transferred to the page, written out, must leave, for a moment or for a long time, a hollowness, an exposure, a vulnerability.

Publishers, book reviewers, teachers of creative writing, editors recognize the signs. The symptoms ape the neurotic and psychotic: paranoia, manic-depressive syndrome, breakdown, hostility and, worst of all, blocks against writing. In most writers the symptoms disappear or are suppressed. In some they are exacerbated by the very trappings of success.

Lockridge's celebrated conflict with his publishers, his suspicions and instructions, his resentments and collisions, were examples of such symptoms. He felt cheated, misused, exploited, anxious and suspicious. If, toward the end, he suppressed these feelings, the anger turned inward and became depression for which neither electric shock therapy nor the goodwill and concern shown by those who loved him, nor even the hope of future writing, could provide solace or respite.

Heggen surely felt some of the same impulses though they rarely came to the surface, muddled and muzzy as he often was from drink. His mode of coping, if it could be called that, attempted to deflect the urgency by humor, or by practical jokes, or by the cloak of seeming not to care. But he did care, and his anger occasionally erupted, directed against collaborators with whom he competed and by whom he felt betrayed.

Yet, in fairness, I think, there is little objective evidence that the wildest concerns of Lockridge about his publishers or of Heggen about his collaborators are borne out here. Houghton Mifflin and its editors not only treated Lockridge fairly but, in view of the confidence they displayed in *Raintree County*—after all, just a first novel—many would say generously. Nor could Heggen's collaborators—themselves ambitious and talented men, flawed in their ways as Heggen was in his—be blamed for his predicament.

The characters emerge then as neither villains nor heroes, nor even solely as protagonists in a moral tale. It is no small accomplishment, considering that a retrospective view invites the playing out of encompassing myths: the Aztec sacrifice of writers to the goddess of American material success, the puritan echo of the Faustian compact, the Freudian explanations of father rivalry and mother appeal.

What the work says to me is not that we have advanced beyond classical tragedy but that, in the fragmented world of the present or recent past, more mysteries remain. Truth no longer seems so manageable. The connections between private fate and public culture are there, and throughout the narrative Leggett recognizes them.

But the assurance is gone. In the effort to be true to the characters and their lives and experiences, causation can only be suggested. That Lockridge and Heggen each may have been motivated to write and to succeed in writing by feelings of shyness and inadequacy, that each may have been plagued by expectations placed on him by his parents, that each may have been unconsciously driven by the need to surpass his father, to earn the place sought in a mother's demands, that the compromises each made (Lockridge to win the MGM prize or Book of the Month acceptance, Heggen to collaborate to assure the success of the adaptation on stage) proved a Faustian pact, that each stored up a sense of betrayal and therefore guilt—all these possibilities have the heft and feel of recognizable truth.

Leggett says that there was nothing accidental about Lockridge's life: "It is true tragedy, the end inevitable, carefully prepared in the beginnings," in his mother's will "to fulfill her father's dream of literary accomplishment, then in the promise and death of her first son, then in vague disappointments by her husband, a second son and daughter and, finally, in Ross's acceptance of her challenge."

And in the case of Heggen, there is evidence of the death wish—in his novel and in a few short stories, in his rebellion against paternal authority (in school, in the Navy, at work for the *Reader's Digest*), in his introjection of his mother's mandate, called from the window of his house as he lay stretched out on the lawn: "Are you going to spend all day on your backside? How do you expect to make anything of yourself?"

The inevitability is there only because we know the end of each story. This gives power to the telling, sharpens the scrambling desperate urge to win which was part of Lockridge's motivation and makes more bitter each sign of success when it fails to assuage the depression, makes more compelling Heggen's search for the answers.

If I have concentrated on these generalities, the text itself is specific. Leggett has tirelessly sought out the evidence of document and witness, so that the chronicles come alive in setting, time, incident and action. We are given access to the two men's lives insofar as it is possible to reconstruct them.

For writers and aspiring writers (and how many of us are not in the latter category?), this book is indispensable reading. The conclusions are not so important as the sense of recognition we feel for fellow human beings whose lives in some way touch our own, not only in their work and private characters, but in their efforts to somehow achieve some meaning.

"Success itself, even when we know it to be fantasy, holds out such promise to us all—fame, money, power and love. They are reasonable promises to the soundest minds, and the compulsion to succeed can become an obsession over which no one has control." Yet, success is an outward thing. Fulfillment is what eluded these two young men. That is the deeper mystery, and it allows us no righteousness or condescension.

September 1, 1974

CARLOS BAKER

Ernest Hemingway: A Life Story

"An enormous fund of misinformation about his life is already in print. Apart from stating the facts about his life and work, no attempt has been made to refute errors that have hitherto passed as truths," Carlos Baker warns us.

Part of the myth and the misinformation came from Hemingway himself, for he was in one of the many roles of his life, "a romantic liar for whom the line between fact and fiction was thinner than a hair, who invented stories for a living and saw no reason to turn off the mechanism when writing letters or conversing with friends and acquaintances."

It is the acceptance of the whole man with his contradictions and aspirations which makes this a great biography. Seven years in the making, the work reflects with clarity and force the meticulous research which went into it. Countless interviews with people who knew him well and slightly from his earliest days to his death, access to some 2,500 letters from Hemingway and as many to him, his own diaries, his unpublished works, inspection of the places which played a part in his life and work, give satisfying detail to the book.

That felicitous phrase from Joyce's *Portrait of the Artist as a Young Man*, "to re-create life out of life . . ." is an accurate statement of the accomplishment. Yet, Prof. Baker tells us, this is not "a definitive biography," and no "thesis" biography. Rather, it is "an approximation," an attempt to record the complexity of a man who was a "romantic activist, the center and in many ways the originator of his own universe."

There are certain scenes, incidents and anecdotes which are probably impossible to relate exactly as happened. One, for example, in Costello's Bar where Hemingway broke a blackthorn stick given to John O'Hara by John Dos Passos has several versions. In the notes (which must be read) John Hersey, who arrived after the incident and was told about it by Costello, says the incident is "a beautiful example of Tolstoy's dictum that as soon as an event has taken place, it becomes as many events as it had witnesses, for they all tell different stories."

Some of the statements have a kind of prescience which may be suspect. Hemingway's grandfather, who died when Ernest was just short of six years old, is quoted as having remarked, just after the boy burst in with the news that he had stopped a runaway horse single-handed, "Mark my words . . . this boy is going to be heard from some day. If he uses his imagination for good purposes, he'll be famous, but if he starts the wrong way, with all his energy, he'll end in jail."

Yet, the charisma, or whatever it was, emanated from the youth and the man. Hemingway, unpublished as a writer and unknown except to a small circle of friends, was given extraordinary introductions to people in Paris by Sherwood Anderson, who referred to him as "a quite wonderful newspaperman" whose "extraordinary talent" would take him far beyond journalism.

Hemingway's writing alone cannot account for the mystique which developed around him, for the influence he brought to bear on the writing of the 20th century. This takes nothing away from it; either its strengths or its occasional weaknesses. His life, his way of life, his personality, his adventures are all part of that staggering influence.

He was born into a period in American life in which the writer had begun to be a heroic figure, a romantic and celebrated personage. Twain and Stephen Crane and Richard Harding Davis and others played this role before him. Hemingway was to give it the ultimate style. It is no accident, for example, that he liked and felt close to Gary Cooper. There was a part of him which was movie star.

His life comported well with the time. Out of the Midwest he came, the Midwest in its insular and conventional ways, but also from the Midwest with its pretensions to art and music (his mother's influence), with its outdoor life of hunting and fishing, its heritage of Huck Finn and Tom Sawyer, its rebellions and ferments, its memory of the Civil War (both his grandfathers had fought and had known the tests of courage and death).

It does not explain everything; nothing explains everything.

But, it is a context. The talent he had, the gift for observation and listening, a sense of the dramatic, an endless appetite for movement, action, contention. From hunting and fishing to boxing, from boxing to war, from war to the bullring, from the bullring back to hunting and big-game fishing. And always he was drawn to the mystery and complexity of human experience: love, cowardice and courage, endurance and luck, that vast cosmic void that Goya called *Nada*. Ultimately, he lived by another aphorism, closely linked to his fiction and his life: *Il faut (d'abord) durer* (It must, first of all, endure).

He learned that the confidence and arrogance of youth, the power and flush of men in the strength of their days, must give way to the destiny of the body aging and the mind going soft. Once in a conversation with an Army psychiatrist on the nature of battle fatigue, Hemingway mocked the doctor, said he knew nothing of brave men, only of neurotics. He was cruel as he could be, and one witness called him gross and cruel, suggested a trace of anti-Semitism (not unknown in other incidents of his life) in his treatment of the doctor.

After Hemingway had rapped psychiatry, the doctor predicted, "You'll be coming to me yet." The prediction came true in 1960 when he went to the Mayo Brothers clinic. It fulfilled a prediction of his own, often repeated to friends: "Whatever we say we will never do we are sure to do sooner or later."

He was a contradictory, paradoxical man. Perhaps all great men must be. Certainly those who invite myth-making, for there is to be found evidence for everything and its opposite in such lives. A discerning biographer does not retreat from this condition. And that is why this work comes so close to bringing the man alive through the mosaic of a thousand pictures, by those who loved, admired, worshipped him, and those who hated him or part of him, or felt betrayed by him.

His life was in many ways an odyssey—Huck Finn and Ulysses combined in a handsome, tall, vivid American, in search of something in Paris or Greece, Italy or Spain, the waters of the Caribbean or the jungles of Africa. From the materials of his own experience—and that of others, for he was a great borrower—he wrought his stories and books. He was a fine journalist. And he wanted something more. He wanted a way of writing which would cut through to the heart of things. He knew much about the process of writing, the agonies and loneliness of putting words on paper. He was constantly fearful that he would lose the gift. Early, before anything much had been published, he wrote of a period in Rapallo: "It was a very bad time and I did not think I could write anymore."

He was brutal. Everyone he knew could be captured and caricatured, if necessary, on paper. For some reason he was especially satirical of those who had helped him. Robert McAlmon was one of these—there were many others. McAlmon saw him "at times . . . deliberately hard-boiled and case-hardened. Again he appeared deliberately innocent, sentimental, the hurt, soft, but fairly sensitive boy trying to conceal hurt, wanting to be brave, not bitter or cynical but being somewhat both, and somehow on the defensive, suspicions lurking in his peering analytic glances at a person to whom he was talking."

Drinking was both release and exposure for him. It could explain the constant contradictions in traits seen at various times by those who knew him: kindness and brutality, candor and disingenuousness, shyness and bragging, toughness and sentimentality, capacity for affection and hostility.

In Italy, he was wounded and it was the beginning of a life-long test of courage and confrontation with death. His actions were heroic, not as heroic as some have made out, nor as exaggerated as others have contended. His legs badly cut by shrapnel, he carried another wounded man 200 yards to safety. When he returned from Italy to his parents' home in Oak Park, the contrast was so great that he could never again be satisfied with the secure and tranquil life of his early years.

"All you have to do is write one true sentence," he decided in Paris in 1922. "Write the truest sentence you know." It had to come out of one's experience. He distrusted rhetoric and college education and high-flown discussions of art. "Artist, art, artistic!" he cried to his friends in Chicago. "Can't we ever hear the last of that stuff?"

Yet, he could not help being in the center of it. He had climbed to the top of the mountain and all around were the young and the hungry writers anxious to excel in life and writing—Mailer and Jones and Irwin Shaw (whose jaw he threatened to break after reading *The Young Lions,* but he didn't when he met him in Costello's), and the college professors writing books about him and his work. He had become king and the crown weighed heavily on him.

The years of fame were filled with absurdities, the Nobel Prize and challenges to duels, moments of respite and the pursuit of hangers-on and publicity seekers. In the end, he had become Papa, old and tired and sick. Andrew Turnbull, biographer of Fitzgerald, spoke with him a year before his death, felt there was something "staged and put on" about the old man, but that there was also "a great dignity" which "flowed from his tall lurching frame and his sad mask of a face."

In the end, the enemy came not as in war, but in the fear of persecution, in depression, in "crack-up" (the same phrase Fitzgerald had used). For a time, he thought he could make it back, for he had been in the black depths before a hundred times. He tried. A note sent to the 9-year-old son of his doctor (the boy was in the hospital) seemed to call up the better past—"I never knew anything about the upper Mississippi before and it is really a very beautiful country and there are plenty of pheasants and ducks in the fall."

But it was not to be. The odyssey ended in the hallway of his home in Idaho where he took his own life. *"Il faut (apres tout) mourir."*

April 27, 1969

WORKS

*"The work of a man for whom art
and life are inextricably melded."*

—R. K.

The Summing Up

A new paperback edition of Somerset Maugham's gave me the excuse to reread this remarkable work. I revise my opinion upward with each reading. . . .

It is, as is most of Maugham's fiction and drama, deceptively simple. The wisdom and perception are not likely to be found in a first reading. It is intended neither as a textbook for writers nor an autobiography; yet, it turns out to be both. "In this book," Maughan writes, "I am going to try to sort out my thoughts on the subjects which have chiefly interested me during the course of my life . . . It has seemed to me that if I should set them down in some sort of order I should see for myself more distinctly what they really were and so might get some kind of coherence into them."

At once we see the difference between Maugham and the predominant mode of 20th-century writers. Experience and observation concern him; introspection is the least of his interests—as a writer. "I saw so many people who excited my fancy, that I had no time to reflect. The experience of the moment was so vivid that I could not attune my mind to introspection."

I think it is this quality, this lack of intellectual and artistic pretention which has thrown so many critics off. We learn in this book that Maugham was not unaware of the requirements for critical acceptance. Indeed, the whole book may be read as a gentle reminder that the storyteller's first concern is to entertain. The deeper levels are there beyond plot and action, dialog and characterization.

He has a sense of perspective about himself. One cannot help contrasting Maugham to, say, such self-advertising writers as Norman Mailer. "I must write," Maugham goes on, "as though I were a person of importance; and indeed, I am—to myself. To myself I am the most important person in the world; though I do not forget that, not even taking into consideration so grand a conception as the Absolute, I am of no consequence whatever. . . . Though I may seem to write as though significance must necessarily be attached to certain of my works, I mean only that they are of moment to me . . . I think few serious writers, by which I do not only mean writers of serious things, can be entirely indifferent to the fate that will befall their works after their death."

Yet, this fate is to an extent out of the hands of writers. What is in the range of their control is experience, natural aptitude, instinct. If Maugham says anything, it is write what you are and what you perceive in the world about you. You cannot be anyone else.

Typical of *The Summing Up* is Maugham's account of his decision to expand his mastery of "the delicate art" of description. At the time he began to write, a florid prose was admired. Richness of texture was sought by means of a jewelled phrase and sentences stiff with exotic epithets.

Walter Pater was the model. Maugham's "common sense" told him that Pater's work was "anaemic stuff."

"But I would not listen to my common sense. I persuaded myself that this was the height of culture and turned a scornful shoulder on the outside world where men shouted and swore, played the fool, wenched and got drunk. I read *Intentions* and *The Picture of Dorian Gray*. I was intoxicated by the colour and rareness of the fantastic words . . . Shocked by the poverty of my own vocabulary, I went to the British Museum and noted down the names of curious jewels, the Byzantine hues of old enamel, the sensual feel of textiles, and made elaborate sentences to bring them in. Fortunately I could never find an opportunity to use them and they lie there yet in an old notebook ready for anyone who has a mind to write nonsense."

He goes on with a sense of candor and honest self-criticism which is refreshing and admirable, reveals gradually the making of a writer. The great lessons here do not lie in dicta or formulae. Rather, it is the style, the way of looking at experience and life, the calculus of experience and fiction, which may illuminate for other writers—and readers as well—what constitutes the problem.

For Maugham, the goals were "lucidity, simplicity, and euphony." For others, these may differ. But the long life of a master story teller is filled with guideposts for that search.

August 2, 1967

Henry Miller

Henry Miller's Book of Friends:
A Tribute to Friends of Long Ago

You can take the boy out of Brooklyn, but you can't take Brooklyn out of the boy. This is particularly true of Henry Miller, the Columbus of the Fourteenth Ward, whose writing has been one long log of reminiscences, who has never run out of experiences to report. Miller is interesting precisely because he is unabashedly interested in himself and what has happened to him, the constant discoverer of new worlds.

Here are the friendships of his youth, a succession of sketches which characteristically are as much about Miller as about those who are its subjects—pals, buddies, idols, rivals, alter egos: Stasiu, Joey and Tony, Cousin Henry, Joe O'Regan, Max Winthrop, Alec Considine and others.

Don't expect more than a tinge of nostalgia and sentiment. At 84, Miller is still the essential reporter—candid, honest, curious, the natural heir to those narcissists, Pepys and Boswell. Miller's friends are special kinds of mirrors and as he looks back at them and into them, seeing himself as shaped, inspired, contrasted with each of them, he recalls the Brooklyn which made him, his biases, his dreams, his loves.

Much of this has been written about before, yet Miller manages to give it a sense of freshness and vigor.

The reason is to be found in Miller's character as a writer. He cannot dissemble. He will not spare himself or others. Sometimes this quality emerges as grotesque or caricatured or self-indulgent. But the more you read of Miller the more you realize that this ingenuousness—this freedom from reserve, restraint, dissimulation, this seeming artlessness and innocence—is engaging and the source of his strength. I am not talking about life. He is as capable of falsehood, cheating, hatred, prejudice, envy and bullying theatrics as he is of loyalty, gratitude, admiration and generosity.

Writing is his art; debts are paid in the best currency, the truth insofar as he can see it and particularly since he has been given the last word.

We begin to see friendship as education, as love, as filling out the vocabulary of life so that books could become more meaningful.

How could you understand malice without meeting Sylvester, the church robber with the face of a cherub by Fra Angelico? Or know the reckless, impetuous criminal without knowing Alfie Melta? How could Miller not admire his cousin Henry, who commanded affection and respect, and though Miller had not yet shown any aptitude for creativity, believed in his worth?

The repayment of all this is to capture and hold the territory and the people. " . . . A life without friends is no life, however snug and secure it may be. When I say friends I mean *friends*. Not anybody and everybody can be your friend. It must be someone as close to you as your skin, someone who imparts color, drama, meaning to your life. Something the other side of love yet including love . . . A friend furnishes you with a thousand eyes, like the goddess Indra. Through your friends you live untold lives. You see in other dimensions. You live upside down and inside out. You are never alone, never will be alone if every last one of your friends should disappear from the face of the earth."

March 4, 1976

HARRY GOLDEN

Only in America

It is an understatement to say that the *Carolina Israelite* is an unusual newspaper. The truth is that this monthly journal is unique.

And the reason that it is unique lies in the personality of its editor and publisher, Harry Golden, a cigar-chewing son of an immigrant, brought up on the Lower East Side, educated in the public schools of New York City and now a resident of Charlotte, N.C.

Mr. Golden's newspaper is printed entirely in English. In its columns you will find no "news," personals, socials or press releases. With the exception of a few "Letters to the Editor" and an occasional book review by one of his sons, the entire paper is written by the editor in the form of editorials ranging in length from 20 words ("How Dr. Samuel Johnson Prepared Oysters") to 3000 words ("Sweet Daddy Grace, the Southern Father Divine").

I have been a subscriber to this personal journal for some years and have often wondered why a collection of Mr. Golden's essays on life, liberty and the pursuit of happiness has not been made into a book. Well, now they have—a marvelous book filled with the special Golden flavor. It's called *Only in America* and reading it will show you why the *Carolina Israelite* is read and enjoyed by the most unlikely people in the most unlikely places.

The title of Mr. Golden's book comes from his favorite phrase: "It could happen only in America." Only in America could a double carpetbagger find his way to the South, speak his mind even on those subjects which the South finds extremely touchy and be accepted as a member of the community even though his creed is nonconformity. And he is accepted: when he wrote an editorial asking "Am I a Tar Heel?" some of the mighty daily papers wrote editorials answering with an emphatic yes! When his offices burned down, the response in aid and well wishes was heartwarming proof of his acceptance. . . .

Whether Golden is writing "Why I never Bawl Out a Waitress"

("The scientists have found out that the farther you go out in space with the telescopes the thicker the gallaxies become, and there are billions and billions as yet uncovered. When you think of this, it's silly to worry whether the waitress brought you string beans instead of limas.") or "They Never Met a Payroll" ("1–Copernicus, 2–Galileo, 3–Newton, 4–Einstein."), he manages to bring in the product of his voracious reading and scholarship.

No topic is outside his ken. He will take on segregation with his Vertical Negro Plan, Jewish snobbishness or gentile snobbishness, death, bread, morals, mother love, Julius Caesar and Pompey, Tammany and the Democratic Party, Galli Curci and bubble gum. You name it—he's written about it.

His reminiscences of life on the Lower East Side are a favorite with his readers, most of whom have never tasted gefilte fish or pickled herring.

Harry Golden reaches across the differences to touch experiences which are universal. Over and over again, his words carry this conviction. It is his creed, simply expressed: "I believe, too, that 'Let us not stick our necks out' or 'Let someone else talk on that subject' are the watchwords of the ghetto, and I do not believe in ghettos: white, black or Puerto Rican."

And as for being a gadfly, Harry Golden writes: "The letters I receive from Jews and Christians have repaid me for my efforts . . . I am as happy as a mouse in a cooky jar."

August 13, 1959

Donald M. Frame, *Trans.*

The Complete Essays of Montaigne

Pascal perhaps best of all defined the source of Montaigne's continuing worth as a writer: "It is not in Montaigne, but in myself, that I find all I see in him."

Pascal did not suggest that Montaigne was a simple mirror in which each of us sees his reflection but a very special kind of glass which compels the viewer to examine his own ideas and thoughts against the challenge and stimulus of another. "His greatest attraction," writes Frame in his introduction to this paperback edition, "is that the book reveals a man and that the man becomes a friend and often another self."

"Another self" is the key phrase. This was the point and purpose of the essays, which are among the best written in the Western world.

On his style much has been said. Perhaps too much; some readers lose sight of his wisdom while looking for the lucidity and brilliance of his writing. But he should be read without too much awareness. He writes freely, informally, with rich and concrete imagery. His prose has muscle and sinew.

These are books to be dipped into for their restorative and even therapeutic quality. They are an antidote to the mushiness and the lack of exactitude which mark so much of present-day writing.

January 20, 1961

ESSAY

"Why a Dearth of Novels Reviewed?"

I have received a number of letters from readers pointing out, with accuracy, that I have not reviewed many novels in the last two or three months. Frankly, many of the novels I have read have not been worth much comment. Fiction offerings have been singularly undistinguished.

This brings up the question of what I look for in a novel. It is first this: entertainment. It must generate interest on that level. A novelist has to earn the attention of his audience. This attention is not his by some right stemming from the fact of writing or publication. There must be in the story, in the characters, in the style (or in all three) that mysterious quality which compels the reader.

Ideally, beyond the story level, there should be the quality of content, vision, wisdom which gives the work an enduring and continuing place in the consciousness of the reader, of many readers. . . .

I want to make it clear that I do not believe the novel is moribund and about to disappear. Such predictions have been made from the beginnings of the novel as we know it in the 18th century all the way to the present. I do not think a cycle of decline is an indication of fatality.

The fact is that we cannot legislate matters of art. For at the core of development is the unpredictable individual, often working in obscurity, who shapes his creation without any real reference to fad or fashion or critical acceptance.

This element in art often eludes us. For we can build up whole systems of criticism, some of which are useful and informative. But criticism itself is basically an act of judgment, operating after the fact.

Because of its nature, the novel lends itself to interpretation by investigators in other fields. One can hardly read in the fields of history, sociology, psychology, anthropology without seeing particular novels or groups of novels cited as evidence for one sort of truth or another.

It is possible to prove almost anything using this method. But, two problems emerge: first, that literary critics are influenced to draw farther and farther away from their traditional function through an essential distortion, i.e. imposing the limit of a psychological or environmental or doctrinal approach.

The second is an exaggeration of the use of the novel as evidence. One simply cannot tidy up the files of literary development. If one trend of the novel in a given period is reflective of audience, values, contemporary ideas, another trend may be in direct opposition to it.

One of the major difficulties is that too many novelists are directly involved in criticism or in teaching (which is an extension of the critical function). I speak of this from personal experience and I do not except myself from the indictment. A critical stance is not without use to a novelist. But, if he is serious about writing, his primary obligation must be neither to his fellow critics nor to some system of esthetics or critical theory. In the end, being a novelist imposes the ultimate obligation of seeking out the reader and providing him with a story which, to borrow from an English poet, will bring old men from their chimney corners and young children from their play.

January 25, 1963

ROSS MACDONALD

The Underground Man

Certain crimes expose the terrors and nightmares of a culture, in the same way that dreams and fantasies reveal the dark terrain of the unconscious. Loeb and Leopold, Sacco and Vanzetti, the Manson case are examples. There are many more.

There is crime fiction and there is fiction about crime. The former is a genre which has produced some superb craftsmen; the latter is something more, a parable of human foible and violence, and some of the best novelists of the last hundred years have examined life and society through the acts and motives of criminals and their pursuers.

Ross Macdonald is one of those novelists who use the form but elevate it into serious literature. He is in a line of writers from Dostoyevsky to Raymond Chandler who have revealed the nether side of humanity and illuminated the worth of life in doing so.

He has been writing his Lew Archer series for two decades now. His latest novel, *The Underground Man*, is even more focused on what has been his major purpose, to examine California as a microcosm of America. In doing so, he has touched universality. The characters here evoke a glint of recognition to Californians. The young and innocent, haunted as O'Neill characters by the trauma of their domestic past, in flight sometimes through drugs and sometimes through a search for renewal in the hills and seas of this vast region; their elders caught in their own tangled histories, of divorce and adultery, of blackmail and greed.

Against the background of hillside inferno, so common here in the sere Southland, Archer with that compassionate cynicism seeks to untangle the web. As Chandler's Marlowe before him, he represents the tough decencies and obsolete chivalry of a man who has seen it all, twice.

The fire is a metaphor, a counterpoint to the purgatory of the soul, created by human beings, endured by them. Natural catastrophe may seem mindless but in this novel it is the catalyst which uncovers the sad and decaying truth. *The Underground Man* is not only a literal title but a figurative one as well. It is a work of art.

Southern California is evoked effectively; no writer since Raymond Chandler has done better in this regard. But I think Macdonald has more amplitude as an observer of life. Lew Archer is far more developed as a protagonist, particularly in the later books. He is closer to Macdonald himself, to his concerns, his thoughtful and penetrating understanding of the California experience.

All of this is free of didacticism. The taut and hard-boiled style remains, but it often carries more. "I followed them downtown," Archer says at the end of the book, "thinking that quite often nowadays the low-life subplots were taking over the tragedies. I gave a more prosaic explanation to a team of police detectives and a stenotypist."

A favorite theme of Macdonald is treated here, with more poignancy than ever. It is not so much the gap of generations, nor even the war between father and son, but that deeper problem in which the life of the young is determined by the patterns of the old: ultimately determined, so that no matter how long the cycles of generations, no matter how fashion or life-style changes, the doom is seeded forever.

The adrenal response to the fire is basic and primitive. It seems against nature to be driving toward it, but Archer must, for the issue is there. "There was only one good thing about the fire. It made people talk about the things that really concerned them." Mood is caught in powerful and effective words. We sense the fire, smell it, see it, feel it. "The flames that from a distance looked like artillery flashes were crashing through the thick chaparral like cavalry."

Occasionally, but rarely, there are moments when Macdonald seems to acknowledge the almost ritual action of the private-eye story. He is hit over the head by a young man who is about to escape on a yacht. "The scene spun away," he writes. Yet, even here, Macdonald avoids triteness. The action is germane. Motives are surprising. What appears to be the kidnapping of a child turns out to be, however wrong-minded, a pathetic effort by a teen-age couple to save the youngster from the world they find abominable.

Is there blame here? Yes, but not in the uninformed and automatic sense. People are responsible for their acts, responsible to the law, which Archer unlike most private detectives in fiction, respects. But there is another kind of responsibility which the rigidities of the law rarely take into account. This is, in the final analysis, a story of crime and punishment. But the crimes are shared and the punishment often built into life itself, in unhappy marriages, in the secret nightmare witness of children to violence and argument, in the endless pattern of private grudge, in love turned to hate; the victims are not only those who are the target of violence. Its fallout corrupts the innocent, exacts an exorbitant price in human suffering.

Lew Archer is not above all this. He has known life and it has slipped him some low blows. Interviewing a man, he says: "A kind of angry brotherhood had been growing between us. It was partly based in the fact, which he didn't know, that my wife had walked out on me and sent me divorce papers through a lawyer. And partly that we were two middle-aged men, and three young people had slipped away over the curve of the world."

It is not the apparatus that touches us so deeply. This is the surface entertainment. What penetrates is precisely what is underneath the town of Santa Teresa, much like Santa Barbara, what is locked in the dens of Northridge tract houses, in the files of juvenile courts, in the high school yearbooks, what takes place behind the fronts of houses in wealthy suburbs, or in ghetto slums. The secret world is Archer's domain and Macdonald's.

Yes, the characters are familiar: real estate men and forest rangers, middle-aged ex-schoolteachers who go away to paint, housekeepers who protect their fuzzy sons, women who marry for money, acquaintances who come out of the past and bring reminders of debts owed and incidents forgotten or buried. They are much like us.

Even the artifacts and machinery, the very nature of Southern California are molded into the story. It is a bulldozer, the ultimate symbol, which uncovers the ancient crime, while the fires blaze. It is a sports car which holds the secret. And the collision of the respectable and the longhairs, the solid people and the dropouts which center contention here. From children, there is no keeping of secrets. Of one young character, Archer observes: "He had to live out his time of trouble as she (his mother) had. And there was no assurance that he would. He belonged to a generation whose elders had been poisoned, like the pelicans, with a kind of moral DDT that damaged the lives of the young."

Where is Archer in all this? Goaded not only by conscience, by a respect for his craft, but something more, he revealed: "The hot breath of vengeance was growing cold in my nostrils as I grew older. I had more concern for a kind of economy in life that would help to preserve the things that were worth preserving."

Critics should not blow their own horns. But perhaps I may be permitted a small peep, for I recognized early the value of Macdonald as a novelist transcending the genre in which he appeared to work. His books are not uniformly good. But the occasional lapse points up his true strength as a novelist. He is a man of sensitivity, sensibility and wisdom, a gifted writer. It is restoring to know that the New York establishment has recognized that something good can come out of California. Many readers out here have known this about Ross Macdonald for years.

March 14, 1971

Philip Durham

Down These Mean Streets a Man Must Go

He began late. His output was relatively small. He worked in a form of literature which most highbrow critics held to be a grimy, cheap neighborhood on the far outskirts of the city of art. Of himself, toward the end of his life, Raymond Chandler wrote:

"I'm a little tired . . . and a little discouraged. Having just read the admirable portrait of Hemingway in the New Yorker I realize I am much too clean to be a genius, much too sober to be a champ and far, far too clumsy with a shotgun to live the good life."

There were those who took him seriously, who sensed the power and the light generated in his work, but only after his death, indeed only after some of his letters had been published did Chandler begin to be discussed in terms he would have appreciated: style, language, craft, theme, point of view. Whether he ever will be considered anything more than an important minor writer is doubtful but in a brilliant critical study, *Down These Mean Streets a Man Must Go* by Philip Durham, Chandler has received the quality of critical attention he deserves.

Of the many points made in the book, perhaps the most important are those which went all but unrecognized in Chandler's own lifetime. First, that his protagonist, Philip Marlowe, the tough, chivalrous, deeply moral private eye, came into literature as the late evocation of a knightly hero, a folk hero who was the symbol of that romantic man of action of the frontier, who expressed some of the notions of justice and responsibility which are part of the texture of our tradition.

Second, the manner in which he accomplished this "magic" of language and situation, the "extended use of the American vernacular . . . a prose that seemed for many to be the nearest one can come to a recognizable American language."

Chandler was no primitive, no natural. He was thoughtful, self-conscious, a close student of literature; his work, in all its range from tales through novels to letters, is strewn with clues to what he wanted to say and how he said it.

There is something else in this work of particular interest to this area. Chandler (though this is a fact more recognized abroad than in America) was one of a small group of writers who used Los Angeles in the regional sense. The setting—from Pasadena to Santa Monica, from Hollywood to the Malibu hills—was crucial to his work. Its places and people provided the stage and characters, and even the poetic mood. It was an ambivalent relationship. At times he loved the place; at other times he hated it. But it was always there. And as George P. Eliot once wrote: "If you want the feel and aspect of Los Angeles and vicinity during the 30s, 40s and early 50s, you could hardly do better than to read his fiction." Certainly, there were few others who equaled Chandler in this. James M. Cain, perhaps.

The interplay then between this hero, Philip Marlowe, and this land, this state of mind (Durham's chapters on "The City" and "The Hero" are superb) is at the core of the fantasies of Los Angeles made real. They combine in the passage, written by Chandler for *The Simple Art of Murder:*

"But down these mean streets a man must go who is not himself mean, who is neither tarnished nor afraid . . . He is the hero; he is everything. He must be a complete man and a common man and yet an unusual man. He must be, to use a rather weathered phrase, a man of honor—by instinct, by inevitability, without thought of it, and certainly without saying it. He must be the best man in his world and a good enough man for any world. I do not care much about his private life; he is neither a eunuch nor a satyr. . . .

" . . . He is a common man or he could not go among common people; he has a sense of character or he would not know his job . . . He talks as a man of his age talks—that is, with rude wit, a lively sense of the grotesque, a disgust for sham, and a contempt for pettiness.

"The story is this man's adventure in search of a hidden truth, and it would be no adventure if it did not happen to a man fit for adventure."

The influence of Chandler has been profound—and not only in this country but abroad (Durham's only *faux pas* in this volume is to dismiss Japan's great mystery writer as "one Edagawa Rampo"— a name which, incidentally, when said aloud sounds like what it is—a Japanese rendering of Edgar Allen Poe)—yet American mystery writers tend to reflect the effect of Chandler rather than the authentic roots of his work.

For he believed in chivalry and in justice, he believed in *noblesse oblige*, in the dignity of man, and his work for the most part reflected it. And later when he grew bitter and disillusioned, Marlowe changed, too. Loneliness was almost too much to bear:

"Let the telephone ring, please. Let there be somebody to call up and plug me into the human race again. Even a cop. Nobody has to like me. I just want to get off this frozen star."

December 11, 1963

David Madden, ed.

Tough Guy Writers of the Thirties

In the light of recent events, Andre Gide's observation in *Imaginary Interviews* that "the American cities and countryside must offer a foretaste of hell" reinforces the impression in European minds that America is a place of unbridled violence.

Headlines and history simply underscore what a certain form in American literature, the so-called hard-boiled or tough-guy novel, always popular abroad, expresses in fictional terms. . . .

Perhaps the foremost critic in the field, Philip Durham (who has been enormously influential both in raising the standard of inquiry and in recruiting, through his teaching, some of the younger critics represented here), has written a longish essay "The Black Mask School," which traces the contribution of the writers for this magazine, edited by the late Joseph T. Shaw, to hard-boiled fiction.

Violence was the hallmark of the best and the worst work to emerge. But as Durham points out, hard-boiled "heroes acted as rugged individualists, while they brought justice to the deserving. The heroes were violent, but their violence was not merely that of sensationalism. It was rather a kind of meaningful violence, sometimes symbolic of a social ethical code or attitude. Sometimes an explicit and implicit criticism of a corrupt society."

It must be remembered, however, that this is paper violence; and it is a facile, common kind of error to assume that because such writers as Chandler, Cain, McCoy, Hammett dealt with violence, they created a climate of violence.

The total effect of this series of studies is to make clear that experience and effect, the projection of imagination, are not equatable with (though certainly they are related to) actual events.

Thomas Sturak in "Horace McCoy's Objective Lyricism" writes of McCoy's observation of dance marathons in the depression. "According to his widow, he was deeply disturbed by the bestiality of these spectacles. All of which was not enough, of course, to explain the evolution of his marathon-dance story into a novel of considerable artistry. As Sartre has said: 'The writer makes books out of words, not out of his sorrows.'"

The influence of these writers on European thought and fiction, particularly the Existentialists, is evident throughout these essays. America is a country of myth to Europeans and has been since the earliest times. From Fenimore Cooper through the Western film, Europeans have been fascinated by what they consider to be the anarchic individualism of the New World.

The tough guy hero seems the apotheosis of this ideal. From the great depression, the detective-gangster-private eye-lone wolf hero emerges, as Madden says, to "develop a hard-boiled attitude that enables [him] to maintain a granite-like dignity against forces that chisel erratically at it."

Deceptively anti-intellectual, the hard-boiled novel at its best, like most literary forms, seeks to make some sense of life in tension. In this, it's at the opposite pole of mindless violence, which it uses as fiction has always used it merely as a vehicle to attract attention.

June 19, 1968

ARTHUR BREMER

An Assassin's Diary: Arthur H. Bremer

I don't feel comfortable reviewing *An Assassin's Diary* because in giving it attention I feel I am drawn into that scenario which was part of his motivation—a motivation shared with Sirhan and, possibly, with Oswald, and beyond that, in the past, with John Wilkes Booth—the assassin's desire to enter history and celebrity by his act.

The alternative is even less attractive. Ignore it. Make believe it doesn't exist. That would be too disingenuous. Bremer's bullets crippled a man in public life. If I were to remain silent, if all of us were to combine to say no—no publicity, no comment, no sales, his act would have had the effect of crippling a process which, on balance, is essential for any community: communications.

Bremer was convicted of attempted murder in Maryland; he faces trial in a federal court on various charges of interfering with an election and violating the civil rights of George Wallace. It is unthinkable to give the would-be assassin the victory of corrupting the right to free expression.

Harding Lemay is a writer whose work I respect, and his introduction is thoughtful although I must differ with many of the conclusions he draws.

I can understand why he says that Bremer was "nurtured" by our society, by "attitudes and responses to reality . . . colored and distorted by those influences that stain the perceptions of an entire population."

A case can be made for the proposition that Bremer, a failure in his life and ambition, seeks celebrity, "future renown," in the new world of mass communications which would magnify his act, by headlines and news film tie him to his victim's prominence, substitute the gun for his impotency which is described over and over again in these pages, "a cry for recognition."

It is no drive for vengeance which prompts me to suggest that the drive to "understand" has subtly overwhelmed the distinctions between act and motivation, between felony and explanation.

Civilization itself exists on the compact, written and unwritten, that there must be minimal respect for each other, and that actions which maim and destroy life are, at their base, more than private. They strike at the very sinew of that compact.

To argue that, in one period or another, civilization itself may be diseased; to quote, as Lemay does, Dostoevsky's remark to his publisher that his protagonist "had submitted to certain strange, incomplete ideas that float on the wind" is to suggest that there is a justification for describing certain kinds of crime as symptomatic and therefore somehow vaguely of a different order.

But when you seek the source of such value systems, you find a network of convenience, some values held, others given over to the vague justifications of existentialism.

Bremer's act certainly has been shaped, partially, by the way we live now. But Lemay's indictment is the essence of fantasy. Blame television, the Vietnamese war, the American penchant for putting prices on everything, blame education for the misspellings and grammatical warpings, blame publishing for his impeded sexual drives.

The fact is that it is precisely this sort of *mea culpa* which becomes part of the distortion which ends in killing and mindless violence. The new communication may only have intensified the impulses in certain individuals but it has certainly produced a distortion in perception. It appears no longer so easy to distinguish reality from fantasy, but certainly we can distinguish the act from the fantasy of the act. *Crime and Punishment*, no matter how convincing, takes lace in print on paper. The shooting of George Wallace really happened.

Carried away by this analysis of Bremer's diary, Lemay writes of the bombings in Vietnam, saying, "I, like hundreds of millions of my contemporaries, shut off the news, turn to a martini or a football game or whatever diversion will neutralize the impulse to take action against what we protest being done in our name. Because we succeed in submerging our rage, we are defined as sane."

This cannot be a throwaway line. It is the whole point, though submerged and all but vitiated in the conclusion: "Society . . . betrayed him by cheapening the values we all live by and robbing him of meaning beyond what we can glean from these pathetic scribblings about his hopes, his fears, and his need for future renown, aspects we all share with him as we share the shame that produced him."

I do not accept this indictment. And not merely because it is unfair and inaccurate, but because it obscures rather than sharpens the moral issues involved. Society is an artifact, useful in generalizing but inevitably the work of men.

It is precisely the shucking off of individual responsibility that we have to deal with. And we won't face it properly until we stop using society as a scapegoat. To elevate Bremer's act as a mindless protest is to contribute to the sickness rather than the cure. It is too facile, too self-indulgent, and we owe more to ourselves and each other than that.

May 4, 1973

HARRY MC PHERSON,

A Political Education

JOHN OSBORNE,

The Third Year of the Nixon Watch

CARL J. BURCKHARDT

Richelieu and His Age

> *God will have life to be real;*
> *we will be damned, but it*
> *shall be theatrical.*
>
> *—Emerson, Journals*

The metaphor of theater to describe politics is an old one and remains apt. There are spectacle, ritual, the elevation of tragedy, the silliness of farce, the contrived sentiments of melodrama. There are character and theme, a certain amount of role-playing and improvisation, illusion and persuasion.

Americans, like Emerson, are likely to use theatrical in the deprecating sense, assuming that authenticity and histrionics are readily separated. The truth is that they merge into each other in performance and most particularly in politics. The cultural bequest of the puritan ethic is a heavy one. We distrust the theater even as it fascinates us.

Yet, reality is not so easy to come by. Politicians of the past and increasingly in the present are obliged, in order to win office, to take account of the audience. For that is where power and opportunity reside. "The politician who once had to learn to flatter kings," George Bernard Shaw wrote in *Man and Superman*, "has now to learn how to fascinate, amuse, coax, humbug, frighten or otherwise strike the fancy of the electorate."

There is a reality in politics but it cannot be penetrated by denying theatricality, but rather by trying to discern the relationship between character and performance. Three recent books deal with just this problem (though not exclusively): *A Political Education* by Harry McPherson, the memoir of an idealistic and intelligent young Texas lawyer who served in Washington as a Senate aide, a Pentagon official, an assistant Secretary of State, and a special counsel to the President from 1956-69; John Osborne's *The Third Year of the Nixon Watch*, part of a continuing review of the performance of President Nixon by the respected White House correspondent of the *New Republic;* and, finally, the long-awaited and massive *Richelieu and His Age* by Carl J. Burckhardt, the Swiss diplomat-historian.

It is far less difficult to bring these books together in a review than might be imagined. They vary in form, style and approach. But in each case, the central effort is to examine performance and character against the setting of politics. Each author is conscious of the theatricality, and each tries to define the reality behind it. The fact is that the books complement each other in very subtle ways. McPherson and Osborne are superior journalists, the first an amateur, the second professional; both had access to the wings of the stage on which political issues great and small challenged action and character. Their works are footnotes to history. Burckhardt is a scholarly historian, whose experience in diplomacy and politics gives his study a present relevance though he carefully distinguishes between the "splendid stage of world affairs" on which Richelieu performed and the stage of the present.

In history and in fiction, Richelieu has come down to us as the very model of the subtle, masterful manipulator. And in this biography there is much to support this view. Burckhardt's rule is a fairly simple one—"what a man says is what he says, not what he is . . ."—and in that distinction, given without automatic value judgments, is the strength of Burckhardt's study. In the end, that is the rule which applies in McPherson's and Osborne's book as well.

For it is not only character and personality which operate in the theater of politics. Event, circumstance, audience, tradition, contention and compromise are often unpredictable parts of the script. The difference between public theater and private drama is often to be found in that other definition of politics as the art of the possible. George Eliot pointed this out in *Middlemarch:* "There are characters which are continually creating collisions for themselves in dramas which nobody is prepared to act with them." In politics, there is no lack of these other characters, and they are usually ready to join the performance.

There is a clue here. The greatest politicians cannot be thought of simply as actors. There is that dimension, of course: Richelieu, the complex man who suppressed the paradoxes of his personality, who overcame his fears and his uncertainties by sheer will, to pursue political influence and power. In McPherson's book, we are confronted with a whole cast of minor and major characters, including Lyndon Johnson, whose public images reflect the same struggle. In Osborne's sketches of President Nixon and some of the men around him, the facile diagnosis of the President as actor gives way to something else. Nixon, in Osborne's view, is not merely acting as a politician, he is a politician.

The clue is this: politicians are rarely merely actors. They are also playwrights, directors and stage managers. Great politicians such as Richelieu contrive somehow to keep all the activities in some sort of complementary pattern.

For those of us in the audience, the electorate, the problem is a different one. We rarely witness the performance directly (even television is a distorting medium through selection and emphasis). We are at the mercy of journalism and public relations. It is no accident that the basic relationship between the politicians and the press is love-hate. The politician cannot exist without the press but the press rarely reflects the day-to-day realities of politics. They are too often the soap opera chapters of a daily or weekly serial.

Osborne is well aware of this and I think his effort to probe not only politics but journalism makes him a critical reviewer. He is even-handed and judicious. Take the defeat of the Foreign Aid bill in early November, 1971. "The notion," Osborne writes, "pumped up and magnified by hostile members of the White House press corps, that Mr. Nixon brought the defeat upon himself was absurd. The countervailing pretense that he had nothing to do with it was also absurd." This unwillingness to find automatic villains and heroes in political sub-drama is an extraordinary departure from most political reporting. Stereotypes are no part of Osborne's journalism. Image is partly contrived and partly the result of something deeper than masks. It is the "disparity between claim and actuality" which constantly concerns him. And he does not exclude himself.

In April of 1971, Osborne wrote: "The announced schedule of Kissinger's 'fact-finding trip' to Asia and Paris was so vague and loose that any fool (I have myself particularly in mind) should have perceived, with all the recent background at hand, that his main destination was Peking. Yet we of the press and, now it turns out, the highest officials of immediately interested governments, notably those in Taiwan and Tokyo, were simply not prepared to believe that *this* President, this man who had made a career of forceful anti-communism, was actually capable of so drastic and dramatic a break not only with past American policy but with his own pattern of attitude and behavior. More important aspects aside, it all provides a lesson in the folly of stereotyping Richard Nixon."

I think that Osborne's real value is precisely his awareness of the theatrical nature of politics, as one component of politics. Thus he is capable, as few reporters are, of subtleties of judgment and evocation, and of admitting that his conclusions are "soggy with ambivalence and short of certainties." At the close of the third year, "Mr. Nixon comes across to me as a President who, in defensive response to the negative view, has constructed a false image of himself and has persuaded himself that it is the true image." Most surprising is that Osborne finds Nixon lacking as an actor. When Dan Rather of CBS, in what Osborne calls "a memorable display of inquisitorial courage and toughness," asked the President why the polls showed many people thought he "failed to inspire confidence and faith and lacked personal warmth and compassion," the President replied: " . . . My strong point is not rhetoric, it isn't showmanship, it isn't big promises—those things that create the glamor and excitement that people call charisma and warmth. My strong point, if I have a strong point, is performance. I always do more than I say. Oh, I don't mean that from time to time I may not have made promises that I was unable to keep, but generally speaking . . . I believe that actions are what count."

Of course, Osborne will not satisfy either the President's partisans or his opponents. Nowhere is the theatrical nature of politics more evident than in this impatience with ambiguity and uncertainty. Our primitive appetites are for the myths, the easy delineations of hero and villain. The value of McPherson's reminiscences lies largely in delivering on the promise of the title. He came to Washington, that "vast stage design," a young Texas liberal, exuberant in his certainties, distrustful of such politicians as Lyndon Johnson. Working there for more than a decade, he witnessed the actors backstage, and there grew a maturation which would no longer support the fable of the good guys and the bad guys. Confronting "the mysteries of authority," the "presence of power begets ambiguity."

By the end of 1968, "I was tired of seeing every dispute turned into an apocalyptic struggle between good and evil, tired of looking at life through a political lens. I needed a respite from my political education—a sabbatical, not a retirement."

I do not at all underrate the book when I call McPherson a spear-carrier. In theater, an observant, thoughtful, sensitive person behind the scenes occupies an unusual position. His literary interests—and an unusually lucid style—his zest for politics and his curiosity make him a surrogate for all of us.

Perhaps it is this empathy, which all of us occasionally must feel, between audience and actors which illuminates the difference between politics in 20th-century America and Richelieu's 17th-century France, and, again surprisingly, also illuminates the similarities. The former is a result of a change in systems which offers more opportunity to participate, and the latter, rooted in human nature, points up the attractions of power and the goad of ambition. Perhaps, without overdoing the parallels, one might see in Nixon's Kissinger the shadow of Richelieu, drawn to the possibility of achievements affecting the future of men and nations, or in the visits to Peking and Moscow, the efforts to redraw the balance of power which was Richelieu's underlying plan for Europe.

The power, of course, is more divided in America than it was in the France of Louis XIII (although even there there was fragmentation and seeking, by an ambitious aristocracy, an emerging middle class, the parties of Protesant and Catholic), and the executive authority today is limited in a time sense by election, balanced by a legislature and a judiciary, and is not absolute.

In human nature, however, and even in the tactics of politics, the changes are not so apparent. There is as much hubris in a senator such as Fulbright as there was in Louis XIII's constant antagonist, Gaston of Orleans. Character counts and that is the center of McPherson's observation as it is in Burckhardt's biography.

But image counts as well. For the first lesson in McPherson's education is that politicians need to win office and keep office. They are different men on the hustings than they are in office. Outsiders may look for surface consistency and authenticity. It is a luxury the politician rarely affords. It is not simply a matter of Lyndon Johnson writing multi-typed letters to every high school and college graduate in Texas or of compromising a civil rights bill somewhere between the fears of the South and the aspirations of the North. In the theater only the critic can display righteousness. Johnson, or any other senator or congressman, could argue even as Richelieu himself might that the first order of politics was to get where you can do something. Richelieu had to persuade a handful of people, and one king, in particular. Modern politicians deal with a turbulent mass.

McPherson translates this into the detail and actuality of political life. It is not so much cynicism or even sophistication which is the result of his education as an increasing and convincing sense of the reality. He analyzes, as Osborne does, and even as Burckhardt, the difference between stereotype and actuality. In the end, the politicians are not so different from ourselves—"men just as ambitious, faulted and responsible."

The illusions are corrected here. Means and ends are reexamined. McPherson's liberal heroes emerge sometimes as rigid men, who seem to have a "stake in losing." His one-time villains, conservative or reactionary, are often the most realistic in awareness of needs. "There seemed no way to settle the (moral) problem of politics once and for all. Perhaps an intense political commitment and moral sensitivity were irreconcilable. If they were, then one could choose one or the other, though one led toward a brutal pragmatism, and the other toward ineffectiveness. Unless—one could choose a third way, and remain, as the modern theologians say, 'in the ambiguity'—acting forcefully, but conscious always that one's knowledge was insufficient and one's heart slightly corrupt. The best political men," McPherson concludes, "seemed to have chosen this way."

The most common answer is to turn away from the spectacle in disgust; but that is no answer at all. The play is not necessarily deterministic. The script is not finally written. Politics can only be theater in the pejorative sense when a sense of reality is surrendered by the audience as well as the players. What all of these books tell us is that it is more effective to get into the act that to quit the theater. The height of illusion is in its slavish acceptance or its automatic rejection.

July 23, 1972

EDWARD BLISS, ED.

In Search of Light:
The Broadcasts of Edward R. Murrow

In a busy and productive life, Edward R. Murrow did not have the time to write the book that Blanche Knopf kept urging him to do. "Somehow," writes Janet Murrow in the dedication to this volume, "he was always too busy with an immediate project to undertake this work."

Also, Murrow may have had trepidation about the challenge of a book. His best work, his pioneering life work, had been in broadcast journalism. He may have had the feeling—one gets this impression from some of his remarks—that radio and television were too ephemeral for the printed page. But if he did, he was wrong. This collection stands as fine, journalistic prose, functional and lucid, stamped with the personality and intellect of a remarkable reporter.

The rhetoric of radio reportage is somewhat different from that of television, and both contrast with the conventions and style of newspaper journalism. The major difference between radio and television journalism is expressed aptly by Edward Bliss in his introduction: "In television, words are tied to pictures; each loses something without the other. Consequently radio scripts read better in book form than television scripts; they are written to stand by themselves."

The bulk of the broadcasts in the book, accordingly, are therefore from Murrow's radio career which overlapped with the beginnings of his television activity. Perhaps this partially explains his television style. He was never merely a narrator; his words were not merely counterpoint to the direct witness of the camera. He was both an interpretative reporter and a commentator, and, therefore, a careful and thoughtful writer.

Writers have long known the difference between the oral language and the written one; and radio was an extension of the oral language. Because the listener could not see, the radio reporter had to provide through language the whole sensory range of witness: color, movement, story. It is significant that both poetry and drama, originally and functionally oral forms, rest heavily on immediacy. The ear forces a certain clarity and directness on the language. The sentences here are mainly declarative and often simple. The effect enhances even the printed word. It is no accident that Somerset Maugham once said that the ultimate test of writing was how it read aloud. It was a test he often used.

What is most impressive about Murrow in print is that he combines the ability to report with a unique style. Those in the future who have never heard the tone and nuance of his language on radio, or even those who have never seen him on television will be able to evoke the man.

His greatest single accomplishment was in World War II. Whether he is describing an air raid from the roof of a London building or the appearance of a mysterious stranger in a British pub (thought to be a spy; the man turned out to be an American reporter, possibly, though he does not say it explicitly, Murrow himself), whether he is describing the terrors of Buchenwald ("I pray you to believe what I have said about Buchenwald. I have reported what I saw and heard, but only part of it. For most of it I have no words.") Or describing V-E Day, he manages to give the immediacy of witness to the reader.

He makes clear the difference between his own opinions and the informed reflection on conditions: "There are no indications," he says on Dec. 3, 1940, "that any British minister is going to urge you to declare war against the Axis, but you must expect repeated references in the press and in public statements to the British belief that a democratic nation at peace cannot render full and effective support to a nation at war, for that is what the majority of thinking people in this country have come to believe. As a reporter I am concerned to report this development, not to evaluate it in terms of personal approval or disapproval."

One comes away with deep respect for the professional but an even deeper regard for the man. For Murrow was never a disembodied voice of a mere television personality. He grew through the turbulent events he reported. That is the measure of a real human being and a sensitive writer.

June 8, 1967

WILLIAM WHITE, ED.

By-Line: Ernest Hemingway, Selected Articles and Dispatches of Four Decades

Some 35 years ago, Ernest Hemingway wrote to his bibliographer, that the "newspaper stuff I have written . . . has nothing to do with the other writing which is entirely apart . . . The first right that a man writing has is the choice of what he will publish. If you have made your living as a newspaperman, learning your trade, writing against deadlines, writing to make stuff timely rather than permanent, no one has any right to dig this stuff up and use it against the stuff you have written to write the best you can."

He was a journeyman journalist almost until the end of his life and a very good one. But the idea that there was a neat division between Hemingway, the newspaperman and correspondent, and Hemingway, the novelist and short story writer, becomes less convincing with the reading of these news stories and dispatches. And this is true even of the earliest pieces written for the *Toronto Star Weekly*.

I am not talking about form, which is the easiest and most obvious compartmentalization. Rather, it is style, selection, perspective and even theme which keeps marring the distinctions. With little change and paraphrase, what Hemingway wrote for *Esquire* in December, 1934, applies as well to journalism as to his fiction:

"Write about what you know and write truly and tell them all where they can place it . . . All good books are alike in that they are truer than if they had really happened and that after you are finished reading one you will feel that all that happened to you, and afterwards it all belongs to you; the good and the bad, the ecstasy, the remorse and sorrow, the people and the places and how the weather was. If you can get so that you can give that to people, then you are a writer. Because that is the hardest thing of all to do."

William White touches on this in his introduction: "Hemingway, no matter what he wrote or why he was writing, or for whom, was always the creative writer: he used his material to suit his imaginative purposes." This strikes hard against one of the hard myths of journalism, that the best of it is "factual and informative" reporting. That is an ideal, rarely achieved in the press of deadlines and the complicated swirl of events.

The reality is that even the best reporter, working as arduously as he can to gather all the facts, can see and hear only so much. It is not that he seeks distortion so much as, in the nature of his position, he lacks perspective. Not only the perspective in time which the historian presumably has, but the perspective in events and in space. On the scene, he can report only what he sees and hears; away from the scene he can only approximate what is going on. He must often rely on a gathering of opinions and interpretations. In the end as the deadline presses inexorably, he writes an approximation of the truth, relying as much on intuition and a sense of pattern as much, I would think, as the creative and imaginative writer.

This may or may not come as a shock to newspaper readers and television viewers. Yet it is urgent that they understand it, for news by its very nature is in flux, a continuing current with a beginning before the lead and an ending after the final paragraph. I am not suggesting that good reporters consciously distort the news. Far from it, they seek to give an approximation of the true events. And even the television sound camera which brings you to the very scene only focuses in the circle of its lens. And its film and sound must be selected and edited, and narrated to place the events you see in context.

Thus, it is unlikely that the reporter, whether he uses words or motion pictures, can ever disappear. In the end we must rely on him as a person, on his ability to shape what he sees and hears into a viable rendering of the truth as it occurred. It is less reassuring than the myth of complete objectivity; but that is the way it is.

And that is one of the reasons Hemingway is a good reporter. First he managed to be at the right place at the right time in a large number of cases. And if he was not at the center of action, he could take from his immediate surroundings something worth knowing, something which illuminated fear or courage, demagoguery or sincerity, life or death.

Second, he could balance generalities with detail, giving some notion of the sweep of events and the sometimes contradictory elements of a specific situation.

Third, he could write in that supple, lucid, authentically Hemingway language which is evocative and compelling. And that was present early in his work as this collection convincingly demonstrates.

In 1924, he calls Mussolini the "biggest bluff in Europe." How does he know?

"The Fascist dictator had announced he would receive the press. Everybody came . . . Mussolini sat at his desk reading a book. His face was contorted into the famous frown. He was registering Dictator. Being an ex-newspaperman himself he knew how many readers would be reached by the accounts the men in the room would write of the interview he was about to give. And he remained absorbed in his book.

"I tiptoed over behind him to see what the book was . . . . It was a French-English dictionary—held upside down."

The range of his writing and of the forms within journalism is vast but within it we sense the presence of an authentic human being, an observer who has the capacity to turn experience into words. That, in the end, is what journalism at its best has in common with literature.

June 4, 1967

Allen Churchill

The Literary Decade

When T. H. White, the British novelist, compared present-day Los Angeles to Elizabethan London, some took it as a compliment, others thought it ridiculous. Where was our Shakespeare, our Marlowe, our Bacon?

I am beginning to understand what he meant. He was not referring to the Golden Age in retrospect, the one contrived out of the great works which were produced in that period, but to the period itself: the turbulence, the turmoil, the combination of *kitsch* and culture, the absurdities and the ideals, the hungers, pretensions, needs of the audience, even the business of art.

This last phrase will certainly cause some concern. Can art be connected to something so mundane as commerce? Well, Shakespeare was not made into a great writer because of the stir of interest in the theater in Elizabethan London. But certainly, he was shaped and given opportunity because people were willing and anxious sometimes to pay to be entertained. He owned a share in the Globe. He was part of that roiling, turbulent, aspiring and even pretentious society.

What puts me in mind of these matters is Allen Churchill's brisk and breezy documentary of the literary scene in the 20s, *The Literary Decade*. This entertaining book has little of the romance and idealization we associate with the period of Fitzgerald, Hemingway and Faulkner, of tragic lives, of lost generations, of what Fitzgerald called that "age of miracles . . . age of art . . . age of excess."

This is a picture of the Golden Age complete with glitter and dross, not only "rather crazy, rather splendid," as Anderson put it, but crass and coarse and crude, not only of the Algonquin Round Table, but of self-serving and posturing literary types such as Burton Rascoe and William Lyon Phelps, not only of the brave publishers such as Scribner's and Liveright but of crossword-puzzle books and suspect such as *Trader Horn* and/or *Cradle of the Deep*, of the Book-of-the-Month Club and the Comstock suppressions, of the Literary Guild and the *Smart Set*.

Examined closely this way, the truths of the age become less comforting and less exact. The Genteel Tradition does not die suddenly as Sinclair Lewis' *Main Street* is published in 1920. For every Willa Cather and Edna St. Vincent Millay, there is an Edna Ferber and an Anita Loos. The popular writers are Joseph Hergesheimer and Michael Arlen, Louis Bromfield and Richard Halliburton.

Literary values are not at the center of this golden age. World War I had opened America to a larger world. Books, buying them, reading them or at least reading the reviews, talking about them (or the gossip about their writers), became a mark of the new cultivation. The elite which had appreciated Edith Wharton and William Dean Howells was under assault of numbers. Before 1920, Burton Rascoe said, "There were only two things for any artist in America to do in those days—stay drunk or commit suicide." Afterwards, they might stay drunk, but there was opportunity and promise, there were royalty checks and adventures, fist fights and feuds. The cult of personality had begun for American literature. As movie-goers sought their stars, readers sought the new literary celebrities. . . .

"In those days," one critic has written, "people talked of the Great American Novel as ministers spoke of the Second Coming." Franklin P. Adams, the columnist for the *New York Tribune*, mentioned the Great American Novel so many times that he abbreviated it to "the G.A.N." and everybody knew what he meant.

We live in the afterglow of the myths created during this period of flux and growth. People still flock to creative writing courses, the means to that glorious translation from the dreariness and anonymity of life to the glamor of gossip columns and talk shows. Reviewers still overpraise first novels. Our authors replicate their heroes. Mailer and Jones echo Hemingway and Wolfe. It is not only a literary influence but a life-style influence. Authors publicize their works *a la* Sinclair Lewis, the press agent who won the Nobel Prize (which at this distance seems the most extravagant fiction to come out of the 20s).

We have chosen to forget the realities of the 20s, concentrating instead on the biographies and reminiscences of the best writers. That is the way of the Golden Age. We remember only the peaks; the troughs are less memorable. But, in truth, these did as much to create the environment, the opportunity and challenge for greatness. The imaginative publishers, the ingenious publicists, the hopes and dreams of the illusions, selling the sizzle and not the steak aided the creation of a ground from which the occasional masterpiece or even important work might emerge.

From Fitzgerald we learn the philosophy of the age: "Not to be sorry, not to loose one cry of regret, to live according to a clear code of honor toward each other, and to seek the moment's happiness as fervently and persistently as possible."

But an age is lived in detail, not generalities. In boozing and envy, in promotion and argument, in insecurity and in grazing ambition. In many ways, the materialism which writers criticized in America was palpable in their own lives. Dreiser could slap the face of his publisher, Liveright, in an argument over the division of movie rights to *An American Tragedy*. And Lewis could take out his rancor on Dreiser in a post-banquet brawl.

The name of the game was making it. The new readership was

buying books and the publishing industry thrived as never before. The search for new novelists was not only a literary matter. There was Maxwell Perkins who could cry out that *Look Homeward, Angel* "must be published!" But there were dozens of others who could feign "wild and honest enthusiasm" and, as in the case of Max Schuster, with *Trader Horn*, "in some mystic way . . . make people consider their lives empty unless they had read the latest Simon & Schuster publication."

Schuster took out a full-page ad: "I am going to buy *Trader Horn* today! I shall set sail for beyond the sun . . . wildest Africa will be my home, swift rivers my daily course . . . Romance will run amuck . . . " It did, selling hundreds of thousands of copies, despite the fact that the book was exposed. It was no memoir, but a melodramatic pastiche touched up by a third-rate novelist.

It kept selling anyway.

There were plenty of overrated works. The novel which inaugurated the decade, Sinclair Lewis' *Main Street*, praised to the skies at the time, in perspective turns out to be a dated and flawed little social novel. Lewis parlayed a modest talent for writing into a vast success by exploiting the public taste. There was no small component of Babbitt in him. He had served an apprenticeship as a flack for a publishing firm and managed to sell himself, unattractive as he was.

The critics fell for it. Lewis met George Jean Nathan and H. L. Mencken one night and let them know his forthcoming novel had "the goods."

"I'm so far ahead of most of the men you two think are good that I'll be gottdamned if it doesn't make me sick to think of it! Just wait till you read the gottdamn thing. You've got a treat coming, Georgie and Hank, and don't you boys make no mistake about that!"

Nathan and Mencken could not wait to get away from that "tall, skinny, paprika-haired . . . numbskull." But the oversell had worked. "Dear George," Mencken wrote his partner, "Grab hold of the barrail, steady yourself, and prepare yourself for a terrible shock! I've just read the book of that Lump we met . . . and, by God, he has done the job!"

It is hard to believe that only a handful of critics held out, calling it puerile and defective. But *Main Street* was praised as a new conception of the American novel. Even books which were merely mentioned in reviews of the Lewis novel began to take off: Sherwood Anderson's *Winesburg, Ohio,* Floyd Dell's *Moon-calf,* Dorothy Canfield Fisher's *Brimming Cup.*

Solid writing also flourished amid the junk. In 1925, at the height of the decade, titles of the year included: A. A. Milne's *When We Were Very Young,* Willa Cather's *The Professor's House,* Hemingway's *In Our Time,* Fitzgerald's *The Great Gatsby,* Sherwood Anderson's *Dark Laughter,* Dreiser's *An American Tragedy.* And that is only a sampling.

There was a ferment, a vibration, a feeling of possibility. Readers yearned to own first editions (publishers obliged by running off special first editions and releasing them ahead of time). There had never been so many writing talents (or claimed writing talents) since the days of the New England Transcendentalists. Writers could understand the remark of Yankee pitcher Waite Hoyt, who said: "It's great to be young and a Yankee." The publishers were ready and waiting to issue books by young men and women who had never had their names on title pages before.

Even poetry prospered. Don Marquis wrote:

> *There's a great poetical 'boom' they say,*
> *(Climb on it, chime on it, brothers of mine!)*
> *'Twixt the dawn and dusk of each lyrical day*
> *There's another school started, and all of them pay.*

Some will find Churchill's account a bit too cynical but this is as much a product of what he must do as a chronicler as of his view of that scene. Telling it how it was is bound to collide with the neat and reassuring myths of a Golden Age. This is the other side: raucous, confusing, turbulent, mercantile, cheap.

June 23, 1972

CARL BODE, ED.

The Young Mencken: The Best of His Work

Puritanism: An attempt to bleach the red blood corpuscles.
–H. L. Mencken

Journalism has a way of ripening quickly and losing its lasting flavor. Not so with these pieces. Mencken has shorn his work of sentiment, never panders to the popular fashions. He is an iconoclast, a curmudgeon, a lover of language, an authentic wit and a brash, brilliant, individual.

In the end, you write who you are. Mencken was a complex man, privately a Victorian, a subscriber to the proprieties, who could not have lashed out at pomposity, hypocrisy, prejudice (in others), and knavery, had he not been secure in himself. He reversed in his own life the predominant mode. Most of his targets looked virtuous from the outside, but were captivated by vice from the inside.

He proclaimed himself "a vulgar fellow," said, "I prefer *Tom Jones* to *The Rosary*, Rabelais to the Elsie books, the Old Testa-ment to the New, the expurgated parts of *Gulliver's Travels* to those that are left. I delight in beef stews, limericks, burlesque shows, New York City and the music of Haydn, that beery and delightful old rascal! I swear in the presence of ladies and archdeacons. When the mercury is about 95 I dine in my shirt sleeves and write poetry naked."

If he found bitter laughter in observing the American scene, the funniest part of it was to see it straight. In his column, "The Free Lance," he would print the press releases from Mayor Thomas Hayes of Baltimore adding at the end HAR, HAR, HAR!

But Mencken, critic of ideas, attitudes and issues, who did more than any other man to influence the writing and thinking of the first part of this century in America, could be equally harsh on himself.

He tried verse and the short story, gave them up when he was merely adroit at the forms. If America needed anything, it was not the "endless amateurishness" of its writers, the work of old maids in pressed pants, its most trying trait a total absence of gusto.

He studies writing by correspondence, writes 52 pages of a novel set in Shakespeare's times, wins commendations from the faculty of the "Cosmopolitan University," for his rich use of expressions like Forsooth! Mencken cuts his losses; he gives up the novel forever as a bad job.

On the *Baltimore Herald* and later the *Sun*, he finds his power as a writer and editor, takes it with him to *Smart Set*. His own prejudices—against religion, against business, against sham, against the illusions of democracy, and above all against puritanism—are supported by his reading, and his reflection.

He very nearly becomes a scholar—*The American Language* is one result. He does become the most vivid and vigorous book and drama reviewer of his time.

These prejudices would harden and Mencken would lose touch with the realities of the 30s and 40s. He would have his wandering in Sinai during the year of America's entry into World War I when his pro-German bias (or perhaps more accurately his skepticism about the propaganda of the Allies) would alienate editors and readers. But these pieces, epigrams, columns, essays, reviews, reportage on politics, hitherto largely uncollected, represent Mencken at his most powerful, and wittiest.

Shaw influenced him and he attributed the Irishman's power to putting "the obvious in terms of the scandalous." Behind his constant and continuous attack on censorship and suppression was the notion that the reformers never knew where to stop.

If outrage is at the source of suppression, it is also, Mencken was quick to realize, an energy which could be harnessed for other purposes. It is suggested that Mencken's famous essay, "The Sahara of the Bozart," which attacked the cultural shortcomings of the South, and drew fiery responses from that region, did much to goad young writers, editors and reporters to prove him wrong.

He starts with his own experience—reading manuscripts: "Boston produces better writing than the Far West; it is suaver, more careful, finer in detail. Los Angeles leads the whole country in quantity; its weekly output surpasses that of Greenwich Village

. . . Chicago leads them all in ideas, originality, vigor; it is the great hatching place of American letters. But the South? The South is almost a complete blank."

The reason: "the astounding orgy of puritanism that goes on in the South—an orgy of repressive legislation not often to be found in the whole history of Christendom." Exaggerated. Certainly. But the pure flame burns and toward the end in "Mark Twain's Americanism," we see the real pedigree of Mencken's journalism.

What Mencken said of Twain, may now be said of him. Twain was so good that the puritans laundered him and made him one of their own. "The truth is that Mark was almost exactly the reverse. Instead of being a mere entertainer of the mob . . . laboriously devoted to the obvious and the uplifting, he was a destructive satirist of the utmost pungency and relentlessness, and the most bitter critic of American platitude and delusions, whether social, political, or religious, that ever lived."

June 13, 1973

EDMUND WILSON

A Window on Russia:
For the Use of Foreign Readers,

To the Finland Station:
A Study in the Writing and Acting of History

For a time after the death of Edmund Wilson, I wished that he might have written a book which could be called *The Education of Edmund Wilson*.

With the posthumous publication of Wilson's *A Window on Russia: For the Use of Foreign Readers* and the reprinting of his pioneering, if not classical, work on social and intellectual history, *To the Finland Station: A Study in the Writing and Acting of History*, I realized that the great critic-journalist had indeed written, in his long and prolific life, a body of works which added up precisely to the sort of statement I wanted.

In these two books, and in the others, what was to be found was the track of a man exploring and expressing that process of education which the dictionary defines as "the act of acquiring or imparting general knowledge and of developing the powers of reasoning and judgment." Though each work dealt with the particular area of knowledge and experience met and mastered by Wilson, the total effect is a kind of Rosetta stone of his quest.

He formulated no specific credo, no theoretical critical position. His preachments were in his practice, eclectic, believing in but not worshipping reason, seeking the felicitous language and following his curiosity, traveling between his times and history, between the life of the intellect and the life of action, becoming as the result of his reading and reflection close to that fleeting ideal of the generalist, the Renaissance man.

He was, in this journey, to be influenced for a time by Marxism, but he was too individual and skeptical to be the slave of system. He was in at least one period taken by Freudianism, long enough to write such essays as that on *The Turn of the Screw* which read like parody. But systems require faith and Wilson was far too much a product of rationalism and the scientific age to be comfortable in ultimate belief.

He wrote: "There is no classical conception of God that can really be made to fit what we know today, in the middle of the 20th century, of the behavior of what we call 'energy' and the behavior of human beings, and of the relation of these to one another. Yet we still use the word in this indolent sense to cover up our inability to account, in a 'rational' way, for the fact that we exist, that the universe exists, and that everything is as it is."

These are resonant and revealing words, not the expression of an atheist but rather that of an agnostic. Reason is not thrown out. Science is not rejected. ". . . We keep on performing experiments which we observe from the rational point of view of the cause that produces the effect, and we know we can find out certain things in this way; techniques for procuring results." But "reason may land us in a cul-de-sac." And science's laws are not "unvarying."

His education brought him precisely to that terrain which exists between chaos and certainty. Wilson is not an either/or critic, except in those areas where data is concerned. For a critic who is most often referred to pejoratively as journalistic, he was a tireless scholar. He prepared himself for each task—studying Russian in middle age to read Russian literature in the original, learning Hebrew to read the Dead Sea Scrolls, addressing himself to different disciplines, psychology, economics, history, anthropology, political science, sociology. Never seeking specialization, he gradually found the synergism of study. One feels that he wrote fiction, poetry, plays, not so much to achieve success as to learn the experience of the creative process, to inform his role as a critic.

From his earlier enthusiasms he kept what he considered useful. He could move away from the dogma of Marxism and retain the notion that economics and history could be a context for understanding literature, he could turn from the excesses of literary psychoanalysis without leaving the insight that individual psychology was a root of creativity. One may detect the other influences from Plato and Aristotle, through Dryden and Johnson, to Zola and Bergson and Howells.

Men make systems and unscrupulous disciples borrow the knowledge of the right from them, he says sarcastically in *To the Finland Station*, "knowing . . . that we are right—we may allow ourselves to exaggerate and simplify."

But, a view of life always goes along with a personality. Wilson was prickly, often extrasensitive. Yet, surprisingly, his literary manner, his journalism if you will, bespeaks a kind of courtesy. Not the phony politeness of the commons room or the overbearing rudeness of the true zealot, but regard and respect for his readers. He never wrote down, never compromised his statement to popularize, was not condescending.

It is his journalism which deserves attention as a form of discourse. Rarely did he pander to the public taste. If he dealt with topical matters, it was to deepen an understanding of them. His decision to opt for journalism rather than an academic career reflects a wholly American belief in the worth of the common reader, a distaste for isolation and narrowness, a commitment to earn the attention of an audience rather than enjoy its captivity in the classroom. If nothing else, both of these books illustrate this quality: scholarship in the service of the broadest kind of instruction.

Wilson has been critical of academic criticism and of the university establishment, and has received his share of criticism in return. But I think it is important to understand the distinction he draws between academic criticism and scholarly criticism. The latter, though he may criticize its content, earns his complete respect. I have never read the adjective "scholarly" used in a deprecating sense by him. Those who are employed in the service of criticism, textual study, translation, historical explication, contribute to the enterprise.

Academic criticism is attacked for its narrowness, its obliteration of the experience of literature and life in favor of nomenclature and categories, a jargon substituting for the precision and grace of language which allows meaning to be rendered into words. . . .

The two books just brought out reveal two of the facets of Wilson's gift. *To the Finland Station* partakes of the critical act, but it is an imposing work of history, tracing through event and biography the roots of the Russian Revolution. It is a work which at once educates and illuminates Wilson's own education. It starts on a day in January, 1842, when the French historian and philosopher Jules Michelet discovered the writings of Giovanni Vico. Significantly, Michelet's interest in Vico (who had written: "The social world is certainly the work of men . . .") brought him to the study of Italian. The parallel with Wilson's way is no accident.

Through Michelet, Renan and Taine, St.-Simon, Fourier, Marx, Engels and Lenin, Wilson's own reading of the 19th century experience is clearly apparent. He brings together ideas and events in a brilliant exposition, "The myths that have made us wonder are projections of a human imagination like our own and, if we look for the key inside ourselves and learn how to read them correctly, they will supply us with a record, inaccessible up to now, of the adventures of men like ourselves. And a record of something more than mere adventures." From Vico's conclusion that "one can and should find [the principles of change] in the modifications of the human intelligence itself," to the arrival of Lenin at the Finland Station is an extraordinary effort to find the interaction of men and ideas.

And even so, Wilson in his 1971 introduction plays the critic of his own work. He does for himself what he has done for others, reminds us that new knowledge makes every work of history and philosophy tentative. He concedes where he has been too "amiable" or where he has placed too little emphasis. He is the first to concede that no writer should be read scripturally. And nowhere is the continuing role of the critic, to amend , to place in context, to seek new information, more clearly indicated. One may still read *Finland Station* today with pleasure and profit for its illustration of method and style but one must remember that it is like all written history, "a being with a definite point of view in any given period."

A Window on Russia illustrates the function of literary criticism in that its emphasis is on the work and spirit of a group of authors. It is in the more obviously journalistic form (although portions of *To the Finland Station* also were first published in periodicals): essays, reviews, notes. Wilson's first function as a critic is evocation. He shows the work as it is, not a substitute for reading the original, but as a guide or window through which to see it. His judgments may be questioned but they are inevitably supported.

In the most celebrated essay of this collection, on Nabokov's translation of Pushkin, he gives the former a lesson in critical writing. On the question of translation, I cannot comment, but his chiding of Nabokov for "flip comment" and his instinct to "take digs" without illustration or example is a masterful job, all the more telling because of Nabokov's habit of committing the same literary misdemeanors over which he invariably attacks other critics.

The essay began a feud between the two men but one cannot help feeling that Wilson felt Nabokov was long overdue for careful criticism. The first paragraph deserves to be quoted: "Vladimir Nabokov's translation of Pushkin's *Eugene Onegin* is something of a disappointment; and the reviewer, though a personal friend of Nabokov—for whom he feels a warm affection sometimes chilled by exasperation—and an admirer of much of his work, does not propose to mask his disappointment. Since Nabokov is in the habit of introducing any job of this kind which he undertakes by an announcement that he is unique and incomparable and that everybody else who has attempted it is an oaf and an ignoramus, incompetent as a linguist and scholar, usually with the implication that he is also a low-class person and a ridiculous personality, Nabokov ought not to complain if the reviewer, though trying not to imitate Nabokov's bad literary manners, does not hesitate to underline his weaknesses."

There is, of course, a quality of snideness but the passage illustrates something about Wilson that is too often overlooked. He despises arrogance, the arrogance of certainty and bad manners. If he himself sounds arrogant on occasion, he has never been spared the test of the critical enterprise. To put one's words forward to be tested, validated or corrected by his peers is the heart of intellectual discourse. The education of Edmund Wilson has taken place in the open and is an example for all of us.

September 17, 1972

VERNON HALL JR.

A Short History of Literary Criticism

Books of literary criticism proliferate in our time. Many of them make the assumption that their readers will know the historical range of literary criticism; some of them suggest that their authors would do well to go back and re-read (if they have read them in the first place) the works which represent the development of critical principles.

A history as brief as this perforce leaves out a great deal. But in criticism as in other disciplines a certain topography forms. There are distinguishable landmarks, personalities and works which rise above the rest.

There are certain themes which run through this work, as indeed they run through any discussion of the critical act and function. First, literary criticism is a paradoxical activity; it is separate, distinct and recognizable on one hand. On the other, it merges with a host of other intellectual activities, philosophy, psychology, history, sociology, anthropology and even, in recent times, particularly, economics.

Second, it is an act of judgment, seeking precedents, standards, and rules. But the derivation of these rules must come in part at least from works of imagination. Imagination thrives on freedom, breaks out of hardened rules and dogma, justifies its own accomplishments. Thus, criticism is from the beginning caught in this tension between the codification of excellence and the artist's indifference to such legislation.

The critical act itself is by its nature the act of an individual, an individual who is partially the product of his time and place, partially the product of his own special environment and personality. Thus criticism itself is in constant flux, torn between objectivity and subjectivity, taste and decorum, past and present, classical and experimental.

From its beginnings with Plato's more or less disorganized remarks about poets and poetry, the critical function has been merged and confused with other issues: the nature of man and the nature of society; the need for moral judgment and instruction; the quality of truth and the function of the imagination. Though these activities of criticism are more complex and confusing than the ones which deal with form and rhetoric, the abstractions of esthetics, the study of language and meter, they are somehow in the end far more satisfying. As we see in this history, the periods which are rule-oriented somehow demonstrate the essential absurdity of literary etiquette. The great critics are invariably those men who deal with art and life, not those who deal with art as the imitation of other, earlier art. I am not suggesting that classic and neo-classic critics are without lessons to offer us. But I am saying that to choose between Aristotle's observation that the play should be long enough to do what it sets out to do and Horace's dogmatic rule that a play should consist of five acts, one must turn to Aristotle, for his remark is closer to the natural process of creation.

It is possible, of course, to go to the other extreme, to assume that artistic freedom is equivalent to artistic ignorance, to argue that the past offers no instruction. And we have seen this response both in the creative act and in criticism. What the artist and the critic, and not least important, the ordinary reader must learn from the past is not only its accomplishment in classic works but the implication of that accomplishment, the how and the why. Such a volume as this introduces us to this past of criticism.

In this volume we trace not only the history of literary criticism but in a very real sense the intellectual history of Western man as expressed by those who see in imaginative writing the mirror of man's flaws and his aspirations.

December 19, 1963

ROLAND BARTHES

Mythologies,
Critical Essays

I suspect that every critic recapitulates in his development the developments of criticism itself. For there are certain basic issues which have challenged and still challenge criticism: the process of expression, its content and effect, the value systems by which it is judged, its art and its science, its significance and mystery, its language and myth.

Roland Barthes, the French critic, has allowed his readers to share vicariously every point of the experience.

"Writing must go hand in hand with silence; to write is in a sense to become as 'still as death,' to become someone to whom the last word is denied; to write is to offer others, from the start, that last word," he says in the preface to critical essays.

There is great respect for the reader in this attitude, but there is even greater respect for form. Barthes has changed; the world has changed. His language might be different today. But "time itself is a form" and we as critical readers are entitled to follow his itinerary. For these are not only essays, reviews, philosophizings on criticism, they are also the record of an intellectual odyssey.

Like most of the exciting critics of this era, Barthes' major struggle is with language itself. "Literature has a peculiar status in that it is made of language, i.e. of a substance which already signifies when literature takes possession of it: Literature must secrete itself in a system which does not belong to it but which nonetheless functions to the same ends as literature, which are: to communicate."

For a man of Barthes' intelligence, curiosity, and erudition, the challenge is clear. To be a critic in the world today (read to be a thinking human being in the world today) one must take the road that so attracted the men of the Renaissance, the ideal of a universal, polymathic man.

At the end of *Mythologies*, he makes this explicit: "a reconciliation between reality and men, between description and explanation, between object and knowledge."

His conversion did not come suddenly. He has come along the path of academic criticism to interpretive criticism; he has experienced and utilized the ideologies and the insights of social science; he has embraced, not slavishly but imaginatively, a new instrumentality, semiology, the science of signs and symbols, and structuralism, the philosophy whose concerns is with form and the rules of functioning, rather than the interpretation of some external value system. The operative concepts are validity rather than truth.

It is an open-ended system. It recognizes the value of classification, the need for data, the use of ideologies to explain, but its real concerns are with questions rather than ultimate answers; it is the equation which is important, rather than the "solution" to a given problem. The sin in structuralism is not falsehood, a possibility inherent always in the difficulty set up by the tensions between object and inquiry, but bad faith or dishonesty.

Thus, the structuralist critic, Barthes writes, recognizes that "At the heart of the critical work [is] the dialog of two histories and two subjectivities, the author's and the critic's. But this dialog is egoistically shifted toward the present; criticism is not an homage to the truth of the past or the truth of 'others'—it is a construction of the intelligibility of our own time."

This is never an easy task, since it requires a constant attention to the precision of language, to one's own motives and history, to one's own age. But, neither is it, as Barthes shows, an impossible task—merely an unending one.

Mythologies is an example of his approach directed through superior journalism.

Highly entertaining and revealing, it touches on everything from striptease to wrestling, from women's magazines to wine as a totem drink.

Critical Essays touches on painting, the novel, film, and literary criticism more explicitly. He is at his most engaging here as "a public experimenter" (his definition of a writer). He can be witty and sarcastic and his remarks are a devastating indictment of the follies and hypocrisies of academic and ideological criticism.

But it is here too that he is at his most passionate and revealing, analyzing the structure of works, dealing with rhetoric ("the amorous dimension of language") showing the critic's task, "a secret practice of the indirect," with great skill, and the critic's growth as an adventure of intellect and imagination.

July 21, 1972

HERMAN HESSE

My Belief: Essays of Life and Art

Herman Hesse may be seen by some as a mystic remote from the world, but the generous collection of his personal essays and critical reviews in *My Belief: Essays on Life and Art* shows another aspect of the man: the professional writer who tried his hand at many forms, and achieved a high degree of excellence in most of them.

This volume will appeal to a wider audience that the Hesse cult. In some ways he is at his best in just such writing as this—literary and cultural criticism, the familiar essay, the development of his personal credo.

Ziolkowski, the editor of these essays, emphasizes the point: " . . . Hesse was never an otherworldly guru, but a professional writer who produced, in the course of an active literary career of some 60 years, a quantity of work so vast that it has yet to be thoroughly cataloged."

I found this volume much more impressive than the recent collection of Hesse's political journalism: *If the War Goes On . . .* His reviews are a pleasure to read, the work of a man for whom art and life are inextricably melded. They deepen as he goes from the young man who in 1910 wrote to a friend that he had read for purposes of review over 300 books that year but that it was his purpose, as he once remarked to Jung, to review only those books about which he could say something favorable; to the old man who, while retaining his enthusiasm for literature and art, rose beyond worldly concerns to attempt an address of the profoundest questions faced by man in the 20th century.

T. S. Eliot recognized this early. He had read Hesse's slender collection of essays *In Sight of Chaos* (1920) and told Hesse he wanted to "spread its reputation." He attempted to do this by including the work in his *Notes to "The Waste Land."* But it was to be decades before the worth of these works was generally realized. Two of the essays here—on Dostoevsky's *The Brothers Karamazov* and *The Idiot*—are taken from Hesse's *In Sight of Chaos.*

We can track the course of Hesse's fiction in the essays and reviews. But they are effective in, and of themselves. Their relevance (no matter how we may tire of that word) comes not from topicality but from depth of penetration. And this in turn is based not simply on his prescience—his early definition of the problems facing Western man in the 20th century—and not even because what he is saying is now part of the popular currency of attitudes—but because Hesse has the true gift of the critical mind, an ability to illuminate the experience of art through life, to achieve that deeper resonance which is struck by a man attempting to demonstrate through experience, language, and learning the possibilities of an enhanced and significant existence.

There are scores of examples. Here is one from *On Little Joys* published in 1905: "Great masses of people these days live out their lives in a dull and loveless stupor. Sensitive persons find our inartistic manner of existence oppressive and painful, and they withdraw from sight. In art and poetry after the brief heyday of realism, dissatisfaction has arisen everywhere, the clearest symptom being nostalgia for the Renaissance and Romanticism."

Whether it is a letter to a young poet, or introductions to collections of European and American literature, or Eastern literature, or an appreciation of music, or reveries, or fantasies, we listen here to an authentic voice.

If there is one single secret to the validity of criticism it is the critic's willingness (parallel to the imperative of the creative writer) to share and reveal the matter of his own life and vision. This is neither arrogance nor pure subjectivity but a kind of honesty and

risk which communicates the magic of the experience. The most
distortion in the critical act comes from the substitution of a
disembodied voice or the detached intellect for the totality of
response which is the way of experiencing art.

February 13, 1974

JOYCE CAROL OATES

The Edge of Impossibility:
Tragic Forms in Literature

The figures of this study are the works of Shakespeare and
Melville, Dostoevski and Chekhov, Yeats, Mann and Ionesco. But
the insights and themes, the wrestling with the nature of tragedy
and comedy, realism and the absurd, come from an artist's reading
rather than a critic's.

Let me restate that. There is no reason why artist and critic
cannot merge. Indeed, it is that special meld which has constantly
reinformed criticism since the days of Horace. How many have
merged the qualities required is indicated by a short list: Dante,
Dryden, Coleridge, James, Tolstoy, Zola, T. S. Eliot.

What the creative writer, particularly the process-conscious
writer, brings to the act of that informed judgment which is
criticism is well-illustrated in these pages. It is a special understanding that no matter how rational, how taxonomic, how con-
textual criticism can be, it must take into account that sense of
dream and mystery which underlies creation itself.

When Miss Oates quotes Husserl, the experience of art "gives
itself as having been there before reflection," a strange and continuing triumph over nothingness, the acclamation of "the mar-

velous in ourselves," the source is made more valuable by her own experience as a writer.

Nowhere in these pages is this made explicit, that is, illustrated by example from her own works. Yet, the implication is everywhere.

For example, the opening words: "We seek the absolute dream. We are forced back continually to an acquiescence in all that is hallucinatory and wasteful, to a rejection of all norms and gods and dreams of 'tragedy' followed by the violent loss of self that signals the start of an artistic effort: an appropriation by destruction or an assimilation into the self of a reality that cannot be named. The art of tragedy grows out of a break between self and community, a sense of isolation . . . The tragic hero dies but is reborn eternally in our dreams; the crudity of our desire for an absolute dream, an absolute key—is redeemed by the beauty that so often surrounds this dream. One can explain the dream but never its beauty."

The point is that these essays published in scholarly or avant-garde journals seem shaped to the decorum and vocabulary of the critical form. But that impression fades under scrutiny. Miss Oates is not merely a professor teaching literature and publishing for her peers. She is an artist seeking validation for her own quest for the absolute, for that "dream within a dream, the dream of absolute truth, the dream that explained everything," as Ionesco wrote in his *Fragments of a Journal*.

No accident that she uses this as a headnote for the book. These essays come not from conventional lectures or from "publish or perish" (at least not in the exact sense of that term), they come from a different kind of selfishness, the selfishness of an artist. Again the words of Ionesco: "I am so very true that I cannot escape from myself. I organize myself. I am the self that organizes myself thus, arranging the same materials in a unique pattern."

Another clue emerges. Miss Oates hardly concerns herself with the issues or concerns of those who have sought to trace the forms of tragedy. That is the work of intellectual historians. Those who argue that tragedy is dead miss the point entirely. The clue emerges in the subtitle. Tragic forms persist for they do not rest solely on any epoch or era. Metamorphosis provides forms; but the tragic impulse does not rest on God or gods, on implacable value systems. The center of tragedy is psychological and perhaps parapsychological. "Suffering is articulated in tragic literature, and so this literature is irresistible, a therapy of the soul . . . We acclaim the marvelous in ourselves."

So supple a view makes it possible to view Melville as the artist who achieved the tragedy of nihilism, or to see Shakespeare's *Troilus and Cressida* as a tragedy of existence, *Antony and Cleopatra* as a tragedy of imagination.

Tragedy will be with us as long as dreams and hallucinations. It is the prophetic artist rather than the reductionist critic which gives Miss Oates the confidence to say: "The abyss will always be open for us, though it begins as a pencil mark, the parody of a crack; the shapes of human beasts—centaurs and satyrs and their remarkable companions—will always be returning with nostalgia to our great cities."

May 5, 1972

ERNEST RAYMOND

Gentle Greaves

JOYCE CAROL OATES

Marriages and Infidelities, Short Stories

"Love," Goethe wrote, "is an ideal thing, marriage a real thing; a confusion of the real with the ideal never goes unpunished." Or, one might add, unexamined.

For love and marriage remain the staples of fiction, a seemingly inexhaustible supply of situations and themes. Ideals change, realities are modified in different ages and epochs. In one period, passion reigns, in another decorum. But neither really disappears.

We look for definitions of love in the works of poetry, philosophy, religion, and we get as many as there are men and women who have written of it. Yet we never get one which satisfies. It is described as madness and the measure of sanity, as bondage and freedom, as sadness and happiness, as a condition, a process, a feeling, an illusion. The "Sovereign Queen of secrets," as Shakespeare called love, still reigns.

Within so many contradictions and paradoxes, love can provide endless combinations and permutations. Marriage, however, inevitably suffers by comparison. For it is an institution so near at hand that any despair, unhappiness, disappointment, is inevitably focused on it. It is the long waking-up after the dream. Love is often the residue of that dream, the flight from reality. Ortega y Gasset writes of sexuality in the following, but it could as easily apply to love:

"Nine-tenths of that which is attributed to sexuality is the work of our magnificent ability to imagine, which is no longer an instinct, but exactly the opposite: a creation." This can be either nightmare or dream—or both.

Marriages and Infidelities, Short Stories by Joyce Carol Oates has the matter and variety of a score of novels, beautifully written, in the end symphonic in its play and replay of a theme of a multitude of loves, and disguises of love in today's world. *Gentle Greaves* by Ernest Raymond is a massive novel, really three novels, which in the tempo and style of another age, the Edwardian years in England, examines three loves, the affection of a child for his father, between a lover and the woman he loves, between a father and his daughter.

There are differences, of course. Raymond writes decorously of a seemingly decorous age. Miss Oates writes with passion and the courage to probe the edge of impossibility, of survival and madness and despair and death. Again, as in her earlier collection, *The Wheel of Love*, she proves her mastery of the conventional short story and then wheels into experimental forms as though the matter is too wild to be contained in traditional ways.

Raymond writes leisurely, with meticulous surface detail of characters whose deepest feelings are often only hinted at, whose lives are concerned with courtesies and rituals and external events such as war and occupations, but who are no less feeling than the strangely troubled characters of Miss Oates' stories. She has chosen the short story, not merely because the taste of her audience has changed, but because, for this attempt to encompass the range of love, the form is eminently suitable.

She will not waste time on the beginnings before the beginnings or the ending after the endings. The short story is eminently the means of attacking directly the point of confluence of forces. Her characters too must deal with the practical occasions of life, of rock concerts and feeding children, of scholarly research and visits to aging parents, of shopping and neighborly chats, but it is the dark, mysterious, dream-like aspect of life which is brought directly to the surface.

In Raymond's novel, darkness exists as well. It begins in the shadows, as life does, and ends in the shadows, as life must. It is part of a larger history, of wars and empires and business, of getting ahead and making do. The story is mainly told by Sir Theodore Allan Mourne, a publisher, a veteran of World War I, in the time of his last years writing a manuscript which will explain to Roberta, his "adopted" daughter, the true details of his life.

The secret, the mystery of her origins, is for the sophisticated readers of this day, the least of the surprises in this book. Roberta is Sir Theodore's daughter by the woman he had always loved, Gentle Greaves, married to another. We know enough now, as if common sense alone was not enough to demolish the myth, that the late Victorians and Edwardians were not so different from ourselves. Love and passion and sexuality inhabited them as they do us. Their feelings, their capacity for mistakes, their honesty, suggest a kinship with our age. It is style rather than substance which has changed.

It is too easy to say from our imagined superiority of knowledge, experience, a sense of reality, that such a novel as this is an anachronism. It may sound sentimental, romantic, even shallow because its handling of sexual matters is not explicit, because its elevation of the ideal of love seems an illusion. Yet, this is not the effect at all. On the contrary, it seems somehow more realistic, even than Miss Oates' uncompromising exploration of the nether world of desire (and despair) and delusion.

One may quarrel with Raymond's attention to detail, the stiffness of his dialog, the cool, practical, predominantly sensible actions of his characters. But, Gentle is not as her name implies, a woman acted upon rather than acting, and Sir Theodore is not only a man of his world.

To us, the conversation between Gentle's husband and her lover, in the hospital as she is dying, seems almost comic until we realize that the gruffness and even the attempt at humor disguises feelings and sensibilities no less insistent than those which burn at the surface of the characters of Miss Oates' stories.

When Sir Theodore writes of the idea of human progress, we may take it that he is speaking of his own experience with Gentle as well. For the characters here still have a sense of the poignant, which is not the same as facile sentimentalizing. "No, things are not made easy for us," he writes. "We are required to know that evil is real and of great power; and before God, these last few years have shown this to us! We are required to look the evil full in the face and endure a death of the spirit that we may rise again with our manhood remade: else is our trust but an easy evasion, empty of truth.

"For some people the contrast between our human aspirations and the world in which we find ourselves is so searing that they cite it in condemnation of the universe. It is not so for me. For me Man's obstinate aspiration is not the condemnation of the universe but its justification."

The surprise is that the evil he refers to is not a sense of sin for his feelings about Gentle. The evil is compounded of the circumstances which made it impossible for them to live out their lives together. He marries another. His life goes on. He can say, without embarrassment of the one woman, Gentle, he has always loved, "Sometimes I am appalled that I can work and be happy for months together without one thought of Gentle, and that when I do think of her there is barely a trace of pain. And that at times I can hardly recall her face anymore. But there is one thing which tells me the love only sleeps, and it is this: Whenever I think of death . . . the prospect, or if you will, the faint chance, of seeing her again fills me with an excitement, a hope, a kind of ecstasy which is no less now than on that delicate and misty morning, 31 years ago . . . "

There are other sorts of satisfactions in this novel, the creation of a world in which the characters and their situations surround us, the old-fashioned experience of a novel which gives us more than brief access to people in the occasions of their lives.

Miss Oates' short stories afford in contrast, satisfactions of another kind. While we watch as an audience in the Raymond novel, the characters in her stories resonate to the way we live now. They are symptomatic. We shiver in anguish as her characters—the troubled housewives, the bored, mute husbands, remote and distant children, lovers waiting in hotel rooms or rented farmhouses, aging fathers and mothers—are attracted or repelled, and play out in passion or in violence the confused longings of their deepest nature.

Almost none of the characters in the stories are contained at their center. The ones who are have retreated from life—into old age, or work, or some strange ritual performance as the widow of a poet in "The Sacred Marriage" who keeps her love alive by a succession of affairs with the scholars who work on her husband's manuscripts and letters.

Decorum, the sense of guilt, the remnants of an older morality, the sense of obligation have not disappeared. But they are no longer at the surface of consciousness. These are haunted people, who have apparently rejected the strictures and who generally act out the deepest urgings of the unconscious. They take great pains to avoid being caught in adultery, in illicit behavior, they often painfully go through the motions of marriage and parenthood. One might assume them free, some through divorce, some through running away.

But the irony is that none of them is free. They are like people in a dream, or nightmare. Their actions rarely produce the reactions they seek. Their grip on reality is often so slight that Miss Oates can achieve the most surreal effects simply by contrasting their inner life with their outer experience.

In the course of the narratives, the old words appear, but their meanings are no longer part of the common language. Love and hate are interchangeable, tenderness and violence often the same,

the private worlds are pockets of agony. The housewife in "Puz-
zle" repeats, "I am not really here." Things do not come together.
She loved the man she married ("The sharp angry pain of love for
him in my own chest"), but she hated the man who became her
husband. "I loved that man, but the man who lived with us, the
man who slept with me, I hated."

Out of the past, come memories of other loves. In "Love and
Death," there is a strange revisiting of another time, a memory of
love, but the experience in memory is strangely without nostalgia,
only a kind of duel between two people who once might have
known each other.

There is extraordinary power here. In a very real sense, the
collection has the impact of a novel, a kaleidoscopic rendering of
the many masks of love. People striving "for sane contact," but
rarely finding it. People opening to one another only to find
punishment, rape, or even death. An illegitimate child appears
from the past, a Victorian theme if there ever was one, and the
father accepts, even welcomes blackmail. He wants to pay. A
young girl walks into a role after the death of the musician she was
going to marry. That emptiness is almost better than the doom of
life.

To call the stories depressing is to short-change the work of one
of the most brilliant writers at work today. Some artists—say, like
Solzhenitsyn—use life to transcend life. Joyce Carol Oates takes
us into the heart of the mysteries and we recognize them as our
own. She pulls us apart: It is for us to bring ourselves together.

September 9, 1972

GUNTHER STUHLMANN, ED.

The Diary of Anaïs Nin, 1931-1934

"*A sorrow made me create a protective cave, the journal. And now I am preparing to abandon this sorrow, this cave,*" Anaïs Nin wrote in November, 1933, at a time when she was in analysis with Dr. Otto Rank. He saw in it a "last defense against analysis. It is like a traffic island you want to stand on . . . I do not want you to analyze the analysis."

Fortunately for literature, Anaïs Nin returned after the analysis to that diary, one of the most remarkable in the history of letters. A portion of it now appears in *The Diary of Anaïs* Nin, 1931-1934 edited with an introduction by Gunther Stuhlmann.

Dr. Rank had said that she was "being kept" by the diary, that it was the "compulsion" of the diary he fought. But the artist within Anaïs Nin sensed that the diary, begun for personal reasons as a child, had evolved as a work in itself, differing in degree and even in style from her novels and stories, satisfying another need in herself, reflecting a special set of truths about herself: "A great passion for accuracy because I know what is lost by the perspective or objectivity of art. My desire to be true to the immediate moment, the immediate mood."

It is a theme which occurs over and over again. "If what Proust says is true, that happiness is the absence of fever, then I will never know happiness. For I am possessed by a fever for knowledge, experience, and creation," Miss Nin writes.

"I think I have an immediate awareness in living which is far more terrible and more painful. There is no time lapse, no distance between me and the present. Instantaneous awareness."

Others talked about the diary, noted the striking difference was her good and close friend Henry Miller. "Elaborate! That is the only way out of these watertight abstractions of yours. Break through them, divest them of their mystery and allow them to flow . . . I think that one of the reasons you have lodged yourself so firmly in the diary is because you fear to test your tangible self with the world. You are producing gems."

Again, Anaïs Nin followed her own intuition. "I think Henry is right about elaborating. But I think he does not understand that it is because I have a natural flow in the diary: what I produce outside is a distillation, the myth, the poem."

No one, not even Miller himself, has produced as discerning and living a portrait of Miller, of Antonin Artaud, of Miller's strangely troubled second wife, June, of dozens of other characters of that period in Paris. "Kill the diary, they say; write novels; but when they look at their portrait, they say: 'That is wonderful.' "

And these portraits are uncompromising; perhaps most uncompromising is the self-portrait. Weakness and strength equally are recorded in a prose so poetic and supple that all comes alive in terror, awe and beauty. After her second analysis (the first with Dr. Rene Allendy turned into an analysis of the analyst), Miss Nin considered becoming an analyst herself. She rejected it. "Just when I have learned not to clutch at the perfume of flowers, not to touch the breath of the dew, not to tear the curtains off, not to extract essences from petals, to let exaltation and dew rise, sweep by, vanish. The perfume of hours distilled only in silence, the heavy perfume of mysteries untouched by human fingers . . . To formulate without destroying with the mind, without tampering, without killing, without withering. That is what I have learned, that delicacy and awe of the senses, that respect for the perfume. It will become my law in writing."

The diary in this portion becomes an odyssey, more powerful than a novel, though possessed of the same elements, beginnings, a middle, a climax, but not an end for we can expect that the remaining volumes will be published. This volume stands on its own. When the rest come along, if they possess the same qualities of insight and perception, the whole will certainly be one of the enduring works of the diary form.

It has been said that each life if traced through its labyrinth of experience contains the elements of a revelation. But, as we see here, there are other elements involved. There must be one who sees in detail, who penetrates below the surface, who connects individual experience to universal truths . . . "Living is the constant motion toward unraveling, a dynamic movement from mystery to mystery."

There is the mystery of femininity and the mystery of identity, the mystery of poetry and the mystery of reality, the mystery of things, places and events. "I want to be the writer who reminds others that these moments exist; I want to prove that there is infinite space, infinite meaning, infinite dimension."

The ultimate test of this diary as a literary accomplishment is this: subtract the well-known names and you will still be interested in the characters and events which remain. For a long time, publication of these diaries has been anticipated. Miss Nin lived through the years which produced a great spasm of creativity. She knew writers, painters, musicians, dancers and actors. She was herself one of the central talents of this period. But unlike other memoirs—those of Sylvia Beach, for example—the interest in this volume does not depend on incidents and anecdotes. It is self-sufficient as a chronicle of a life lived with extraordinary intensity and sensitivity, recorded with great empathy and luminous understanding.

She began to write this diary as a child, to record for her father, the Spanish musician Joaquin Nin, who had deserted his family, their journey to America. She sought through this to win him back. (Some of the most touching scenes in the book deal with her relationship with her father in the years covered.) The journal became an island, a refuge. If it remained solely that, it would be of less interest than it is.

But it began to change. As she emerged into life, attempting to find herself, it gradually became something more than a protection against the world. In it she was able to discern in retrospect the thousand fragmented selves which make up a deep and sensitive person. Her face for the world to see was that of a beautiful woman, one of the most beautiful of her time. In these pages we see her despair, her shyness, her uncertainty, her enslavement to a past. But as the diary goes on, the identities become fused, meaningful and accepting of truths. Yet, even at the end, in 1934, as she is about to leave for America, after three crucial and exciting years, mysteries still remain. We live with her through relationships and friendships, analysis and the desperate experience of losing her prematurely born infant.

Of special interest is what she has to say to women. Few women diarists since the 18th century have so eloquently expressed the core of femininity. "We love best those who are, or act for us, a self we do not wish to be or act out," she writes near the end. She brings out in others not merely an extension of herself but, through a kind of catalysis, illumination. Even the tortured Artaud, haunted, driven by a sense of persecution, expresses this: "With most people you can only talk about ideas, not the channel through which these ideas pass, the atmosphere in which they bathe, the subtle essence which escapes as one clothes them."

All this is done without the loss of femininity no more than the lens loses its substance when the light passes through it. With this initial publication, Miss Nin, already assured of a place in contemporary literature, makes this doubly secure.

April 17, 1966

PHILIP K. JASON, ED.

Anaïs Nin Reader

"What I wanted to teach you," Anaïs Nin wrote in "Collages," giving the words to Varda, an older painter, "is contained in one page of the dictionary. It is all words beginning with *trans:* transfigure, transport, transcend, translucent, transgression, transform, transmit, transmute, transpire, and all the trans-Siberian voyages."

All of Miss Nin's writing is part of a single, larger transaction—between dream and reality, the unconscious and the conscious, the symbolic and the familiar. What gives it unity is the personality, its cluster of sensibilities reaching outward from the dream. The symbol of the labyrinth she so often uses is felicitous and many-leveled. One can enter it through the diaries, the stories, the novels, and even her nonfiction. . . .

Some critics have found it easier to dismiss Miss Nin as a cultic figure but in this they reveal more of their weaknesses than hers. For the armor they wear, breastplate and helmet, shields the areas of their own fears, and misunderstandings.

What they have not seen is that the artist need not be imprisoned by form, by convention, by tradition, and perhaps most important of all, refuses to be intimidated by a criticism which claims to be rational but in the end is more victim of repression and neurosis than the art which attempts to transcend the physical and reach the metaphysical.

In this sense, those who came to admire her in the early days before the publication of her diaries represented a respect for the courage and candor which is at the base of Miss Nin's writing. They did not reject the intimacy she offered, recognizing the dream-like world of her prose-poems and fictions was not a flight from reality but an effort to find the interdependence and interaction between dream and life, dream and action.

Miss Nin did not offer herself as the sacred figure of a cult but as the representative in art of a search with which others could identify.

That this search and odyssey was not handed down from above but was fought for and experienced in the real world is the ultimate lesson of this collection.

"The creative personality never remains fixed on the first world it discovers. It never resigns itself to anything. That is the deepest meaning of rebellion, not the wearing of different clothes, haircuts or adopting other cultures."

The diaries made that clearest of all. But when the diaries are read as they should be read, i.e., along with the creative writing, we begin to see the real challenge of the search. One can be a camera and tape recorder, record, report a world. But that "discounts all possibilities of change, of transformations . . . The poet reveals the differences which can rescue man from automatism."

The single brief entry of the diary of 1936, in Fez and Cadiz, illuminates a moment in which the poet escapes the bonds of introspection and is but one evidence that Miss Nin's writing is an account, evocative and perceiving, of the capacity for growth and discovery.

I do not suggest that her experience is the categorical imperative for all writers. Indeed, I take it as the central point of this book and the complex edifice of her work—the diary as laboratory, the dream and reverie, vision and hallucination as the materials of fiction, the symbol as a unity and synthesis of the forms of reality—as the way in which a writer, one writer, has demonstrated that "passageways" can be opened between the world and the "spiritual underground" and kept open.

The result of such a search is in these pages. "The total death of the novel was always being announced," she writes, "when what should have been observed was the death of certain forms of the novel. People cling to dead forms."

It turns out then that some of the critics were more cultic than Miss Nin. When she wrote, in her preface to Bettina Knapp's *Antonin Artaud*, she might have been referring to them:

"When a revolutionary spirit confronts his contemporaries, the violence of his contempt for banalities, for the dead weight of worn-out traditions, for dead symbols as D. H. Lawrence called them, causes antagonism and resistance. Fear paralyzes understanding."

Increasingly and deservedly she has won attention. Her art is resonant, speaks of the hunger for values and for health, celebrates the truths of the inner life, of perception, as against the "objective" and documentary, traces the deeper areas which inform the drives toward emancipation today.

There are no slogans here, no banalities, only a belief in the restorative value of experience, the new-old language of symbolism.

As Goethe said of *Wilhelm Meister*, we may say "People seek a central point: That is hard, and not even right. I should think a rich, manifold life, brought close to our eyes, would be enough without any express tendency; which, after all, is only for the intellect."

Miss Nin is not against the intellect any more than she is against the surface of the sea. She is against those who merely float in tiny boats constructed of their own fears. She has the courage of those who dive beneath, to the depths.

April 27, 1973

"Connects the I with Thou."
　　　—R. K.

"On the Eve of a Sabbatical"

Beginning next week and continuing for a year or so, I wil be in London to work on a research. The task I hope to complete in London (where most of my research will be done in the excellent library and manuscript collection of the British Museum) is one which had its origin in the work which I have done for *The Times* as book columnist and book editor for the last several years.

It also grows out of my own preoccupation with the form and purpose of the novel as one who has been concerned both as critic and novelist. Some of these ideas are tested in my own novel, *Madeleine Austrian*, which will be published by Simon & Schuster this fall.

In it I have attempted to return to some of the values which have been slighted in the modern novel with its emphasis on realism as an end in itself.

To continue this investigation and to crystallize these ideas, I plan to do a critical and historical study of the English-language novel. It is time and past to question some of the theories which have become dogma in our time. Others, notably Edmund Fuller and Jacques Barzun, have been engaged in similar and parallel examinations. Out of an intensive re-examination of the 18th-century beginnings of the novel and its spectacular development in the 19th century, I hope to find both a new set of critical standards and the direction which a renaissance of the novel may take.

Any art form must reflect the culture and values which make up its environment. The novel is a specially sensitive indicator of modern times. It is a by-product of the phenomenal growth of mass literacy in the last 200 years. It offers the greatest scope of experiment and type. Because of this freedom, the novel has been a reliable diagnostic device for social, philosophical and psychological theories at work in our civilization.

By the end of the last century, two theories of fiction had received their definition and statement: realism, or more properly psychological realism, by Henry James, whose eloquence and cognizance of the problems of craft and technique were unmatched in modern times; and naturalism by Emile Zola, who under the influence of the scientific method, saw in the novel a crucible through which the writer might examine under controlled circumstances the problems of man.

The impact of these developments was to concentrate on depicting man and the world as they really were. Thus, the critical standard applied was in terms of this realism: characters were "dimensional and credible"; situations were recognizable and believable. In sum, the measure of accomplishment became parallel to that of photography. Did characters look and act as they really did in life? But the imaginative core of fiction, the traditional cosmic setting, the context of values for the most part had disappeared or were atrophied.

The focus of concentration of psychological realism was cut down to the size of man dwarfed by the pressures of a mass society. Heroism was denied; the traditional mythos fragmented. Entertainment, in its oldest sense—taking over the mind and imagination of the reader—was frowned upon.

Somewhere in the past of the novel and the even deeper past of those forms whose values the novel inherited are to be found the shape and suggestion of a new and invigorating rebirth of fiction. One or two examples may suffice. Could Don Quixote or Captain Ahab be measured by any of the life-size standards imposed today? Could *War and Peace* or *Billy Budd* or *Madame Bovary* be produced by contemporary writers?

I do not suggest that realism is the villain of the piece but only that it has been substituted for all the potential and proven values of the fictional tradition. This is a vast field of inquiry and I do not know at this moment all or perhaps any of the answers. That is precisely why I feel myself compelled to devote the time and effort necessary to delve more deeply. I look forward to this challenge and hope to return with a new and deeper perspective on these matters.

July 24, 1960

ESSAY

"The Function of the Paperback"

As I read more and more original novels in paperback, it strikes me that this method of publishing has replaced some of the older media of training, experimentation and exploration in fiction.

Years ago the pulp magazines and the avant-garde magazines provided the two areas in which writers could prepare. Now the pulps are gone and the avant-garde is for the most part languishing. Paperback originals, with their demand for action and movement, their need to satisfy and compel the reader, their freedom of subject matter, have moved in to fulfill this need. . . .

March 11, 1960

WILSON MIZENER,

The Sense of Life in the Modern Novel

MARCUS KLEIN,

After Alienation

FREDERICK J. HOFFMAN

The Mortal No: Death and the Modern Imagination

I am beset by a kind of fantasy. I see men, healthy, well-fed, hefty, riding small creatures up a steep and rutted path. From the distance I cannot tell whether the beasts are lions or burros; I cannot tell whether, in fact, the men are separate from the creatures they ride. Are they liontaurs or burrotaurs?

The creatures emit weak and halting sounds, difficult to comprehend; the riders make orations, wise, eloquent and powerful. Certainly, their remarks make more sense than the cries of the beasts.

When I come out of this fantasy and try to make sense of it, I realize that the novel has been captured and tamed, its makers seduced or intimidated by the critics. I don't know how or why this has happened. But I can make some guesses. With rare exception, the functions of the novelist and the critic have merged. At the risk of oversimplification, what began as separate and even antagonistic functions; the novelist's goal of entertaining, the critic's goal of assessing and explaining, has become a kind of Gallagher-and-Shean vaudeville act. Sometimes, the dual role is played by the same individual, the novelist-critic, the critic-novelist. In other cases, the novelists, lions grown mangy and toothless, have been brought in for display in the menageries of English departments. The position is undeniably attractive, secure with tenure, protected from the risk of the jungle of ordinary readers, given the meat of love and acceptance on classroom and lecture-hall schedule.

And even if the post is not made official, there is feeding in fellowships, grants and subsidies, administered largely by the critics and scholars who must be impressed. What does it matter if Wright Morris or Herbert Gold or Harvey Swados are capable of boring the average reader to the point at which even television is to be preferred, so long as these writers offer convenient starting points for the *pilpul* of the critics.

So powerful is this tug toward theory and critical abstraction, that most new writers are far more articulate and interesting when they write about the mode, manner and method of their fictions, than when they write the fiction itself. It has gotten so that the interviews with writers in *Playboy* and *Time* magazine, not to speak of the autobiographical data they supply publishers, are far more compelling than the stories or novels they write. Everybody is aware of the process; few are concerned with the product.

This concern with process, redolent as it is of campus bull-sessions and of the adolescent reading of Henry James and Joseph

Conrad (not their stories or novels, but their prefaces, introductions and letters), is not the whole story. Much more of it comes from another function of criticism which is at its core justifiable and even important but which has, in the order of things, come to carry a burden it was never designed to bear.

Literature from its very beginnings has been oracular and symptomatic. The novel is no exception. As the prime literary form of modern times, the novel has been used by psychologists and philosopers, historians and theologians, to explain or amplify all sorts of insights. This is a legitimate area of criticism but it must be, I submit, only a by-product of the novel. Almost invariably when this didactic or metaphysical function usurps or preconditions the novel, it is the novel quality which suffers. *Uncle Tom's Cabin* undoubtedly had a great effect on the attitudes of readers but this by no means is the same as saying it was a great novel.

I do not want to give the impression that I am attacking the legitimate functions of criticism. Such a work as Frederic J. Hoffman's *The Mortal No: Death and the Modern Imagination* exemplifies the power and depth of certain scholarly criticism, properly concerned with issues of importance, with meaning, with rhetorical and aesthetic considerations. V. S. Pritchett illuminates another aspect of criticism, the wide-ranging, informal essay, the response of the gifted critical reader.

It is not therefore the critical function which can be blamed, but a fugue of conditions which make the critical stance attractive and even overwhelming to most novelists. In an age of voided belief and increasing uncertainty, critics retain some contact with tradition and a past. In an age of chaos and absurdity, critics are at least trying to elicit some pattern and meaning. In an age of insecurity, the critics are members of a community which offers some security. Critics represent some authority, some establishment, some influence. And finally, the unavoidable fact is that much of the writing of critics, in style, power and vitality, is simply better than the writing in most novels.

Hoffman's examination of the metaphor and meaning of death in the modern novel, his discussion of the response of writers as faith in transcendence over the fact of death declines, his examination of grace, violence and self, becomes, in simple fact, far more interesting and engaging to the reader than most novels published this year or, even, in the last 10 years. One might paraphrase Saville here, "The inquiry into a story is another story." And indeed, as things now stand, a more interesting story.

Marcus Klein tells us more about the age in which we live than most social novelists. In this, he is performing a useful function. He sees something new in the five writers he has chosen—Saul Bellow, Ralph Ellison, James Baldwin, Wright Morris, Bernard Malamud—something which has changed. They represent accommodation, rather than alienation. Allowing for the semantic adjustments, Klein's notion of accommodation is "that simultaneous engagement and disengagement which is the characteristic movement of the novel in these past years." He goes on: "The hero begins in freedom of the self and discovers that he is isolated. The hero chooses community—he assumes racial obligations, or he declares himself a patriot, or he makes love—and he discovers that he has sacrificed his identity, and his adventures begin all over again."

There is something missing: "not only the exhilaration of assault on the smug and somnolent community, but the conscience that such assault once implied. Once, to be an alienated artist-intellectual was to have clear and passionate convictions about the nature of good and evil." So, says Klein, accommodation "is restoration and love in their ordinary domestic, painfully contingent instances, and it makes up in plain necessity what it lacks in conscience."

The citation of evidence from the novels bears out at least to some extent (there is contrary evidence to be found in the work of at least two of the writers dealt with) the diagnosis. What is more interesting is the almost incidental treatment of alienation and its suggestion that a good many of the writers mentioned in the introduction are as much concerned with fighting critical battles as with writing. This suggests perhaps the central problem of the novelist in an age so overwhelmingly critical. As Philistinian as it may sound, the novelist ought to submerge the intellect as much as he can when he is writing. The term artist-intellectual is as senseless as those words Walter Winchell used to make up. Intellect is not excluded from the product or process of art but it must blend in imperceptibly. Intellect is essential to art. Indeed, in the process itself it can diminish and inhibit the imaginative. At the very best, it is something to be experienced.

Though I am no great follower of Wilson Mizener, and I disagree with many points he makes about the nature of realism and the expression of values in the novel (a position similar to the theory of the imagists in poetry) in *The Sense of Life in the Modern Novel*, I must concede that he understands the nature of the influence exerted by the critic on the novelist. " . . . Though it is true that good novelists are not writers who put into practice the theories of the novel dear to the critics of their time, as true that novelists are much more likely to be influenced by models that are analyzed and given prominence by the criticism of their time than by any other models, even those that may be far more congenial to their talents."

The critic's function is judgment, elucidation and the application of standards. He must deal with the tangible product, to elicit from it such wisdom as he can.

We have not mentioned the third important element in the triad. The reader. The novelist's concern must be primarily directed to him. Whatever else the novel may do, its primary purpose is to entertain. That's where it all started and the lack of entertainment may finish the novel. Klein speaks disparagingly of "mere entertainment" as one of the possible ends of alienation. One can only sigh and wish that in this he were right. Without entertainment, at least on its surface level, only critics can keep a novel alive by pumping in metaphysical oxygen. Both Pritchett and Mizener recognized that need. Pritchett on the 18th-century novelists should be required reading for novelists. Mizener seconds E. M. Forster's remark that the one indispensable element of the novel is the story.

And unfortunately, it is the story, the old, primitive compelling part of the novel, which is disappearing. And I wonder whether the decline in the novel is as simple as that. How many novelists are content with being mere tellers of tales?

July 19, 1964

ANTHONY WEST

Principles and Persuasions

If Anthony West's new book *Principles and Persuasions* were to be reviewed following his own technique, we might dismiss the volume as "interesting and stimulating" and then blandly go on to a discussion of the following possibilities:

Anthony West's personal history, his life and psyche in relationship to his writing and the Bloomsbury circle.

Or, a history of the *New Yorker* and its influence on the American short story.

Or, criticism of literature from Dryden through Dr. Johnson to Nancy Spain.

Or, the curious adventures of expatriate Englishmen in America from Smithson to Alistair Cooke.

Principles and Persuasions deserves a different kind of review, however, than Anthony West customarily gives those books which come before him. It is a collection of his essay-reviews which have appeared in the *New Yorker* from time to time. Along with it comes an introduction in the form of an explanation of his theory of criticism.

The introduction deserves special attention. In it West says he is not apologetic for his "negative" and "destructive" criticism. There are essentially two justifications, he writes. First is his concern to tear away the honeysuckle vine which has grown up about writers of the past. This he calls biographical criticism: "often destructive of a pose, and of values fabricated to sustain it, but . . . a soundly creative technique when it comes to literary assessments."

Thus, to West it is "simply grotesque to treat George Eliot's work as the disinterested product of a morally healthy personality and as a valid interpretation of the life of the time; but as a creation of the psychological necessities of an essentially second-rate mind driven by ruthless egotism it is of the greatest interest."

Now, no one would argue that a knowledge of the writer's life and personality is of assistance in understanding and assessing his work. But there is a serious question whether a work ought to be judged on its own merits and values rather than on an amateur psychologist's diagnosis.

For many writers of the past, whose lives are relatively obscure, Chaucer and Shakespeare, it is almost impossible to determine whether they "give a truthful interpretation of their experience." We do not know "how much [their] work is a contribution to knowledge, and by how much it is a simple reflection of (their) psychological necessities."

Further, it would seem dangerous to assume as West does that truth in an ultimate sense is to be measured by the "psychological necessities," whatever they may be. If this is applicable to nonfiction where objective standards may be utilized (and there is a substantial question here), it is certainly not as applicable to fiction where the writer's view of the world is essentially subjective and properly so.

West's second justification for negative and destructive criticism is that literature has become "a branch of the entertainment industry." The critic, he says, "must keep a sharp edge on words, and . . . maintain standards by occasionally exposing the commercial products that pass for contributions to our cultural inheritance to the full weight of aesthetic and ideological criticism."

Again, there is not much to argue with here except to inquire whether West himself practices what he so eloquently preaches. The answer is not always. He appears to be surprised that literature has become part of the entertainment industry. We would suggest that it always has been and that the author go to a sturdy dictionary to find the definition of entertainment.

Now to the reviews themselves. They are of two kinds. First, the kind which uses the book as an excuse for West to display his own erudition and it must be granted that he is a sort of literary Teddy Nadler. Second, the kind in which West uses the book as an excuse to reveal his own "psychological necessities." Neither type does much to assess the book reviewed.

West is a good essayist but his book reviews leave a good deal to be desired. He defends his pugnacious attitude by saying, "pap is pap and not good red meat." And with this truism we must agree. West's collection is neither pap nor good red meat but gristle which toughens the teeth and gives little nourishment.

March 8, 1957

NORMAN MAILER

Advertisements for Myself

My nomination for the sickest book of the year is that self-selected anthology of agony and anger, *Advertisements for Myself*. In the words of the hip-bop-beat boys, "Man, like he's flipped."

The book, whose dust jacket is adorned with not only one, not two, but five pictures of Mr. Mailer (a fact mentioned only for symptomatic purposes), is a collection of just about everything short he has ever written, fragments of two of his three novels and a chunk of his new novel. He would have been better advised to have skipped this book and gone on to the completion of the new novel.

In addition to his own work, some reviews on his work and some letters to the editor prompted by certain columns he wrote for a Greenwich Village newspaper, Mr. Mailer provides a running commentary in the form of prefaces which reveal him as a man of grotesque and frightening egomania, one who cannot take criticism but can certainly hand it out (not only to his critics but to just about every writer of stature in America as well as to his contemporaries), one who affects to be contemptuous of success but yearns after it with more appetite than the squares he despises.

Despite the thunderous rages, Mr. Mailer emerges as the advocate-victim of the system which he keeps telling us he hates. Book reviewers are incompetent (except those who reviewed his books favorably). Readers have no taste (but his own test of success is the sale of tens of thousands). His problem is that he read and believed the favorable reviews of *The Naked and the Dead* and obviously assumed that a runaway best seller is some sort of reliable index to the quality and greatness of a work. . . .

He fell into the man-trap of 20th-century American letters: the assumption that a writer is more important as a public personality than his writings are as literature. Curly-headed, tough, dirty-speaking, his image appealed to the star-makers. When his writing couldn't make it, he became angry at himself and at his audience.

For all his loud talk and his grandiose efforts to shock, he appears arrested at that childish state in which the juvenile aware-ness, discovering itself, assumes that it is not only the center of the universe; it is the universe.

The sad part is that Norman Mailer has not yet demonstrated any portion of that empathy and understanding necessary to take him out of his intense self-concern into the universe inhabited by other people. As a case history, *Advertisements for Myself* has a certain value; as a statement by an unhappy young writer it is largely a waste of time.

December 1, 1959

DONALD BARTHELME

City Life

Donald Barthelme is a critic's writer, particularly those critics who are less concerned with the experience of reading fiction than with the function of interpretation or that cerebral game of tracing trends and influences.

I first read some of the fictions which appear in his newest collection, *City Life*, in the *New Yorker* magazine. He is an extraor-dinarily gifted writer—which is to say that he can render experi-ence into words, communicating not only the surface event but the shape of the meaning and the penumbra of effect.

For critics who are interested in exploiting a writer to de-monstrate their own cerebral accomplishments, he offers unusual opportunity. For the common reader, there is a good deal less profit.

It was another experimental writer, Virginia Woolf, who spoke on behalf of those private people, citing that sentence from Dr. Johnson's *Life of Gray*: " . . . I rejoice to concur with the common reader; for by the common sense of readers, uncorrupted by literary prejudices, after all the refinements of subtility and the dogmatism of learning, must be decided finally all claim to poetical honors."

Barthelme has been praised highly by those younger academics who see him in the tradition of Borges and Kafka (they might well have said Sterne also), who see parallels to Barth and Robbes-Grillet, praise his elimination of ironic use of "the realistic matrix in which most works of fiction are embedded—the life-like quality that gives them credibility and coherence, the thematic explicitness that gives them the gratifying feel of significance," as Morris Dickstein wrote in the *New York Times Book Review*.

But this same critic also spoke of the "exhaustion of traditional forms," giving as an example Bellow's *Mr. Sammler's Planet*. And that is where I get off the train. Barthelme's experimentation with language, and more directly his abandonment of sequence and causality, his flight all the way to the antithesis of the explicit, is just too much.

Prof. Dickstein digs this, largely because it enables him to say such magisterial things as "One story that must be mentioned is 'Brain Damage,' which has no story at all but is a superb justification of Barthelme's fragmentary and surrealist method—he brings to mind the painter Magritte as much as he does any writer. It is one of the best pieces on non-sequential prose I've ever read."

I won't go into Prof. Dickstein's spasm about Barthelme's use of the abbreviation etc. in "Views of My Father Weeping" except to quote this sentence: "The story concludes, staggeringly, on the word 'etc.,' as if to say, you've heard all this before, fill in the blanks."

This is really the point. Some critics want to fill in the blanks for reasons other than the kind of entertainment the common reader seeks. Where the function is commentary, the more cryptic or provocative or even fragmentary the work, the more opportunity for the critic to expand and leap in interpretation.

Take this passage in a story called "Paraguay": "Behind the wall there is a field of red snow . . . I said to Jean Mueller, 'What is the point of this red snow?' . . . 'Like any other snow, it invites contemplation and walking about in.' . . . It had a red glow as if lighted from beneath. It seemed to proclaim itself a mystery, but one there was no point in solving—an ongoing low-grade mystery."

The potential is endless, but if the reader is not motivated to solve the mystery, then the experience lacks any kind of closure.

Barthelme strikes me as a very self-indulgent writer, demonstrating his talent impressively in such stories as the title one, brilliant, subtle, dreamlike, frightening, relating the experiences of detached and detachable human beings in the parapsychological space of the "exquisite mysterious muck, (which) heaves and palpitates . . . is multi-directional, and has a mayor," and then going off into the oddments of "Brain Damage" which is a preachment without parables.

In the end, the critic has to weigh the extent to which satisfactions are balanced with dissatisfactions for himself and his needs, but he also has an obligation to speculate about the common reader. In this book, the pleasures traditionally sought in fiction are rarely found.

June 15, 1970

LAWRENCE STERNE

Tristram Shandy

It will come as no surprise to readers of this column that if I were backed to the wall and asked to choose a single novel which I considered to be the best, the most interesting, the most experimental, I should have to choose Laurence Sterne's *Tristram Shandy*. Fortunately, I am not driven to such extremes. But I cannot forebear mentioning a new paperback edition of this work.

What appeals to me most about this novel is that it contains within its rambling structure just about every technique that has ever been thought of in connection with the novel. Prof. Weales suggests one that I had not thought of before, that "for all that is novelistic about it—it is anti-novel as much as it is anti-book." He is, of course, right as even Robbes-Grillet and Nathalie Sarraute will have to admit. So Sterne's record as the first innovator of all still stands.

I must warn those who despise sex to avoid reading this novel, as well as those who feel foolish when laughing. And while I am in a warning mood, I might as well alert those who wish crystal clarity in narration, stark realism, and profound moral strictures.

Perhaps my own affinity for this mad novel comes from my student days when I read that Samuel Richardson attacked it as filled with "unaccountable wildness; whimsical incoherencies; uncommon indecencies . . ." Richardson, in his work, was of the order described by Tristram himself: "Of all the cants which are canted in this canting world—though the cant of hypocrites may be the worst—" [and here I am about to stop for obvious reasons] "the cant of criticism is the most tormenting!"

November 13, 1962

John O'Hara

Assembly

I'll take O'Hara anytime.

I'll take him over the assorted literary ward heelers, the critical lap dogs, the academic pets who can't hammer out anything more than non-story fragments and long prose fashioned, like some alleged modern sculpture, out of junk. I'll take him over the pampered, puffed-up darlings who are long on favorable reviews but short on the stuff that attracts readers.

I'm beginning to feel a real sense of gratification when I see the New York reviewers concoct elaborate theories about John O'Hara short being better than John O'Hara long. They're just writhing, of course.

While these hyenas are yipping, John O'Hara is writing. His new collection of short stories *Assembly* is first-rate. There isn't a bad story in the 26. Ten of them appeared in the *New Yorker*. Two of them approach novella length. All of them illustrate the tremendous virtuosity which indicates not only a master's skill but also the kind of growth and variety which is the mark of brilliance in a writer.

After 11 years away from the short story, O'Hara went back to it. (Most of these stories, as he tells us, were written during the summer of 1960.) What brought him back to the short story was an "urge." He calls it an "apparently inexhaustible urge to express an unlimited supply of short story ideas." That is, not as some of his detractors would suggest, a need to shorten and compress, but materials which by their nature and characters demanded the short story form rather than the novel.

Only those who try to break O'Hara into two parts—to make of him some kind of schizoid character—can maintain the position that he is a better short story writer than a novelist. It is necessary to dispose of that fiction because it has become the rationalization of many reviewers when dealing with his work. The short story and the novel are two separate and distinct literary forms. For the real writer, i.e. one who recognizes this distinction, the short story is not a novel boiled down and distilled into a few pages and the novel is not a short story padded and fattened with literary cholesterol until it is large enough to make a hefty book.

O'Hara knows the difference. It is the difference, if we have to look for ordinary similes, between a jab and a left hook, a compact car and a limousine.

What you read here, then, are short stories, not digested novels. They are not dashed off. They are made to be read at one sitting, to stir you into attention and to sustain that attention, to give you an illusion of the beginning before the beginning and the ending after the end.

December 6, 1961

RUPERT HART-DAVIS, ED.

The Letters of Oscar Wilde

"A publishing event of major literary importance" is a phrase cheapened and nearly made devoid of value by the dust jacket copy writers. But it is perfectly applicable to *The Letters of Oscar Wilde*, edited by Rupert Hart-Davis. This is a work of superb scholarship, a contribution not only to literature but that relatively rare example of scholarship which should appeal to the lay reader.

If Rupert Hart-Davis deserves praise for the honesty and courage, the completeness of his search (1,098 of the Wilde letters are published in the volume with only three slight deletions; the remaining 200 are brief notes of no literary or biographical interest), it is the inimitable style and the complex character of Wilde which makes fascinating reading.

We see Wilde in this collection not only in his posturing eloquence but in such searing honesty (however self-pitying it becomes at times) that this volume comes closer to the essential Wilde than any biography yet attempted.

Wilde's notoriety in the scandalous Queensberry trials, the smashing of the literary idol who went from tremendous success to a shattering prison term, the caricature who became a tragic figure—all of these account for the tremendous and continuing public interest in the man. Some of his work has an unquestioned place in English literature. Yet with everything that has been written about Wilde—the studies, the biographies, the plays and motion pictures based on his trial and punishment—there remains a good deal more to be said. And in this book, the missing portions are supplied.

We begin to get an approximation of the extent of Hart-Davis' task when we realize that Wilde's letters were dispersed all over the world in private and public collections.

Efforts had been made before to collect and publish the Wilde letters. But this is the first complete publication. Such a collection would be important under any circumstances for a figure of

Wilde's stature in English literature. It has an enhanced importance because of the special nature of Wilde's talent. As he recognized, his talent was in life even more than in work. He was a conversationalist. And as Hart-Davis says, " . . . The art of the talker, like that of the actor, dies with the artist and can seldom be recaptured from the written word. Perhaps the nearest approach to it is by way of letters, particularly those written to intimate friends without thought of publication."

There are two kinds of letters here. The first are those which appear before the end of the disastrous trial. Almost the last of these is to his good friend Ada Leverson, whom he called fondly "the Sphinx," in which the mask of cleverness, self-conscious glibness is still worn. Ironically, he mentions that a fortuneteller has prophesied complete triumph. But the mask is slipping. The letters are tinged with the anticipation of doom. To his wife on the 5th of April, 1895, he writes a desperate little warning, "Allow no one to enter my bedroom or sitting room—except servants— today. See no one but your friends." After this, the voice becomes constricted and emotional, filled with terrors; it is the voice of the tragic hero in the fifth act.

There is no time for posturing. The hubris is exposed and punished. In the years between 1895 and 1897 while he is in prison, we see a spirit and a soul in torment. After he is released and goes into exile, there is an epilogue, not a very admirable or attractive one, in which he seems to become both a mockery of what he was prior to the trial and what he seemed to become in the catharsis of his agony. In these letters from 1897 to his death in November, 1900, he has become a pathetic figure, mooching money, attempting to resurrect the disastrous relationship with Douglas, writing with only a shadow of his old eloquence and fire. Death, when it finally came, was a blessing.

For me, the letters between 1895 and 1897 have an almost unbearable power. They are, naturally, the most revealing. But not merely in detail. Rather in insight, self-analysis, perception. Of particular interest, from every point of view, is the long (nearly 100 pages in the book) letter written in January and March, 1897, addressed to Lord Alfred Douglas from Reading Gaol, but not posted. From this letter was drawn *De Profundis*, possibly the most important work ever to be published under Wilde's name. Yet, *De Profundis* amounted to less than half the writing which appears in this letter and contained no reference to Douglas. The manuscript of the letter was presented to the British Museum by Wilde's faithful friend, Robert Ross, in 1908, on condition that no one be allowed to see it for 50 years. This is the first time, then, the letter has appeared in print exactly as Wilde wrote it. This alone would be a literary event of the first magnitude. There is an awesome power in these words. No shred of illusion or self protection remains.

The letter is nominally addressed to Douglas but it is really Wilder's letter to himself and posterity. That it is one of the most searing indictments of a human being ever written is only part of the truth. But it does not only demolish Douglas, the cruelty, the thoughtlessness, the betrayal. It demolishes Wilde himself in one of the most unsparing documents I have ever read. But there is not only the explanation of the relationship, not merely a masochistic revelation, there are hints of what Wilde might have become in the world of letters had not these events tarnished him and made him a symbol for another aspect of human life.

For it is not the element of homosexuality which is important in these lines. This is perhaps what has kept a certain curiosity alive. In the end, it obscured some very important things about Wilde in terms of the very direction of literature. His personality kept getting in the way but Wilde might have emerged as the spokesman and theorist of an important balancing element in the literary currents of the turn of the century. To some extent, he does serve as the spokesman for what is glibly called "art for art's sake" and in survey courses he is a convenient cartoon with his long hair, his velvet jacket and his lily of the valley. But this is only a faddish thing.

Where he might have served, had he not been destroyed as a serious literary influence, had he not been simply a symbol of aberrance, he might have served as a rallying point for an older current in literature, an aesthetic which might have kept alive certain values which were overrun by the surge of realism and naturalism.

Lest you think I am making too much of this, I would point out that the *De Profundis* letter not only covers Wilde's personal life and response, it is, in fact, a manifesto of the imaginative in art. He realizes that his own behavior, his own weakness (he spoke of his proclivities as a mania) had undermined his claim as a spokesman. "As regards the other subject, the relation of the artistic life to conduct, it will no doubt seem strange to you that I should select it. People point to Reading Gaol and say, 'There is where the artistic life leads a man.' " He never lost his sense of the sarcastic.

The point, here, in this writing, is precisely the opposite. Too many critics and commentators have leaped to the facile connection. But the point which Wilde makes is precisely the opposite. He considers his life a failure not because of art but because of his human flaw. It is not the art which betrayed him but the sensual, material side of his life.

It is precisely in passing from romance to realism, to the fascination of "the gutter and the things that live in it" that brought his downfall. "The real fool, such as the gods mock and mar, is he who does not know himself." As "incomplete, imperfect," as he recognizes himself to be, he defends without shame not what he has done, but what he might have done with his art. "The past, the present and the future are but one moment in the sight of God, in whose sight we should try to live. Time and space, succession and extension, are merely accidental conditions of thought. The imagination can transcend them, and move in a free sphere of ideal existences. Things, also, are in their essence what we choose to make them."

Here we get a clue to the deeper tragedy. Not the gossip, not the scandal, not the lurid and distasteful exposés, but the image of a man not merely punished by prison and disgrace but punished by the ultimate betrayal of a vision which he could not realize.

October 21, 1962

CAROLYN G. HEILBRUN

Toward a Recognition of Androgyny

> *The dark area (Yin) of the inner circle contains a white dot and the*
> *light area (Yang) contains a black dot; this teaches that even in the*
> *purest state each pole contains the seed of the other.*
>
> *–Alfred Douglas, on the I Ching*

That graceful circle symbol of Yin and Yang, feminine and masculine, curving into each other, containing the seeds of each other, is a very old expression of the ideal which Carolyn G. Heilbrun examines in *Toward a Recogniton of Androgyny*. In this book of three essays she seeks to ameliorate the word itself, which derives from the Greek *andro* (male) and *gyn* (female) and to her suggests a spirit of reconciliation between the sexes.

The residue of revulsion against the word, often used as a simile for hermaphroditism, "an anomalous physical condition," she says, stems from the polarization of sexual roles which is predominant in the Judaeo-Christian tradition and reached its strongest point in the patriarchy of the Victorian period.

Exploring myth and literature in search of expressions of the androgynous ideal, she finds a richness of signals, in Virginia Woolf's phrase, "pointing to a force in things which one has overlooked." The first essay, indeed, is called "The Hidden River of Androgyny."

She began writing these pieces in 1964 when the caricatures of sexuality were much firmer than they are today, less than 10 years later. What could have been a highly controversial book is overtaken by a swift change in attitudes, at least public attitudes, though the shift may be more apparent than real.

The conditioning of centuries—which saw the "masculine" as forceful, competent, competitive, controlling, vigorous, unsentimental and occasionally violent; the "feminine" as tender, genteel, intuitive, passive, unaggressive, submissive and weak—does not easily give way.

Few today will quarrel with Miss Heilbrun's concept of the

liberating possibilities of androgyny, particularly as it expresses a notion which has the power of an idea whose time has arrived.

The most useful part of her study is to remind us that the idea had an ancient and persistent pedigree, that its expression in literature has been the result of the efforts of individual artists, of both men and women to transcend the "prison of gender."

" . . . Recognition, not revolution, is the object of this essay. My method is to use the vast world of myth and literature as a universe in which to seek out the sometimes obscure signs of androgyny. My hope is that the occasional interpretation I bring to the literature of the past will suggest new ways of responding to the circumstances of our own lives and the literature of our times."

The marvelous thing about literary criticism is a reflection of literature itself, its variety and complexity. Depending on the lens the critic uses to examine the works of the past, new perceptions are bound to appear.

This volume is a good example both of the values and weaknesses of that function. Miss Heilbrun is aware of this, and nowhere does she make it clearer than in her essay, "The Woman as Hero." Discussing *Wuthering Heights*, she says, "The androgynous view of the novel is not meant to supplant but to accompany other interpretations. . . ."

This enables her to recognize Tolstoy as a great novelist, though he "failed so absolutely to embody in his great work any androgynous quality whatever," defining the source of his greatness as the writer of works which, "in the words of Lionel Trilling, give 'the novel its norm and standard, not of art but of reality.' "

The suggestion is that with androgyny, art is not only possible but probable, without it the result is inevitably a form of reportage of fidelity to what is and not what may be. The redeeming quality of Miss Heilbrun as a critic is that though she flirts with a kind of polarization she avoids, in most situations, becoming the prisoner of theory.

The flaw in the study lies not in the concept of androgyny which refreshes and invigorates literary criticism with a new relevance, but in the occasional distortions it promotes.

Social vision is important, but it does not always guarantee the emergence of greatness, either in critics or in creative writers.

This, despite Coleridge's observation, " . . . a great mind must be androgynous."

March 26, 1973

Helen Gurley Brown

Sex and the Single Girl

Sex and the Single Girl is about as tasteless a book as I have read this year. I'm sure it wasn't intended that way; it just happened. It is, in fact, hardly a book at all but a collection of burblings, printed, bound and provided with a dust jacket.

It has what is called in a part of the book world (the part where books are referred to as "projects") a selling title. But the price is far too expensive for a title: 99 cents a word, excluding retail tax. After the title, the text goes to pieces.

Miss Brown (a courtesy title since she has left the single life for matrimony) has produced a pastiche of hints, diets, tricks designed to hunt and trap the male who is regarded as the natural but necessary prey of women. The style is a conbination of beauty parlor gossip ("Betty took up oil painting, without ever having drawn a line in her life, and it transformed her previously dull weekend into a Gauguin-like fiesta") and what is called in advertising creative copy writing ("You 'can' have something else with make-up . . . an interesting face, an alive face, a sexy face").

Her purpose is manipulation. It is based on the assumption that the sizzle sells the steak. Most of all I detect a thorough contempt for men who are the marionettes of this manipulation. There is the assumption that they are blind to artifice and shrewdness, that they are pushovers for the clever and designing woman.

I very nearly said the "designed" woman. Miss Brown provides the blueprint of a female so phony that the man who cannot see through the mask and affectation deserves his fate. The point is that she reduces to ritual that which should be natural, to the spurious that which should be authentic. Indeed, everything is front.

The pathetic thing is that Miss Brown doesn't seem to realize it. She rushes breathlessly from punchy paragraph to compressed exposure, a creature of the advertising age, endorsing the phoniness and hard-soft-subliminal sell which substitutes for individuality, candor, sincerity. What she describes as sex is not sex at all but a kind of utility. Perhaps futility would be a better word.

Love, honesty, romance, the glow of an authentic emotion is not, and couldn't be here. She goes so far as to recommend that a single girl "borrow" children. And somehow this sums it up— decorate the apartment, get the right travel posters, put magazines in the bathroom, find the right perfume, get the proper props—it's all a masquerade anyway.

"The question is," she writes, "is your image coming through?" She ought to look up the word in the dictionary (a process which would have helped the book in general). I'm tired of the image coming through. I think most human beings, single girls included, would be delighted to abandon the image and start dealing with real people again.

The case studies who clutter up this book are about as uninspiring as a bunch of wax dummies. Poses are calculated; lighting is calculated; raises are calculated. "The charm that brings him to your side after five will enlist him in your behalf at the six-months' salary review," she writes after assuring us that she became the highest-paid advertising woman in Los Angeles, at least for a while.

Matrimony has placed her in a dilemma of equities. For single women, she still recommends playing around with married men. Among the cons of such an arrangement:

"He almost never gets a divorce.

"He is practically useless on Saturday nights, Sundays, holidays and, nine times out of ten, on your birthday.

"You can't introduce him around as your beau.

"He never introduces you to his boss or other influential figures in his life."

The pros outweigh:

"He can be your devoted slave and remain 'faithful' to you for years.

"He will love you more passionately than the woman he married, and prefer your company to hers.

"He is often generous with gifts and money. If he isn't, you can explain the facts of life."

Miss Brown's concern with presents, money and other "spoils" of the single life reappear throughout the book. If candor and precision were the rule, she might prefer another word.

She uses her own experiences throughout the book. But now that she is married, her "cavalier" attitude toward wives seems somewhat changed. She went with her husband to a Sunset Strip coffee house, crowded with lovely young starlets. It was his birthday so she let him stay exactly one hour. I assume we may expect a sequel on *Sex and the Married Woman*.

July 6, 1962

ELIZABETH TAYLOR

Elizabeth Taylor: An Informal Memoir

"This book is probably best described not as an autobiography—that's much too pretentious—but as a long, slightly overcozy conversation with a garrulous broad named Betty Burton."

Betty Burton? Think a minute. Elizabeth Burton. Elizabeth Taylor Burton. Elizabeth Taylor. That's it. She has written a book. I *believe* she has written it herself. It is called *Elizabeth Taylor: An Informal Memoir*. For those who are knocked out by the styrofoam style of fan magazines, this airy overview of Miss Taylor's life may hold some interest. For me, the effect was expressed best by Miss Taylor herself: "The public me, the one named Elizabeth Taylor, has become a lot of hokum and fabrication—a bunch of drivel—and I find her slightly revolting."

Mind you, I am not talking about the circumstances of Miss Taylor's public and private life. I will leave it to others to make those judgments. The point which struck me is that the real Miss Taylor is just as much of a pompous, matronly, cliche-captive bore as the public Miss Taylor. If we are to judge her by this book, we can only find her guilty of shallowness, poor taste, poor writing, and vanity, which are misdemeanors in today's world and as common as traffic violations.

We are just as much at fault in this transaction as she is. After all, we buy the books. We participate in the ritual which elevates quite ordinary, banal human beings to the status of worshipped icons. We attribute mystery, value, awe and depth to our stars. And this should tell us more about ourselves than this book tells about Miss Taylor.

What does emerge here is the partial self-portrait of a woman who embodies some strikingly median traits. And I am not questioning her sincerity here. I think that she is aware of the phoniness. But she may be a captive of the belief that beneath the tinsel there is something of substance. Judging from this book, I doubt it.

At the end of the book, she writes: "I have often wondered what kind of a person I would be today if I did not have these enormous guilts—if everything had gone easily and I had not made such horrific mistakes. I think I would have been the most awful, pontifical Goody Two Shoes. I was really so smug, so sweet, so good, so spoiled—so intolerant of anybody else's downfall."

She disapproves of those who make conjectures about the private lives of movie stars. But the point here is that the whole book is evidence that underneath it all, Miss Taylor is smug, spoiled, selfish, and, in the end, tedious. She is also a handsome woman with a modest talent for acting in films. Most of all, despite her constant protestations, she is a prisoner of her own myth. Had she not been an actress, she would most certainly have been the apotheosis of the movie fan. In fact, beneath all the veneer of sophistication, that is what she is: a namedropper, a believer in the Hollywood legend of love and romance, a housewife elevated, beyond her wildest Walter Mitty fantasies, to the heaven of Hollywood.

December 3, 1965

ERROL FLYNN

My Wicked, Wicked Ways

Errol Flynn's autobiography has that commodity which is evidently highly prized in the current market for show business exposes. It is revealing, candid and lusty; Flynn names names and places. And if you are interested in the low life in the high places of Hollywood, you won't be disappointed. But the book is more revealing, perhaps unintentionally, in other, more important, matters, which I would, for lack of a better term, call the pathos of prominence. This is a disease, or perhaps more accurately, a symptom of our times. A society reveals itself by its hero-symbols. And Flynn, for a good part of his life and for a good many people, was such a symbol.

This volume, which to the best of my information, was not ghost-written, reflects no little writing talent. For all its sprawling formlessness, it is an honest effort to probe Flynn's own character and personality, an honest attempt to understand the forces by which he was driven and against which he contended. He was a mediocre actor, a fact which he recognized although he was not without his dreams of true greatness in the theater. A combination of accident and luck brought him to Hollywood. He was a handsome and athletic man.

The films needed a dashing personality; in whatever mysterious way these things happen, he answered that need. "All my life the one thing I feared most was mediocrity—and my whole living effort was to oppose ever being or becoming a mediocrity. I did not wish to live in a mediocre way, nor to be regarded artistically as a mediocrity. This was to me the cardinal sin, to be middling was to be nothing," he writes.

An important factor entered his experience. Flynn had always liked women, excitement, trouble. But Hollywood catapulted him into another world. Suddenly he was in the spotlight, making a great deal of money, receiving adulation, meeting other prominent people. He was unequipped as most of the celluloid heroes are unequipped for this burden of modern fame.

It was empty and he was empty, a hollow man, playing hollow roles in a succession of adventure films which offered no satisfaction, no sense of accomplishment. If numbers create these modern idols, numbers destroy them. Everything they do becomes a matter of public interest, morbid or otherwise. Flynn had his share of these experiences: marriages which could not possibly survive the demands made on them; the lack of privacy; adoration which cannot possibly evoke in the admired any sense of real worthiness; the punitive legend which pursues those the mass sets up in order to destroy. For the matinee hero, we know unconsciously, is necessarily unreal. The symbol who reflects the urge of a community which wants a hollow hero must inevitably succumb to the corruption of that adulation.

It reminds one of the young men and women who, were chosen as human sacrifices to the gods of the Aztecs, raised up, praised, given every comfort, only to be destroyed.

January 17, 1960

HAROLD GILLIAM

The San Francisco Experience

Harold Gilliam, the naturalist and conservationist, first came to the Bay Area as a student at Berkeley three decades ago. I think it fair to say that it was love at first sight—and many who share that love will understand Gilliam's *The San Francisco Experience*.

If feeling is at the base of the book, it is no uncritical celebration of that city and its hinterland and bayscape, "like some modern Camelot." This is not a work of puppy love or boosterism, but a series of essays and stories, combining history and geography, nature and man's artifacts, in an effort to communicate emotion and information. It is a work worthy of that remarkable, even superlative city.

There is something about the work of a naturalist which encourages and even demands a poet's sensibility and his gift for rendering experience into words. Gilliam possesses these in gratifying measure. As a scientist, he knows weather and terrain and the cycle of life, but Gilliam is also committed to seeking significance and wholeness, to defining and penetrating the interaction between men and environment which forms experience.

Many of these essays are expanded from their original publication in the *San Francisco Chronicle*. But, as attractive as are the parts, the whole is something more than their sum. The achievement of this sense of life and reality is worth some examination.

Gilliam may occasionally deal with abstractions and generalizations, but the triumph is in detail and evocation of individual experience. The men and women presented here are contemporary—coast guardsmen and vineyard foremen, airline pilots and tugboat captains, commuters and artists—or historical personages—bridge builders and poets, architects and Spanish explorers, Indians and merchants.

Natural phenomena may be explained scientifically but they are also evoked. The scientist's knowledge melded with the poet's metaphor. One may go from the giant Tamalpais, seen magically from the distance, to the closest look at its creeks and meadows, the sounds of water flowing, and the spider's web spun between three blades of grass, or follow the red-tailed hawk in his flight against the backdrop of bridge towers and skyscrapers and the observatory on Mt. Hamilton.

Perhaps most important is the question of significance. One may experience the sights and sounds, the taste and smell of a complex city, made by man in the complex theater of a heroic, sometimes perilous nature. But it is precisely the quest of humanity to go beyond awareness into perception.

Does this experience tell us something? What is its meaning? At the heart of the book is something close to the demand of art: that deeper intuition of a particular moment or setting captured in its essence and made universal.

Such epiphanies are rare and yet periodically we sense them in this book. Sometimes as in the account of the Berkeley fire, the destructiveness of which cannot compare with the man-made violence of recent years in that community. Occasionally, in the verses of a Robert Frost, who caught the ominous tragic potential of Lobos Creek:

> *The shattered water made a misty din.*
> *Great waves looked over others coming in,*
> *And thought of doing something to the shore*
> *That water never did to land before.*
> *The clouds were low and hairy in the skies . . .*
> *It looked as if a night of dark intent*
> *Was coming, and not only a night, an age . . .*

The city has not wiped out the land though natural catastrophes such as earthquake vie with manmade catastrophes such as pollution. Grand View Peak somehow survives the bulldozers and the builders, an extraordinary haven for wildlife and plants, a meeting place of inland and marine weather, forming on occasion, a giant apparition of fogs and mists, the ghost which residents report seeing.

Typically, Gilliam has seen it too although he knows it is a perfectly natural phenomenon. He relates it to a similar incident reported by John Muir at Half Dome.

There is much more here, a heroic effort to capture the complexity and significance of the San Francisco experience. There are no glib, final answers. As a student, Gilliam raced to the impulsive notion that such a superlative environment could produce superlative people. Then he drew back from this romantic theory.

Now he is no longer certain that within this arena of the Bay Area some quality of energy and innovation, ferment and challenge, is charged by the nature of the land and weather, the history and the tragedy.

April 25, 1972

John Lennon

John Lennon in His Own Write

Beatlemania is a gentle lunacy, ad leest I think it were. Farther am I of a beatle awtor, ten of age. My books I reed; she her beatles collects, records and bubble gum cards, pitchers of robin-nested headed Liddypool ya-ya-ya ringers and singers.

Between the tew of us is a mersey-full chasm of years: I short-haired and tome-full in my study; she wildhaired and on the tellyphone retelling gossip of paul and george and john (the married one) and ringo, listening to the ya-ya-ya rolling over Beethoven. Never the skein would meet.

Except, thus john (the married one, arty-writty one) writ and drawed a book. Then, suddenly I was sub-one in mine own howshold again. For the publisher send to be this book, *John Lennon in His Own Write*, ya-ya-ya-ya. Not only that but paul writ an introduction. It was sprigtime again. My bittle dauthor came to me and:

"Dad, yew dew review books?"

"Ya-ya-ya," I sid, "so yew can buy beatle records."

"Are yew going to write about john's book? It's so cute."

"I dare not sink of reviewing that book, if it is a book," I said.

"Please be serious, for a moment," she said.

That hid me. My own dauthor turning cereal—about books.

"The Times Literary Sublimate of London," she said, "wrote that John's volume is 'worth the attention of anyone who fears the impoverishment of the English language or the British imagination.' "

"Yew r kidding," pled I.

"No. It's says so right here."

So it did.

"And the *London Daily Mail:* 'What might at first glance seem just nutty as a fruitcake is planted with anarchist bombs popping damagingly under straitlaced notions.' "

"Bud yew see that English reviewers dew not have to signify their name on their review. I will have to live under a crowd of suspicion if I revue that book. In fact, I may nod have a job if I did and my heir might nod grow and I am tone-deaf," I said.

"If you could review this book," she hesitated (and I new that English reviewers had had beatle dauthors), "then when they come to Los Angeles maybe I could get a ticket to the Hollywood Bowl."

"Suppose I did not like this book," I asked.

"Oh Dad!"

"Well, I mean, it is a question of ethics. I cannot be bought. It is a well-known fact."

"You would sacrifice your ownly daughter's happiness, her future, everything."

Put that way, what would yew have done?

Here follows a revue of john's own write:

John Lennon is the natural heir of the Victorian nonsense writers. One senses in these parodies, poems and word ploys, the spirit of Edward Lear and, in an earthier way, the touch of Lewis Carroll. His drawings are deft and untutored, suggesting a younger Thurber.

The touch is puerile, even pre-adolescent, the marvelous and pure silliness of the very young yet with a touch of sadness and a wisdom of one "bored on the 19th of October 1940 when, I believe, the Nasties were still booming us led by Madalf Heatlump . . ." The rhythm of the poems is that of the interrupted nursery rhyme:

"*I'm a moldy moldy man*
I'm moldy thru and thru
I'm a moldy moldy man
You would not think it true."

As for technique, we find certain clues in "All Aboard Speeching":
"For sample, the word frenetically wrote, must be charged grammatically with vowel pronounced strangely . . ."
Or. "Speak you Clear and Nasal, for distance . . ."
The fragmentation of experience is expressed in the unconscious yearning toward the secure poverty of pre-11-plus school days:

"*He is putting it lithely when he says*
Quobble in the Grass,
Strab he down the soddielfays
Amo amat amass . . ."

Now that was the whey I yewsed to writ revues. From now on, I know lunger feer the impauverichment of the Inglis lengwidz, that old moldy figyour of speech. I am lunched on my new style: ya-ya-ya.

May 8, 1964

ESSAY

"Paris Students Topple Ivory Tower"

PARIS—Some are calling it "La Revolution Culturelle a la Chinoise." Francois Mitterand, one of the leaders of the opposition, describes the events of the last 12 days as "La Revolte de la Jeunesse."

These assessments may be premature. But there is no question that the student demonstrations here represent a historic departure. For the first time, student unrest has triggered a powerful and for the moment unified response in France. In years past, student demonstrations were regarded as a natural concomitant of life in the Latin Quarter or as a result of initial pressures from other sectors; political, economic or social.

Few could have predicted that a minor disciplinary incident at the suburban campus of Nanterre, the call for police assistance by the rector of the Sorbonne, would have escalated so quickly into a major confrontation, attended by scenes of conflict which for many recalled the days when the French underground emerged to challenge the German occupation troops in Paris.

If it is a revolt, it has come before it has had a chance to decide on its goals. The students and most of the professors in the universities, the Grandes Ecoles, the Lycees, want a reform and renewal of the system which they contend is out of touch with the real world. The nature of that reform is not yet apparent and such policies as the Fifth Republic (which has called education "the most prior priority") has pursued are themselves a part of the malaise. One writer, Francois Nourrissier, says:

"The task of summing up . . . the traditions, incoherencies, successes, shortcomings and present evolution of the French educational system calls for something like prestidigitation. How is one to describe an academic system which is being reformed so rapidly that the students themselves do not know in December what examinations they will be expected to take in June, or if they will take any . . . ?"

Nor were there any specific answers given when students, having won their immediate demands—release of those arrested, withdrawal of the police from the Latin Quarter, reopening of the Sorbonne—met in the great amphitheater in a scene reminiscent of the days of the French Revolution. There were plenty of slogans and eloquent speeches, a profusion of slogans: restructure the university; change the system; make it more relevant.

Outside, the hundreds of thousands of marchers in the giant demonstration of the day of the general strike shouted other slogans: "The power is in the streets." But the most thoughtful in the universities, in the political opposition, in the government, know that the meaningful reform in education, which all concede is badly needed, will come from dialog and study, consultation with students and professors.

If, as is generally conceded, the system is swamped by numbers, archaic curriculum, suffering a lowering of standards (with some exceptions), unrealistic, chaotic, if students feel alienated, confused, angry, is there a difference between the French student demonstrations and, say, those at Columbia or UC Berkeley?

There is. With its highly centralized school system, the target becomes clearer. Little time was spent in criticizing rector Jean Roche; the demonstrations quickly soared to the source of policy and power: the government. And today in France, there is hardly a family which does not have a son or daughter in higher education or in the Lycees with the hope of going on.

That is why the French student demonstrations can be called revolutionary. As the demonstrations began, students marching down the middle-class streets such as Rue de Rennes received cheers from the windows; flowers were thrown to them. In the conflict at Gaye-Lussac, householders lowered pails of water to those suffering through the tear gas attacks, at great risk offered refuge and asylum to those attempting to flee.

And the inept use of force helped to solidify public sentiment. The callous and unselective brutality of the gendarmeries, particularly the hated Compagnies Republicaine de Securite, whose actions against student and public alike became an important factor in mobilizing support of the student movement. (In one poll, 61⅔ of those questioned expressed support and admiration for the students.)

This, in itself, was a victory. For one of the great complaints of French students is their feeling that they are unappreciated, that their work in the lockstep system is some sort of game, that they are kept infantile and dependent through long years of study and treated accordingly.

A hangover of other years when the student body was composed of privileged youngsters, this is galling to men and women who work with zeal, are often married and the parents of children before their long education is ended.

This time, the student unrest touched the conscience of France, exposed its fears and insecurities, jarred its considerable sense of justice. Parisians saw for themselves the behavior of a majority of the students, particularly during the four days of marching between the two violent confrontations, in which these youngsters and many of their teachers meticulously avoided provoking any incident, sought to recover their police-occupied university.

And they also saw, pastors, professors, lawyers, doctors and ordinary citizens, incidents of what *Le Monde* editor Jacques Fauvet called "blind and useless brutalities." Tear gas and truncheons used indiscriminately, foreign students pulled out of cafes and beaten far from the scenes of the demonstrations. I saw many of them myself.

On the other hand, the students, the vast majority—displayed moderation. Their marshals and monitors directed traffic, linked hands to keep the demonstrators from the police, persuaded, in most instances, the more extreme of them from causing incidents.

There are, of course, parallels in the student unrest here with those in ferment elsewhere. But at their deepest root, they reflect a meld of economic and social problems which must be faced by the French. Even with the new prosperity, suitable jobs for the 600,000 crowding the strained facilities of higher education do not appear in the offing. They feel their education, particularly in the faculty of letters, does not equip them for the work they may be called upon to do. To borrow the phrase of novelist Alain-Fournier, these young people see nothing but "the ancient obstructed path" ahead.

They feel remote from the real world; separated from most of their professors, who lecture to as many as 3,000 crammed into amphitheaters. There is no discussion, no time for questions. The ferocious competition for grades and places, says one observer, forces the student into a choice between "apathy and violence," with mediocrity as the middle course.

There are many professors, among them Nobel laureates, who have joined the students in urging deep reforms. Few of them have been consulted by the government in its previous efforts.

It is ironic that Nanterre, which was to have been a model American campus, new, spacious and well-equipped, should have provided the spark which ignited the explosion. But Nanterre had all of the problems of the Sorbonne without the mitigation of life in the Latin Quarter.

When Rector Roche called in the police, the moderate and patient students had had it. All the bitterness and anguish which I heard in the conversations with friends in the university erupted. The Sorbonne is an old university, its traditions dating back to the Middle Ages. Part of that tradition was its independence of civil authority. In times past, those wanted by the law could find asylum in the precincts of the university.

To see squads of black-uniformed, black-helmeted police take over the heart of their university brought an intense emotional response, as one student put it, "in the pits of our stomachs." Locked out, large numbers of uncommitted students joined in the demonstrations. The U.N.E.F. (the National Federation of University Students) threw its considerable weight on the side of manifestation, attempted to take control from the hard-core extremist student groups.

The early charge that the demonstrations were simply designed to embarrass the government while it hosted the peace talks between the United States and North Vietnam just would not hold up. To be sure, there were a few Maoist supporters, who might want this, and some anarchists who would do anything to grind the system to a halt. But it is significant that demonstrations on the Vietnam war could only bring a few thousand to the streets.

On Monday, there were from 200,000 to 800,000 (the first an official estimate, the second an estimate by the leaders of the demonstration) demonstrating, and slogans on the international situation were not in evidence.

Daniel Cohn-Bendit, the young German self-proclaimed anarchist tapped the vast reservoir of discontent which already existed. One professor put it this way: "It is here where students learn to be critical of the institutions which exist. But too often this is just an intellectual exercise. Going into the streets was doing something. Action satisfies."

Another professor of physics at the Faculty of Science (which is among the most active in pressing for reforms) pointed out that explosive pressures are built up in pipes which have no safety valve.

There was no safety valve. The government and the administration of the university seemed unresponsive. There was public apathy. (And even opposition—the French Communist Party, dinosaur-like, came late to the conclusion that students had justified grievances. Until a few days ago, their press scoffed at the "*fils a papa*," their reference to the petit-bourgeois nature of the students. Now, they are attempting to exploit the situation.) And the inept use of police force helped to gain them adherents. *The Times* of London summed it up: "Civilized, modern societies should not educate the elite of their children by beating them over the heads with clubs and by blinding them with tear gas."

Among the hundreds beaten and gassed are the brightest youth in France; courageous, intelligent, creative. The irony has not been lost on any side in the conflict. One bearded Frenchman in his 50s told me: "They represent the best of France." Moments later, a squad of CRS came by. "Look at them. They are the past. And they did not do so well against the Germans, the Algerians, the Indo-Chinese. Perhaps they feel more confident against unarmed students." He hesitated for a moment. "Perhaps if we had these students in the 40s, it would have been a different story."

At Rue Gay-Lussac, in the fire and the mists of gas, one could see what the meant; these youngsters were brave and dedicated under the barrage of gas and concussion grenades. And they brought a response from others: doctors attempting to help the injured in the melee, residents coming out of the safety of their apartments to hold the unconscious in their arms, women taxi drivers driving up to the barricades to evacuate the injured.

The years of drudgery and dependence, the years of feeling faceless ended. It was not what the students wanted or intended; far from the decorous environment of study. But, as one said: "At least we are doing something."

May 19, 1968

FLORIDA SCOTT-MAXWELL

The Measure of My days

These are the notebooks of a woman in her 80s, a writer who has been in her long and active life dedicated to such causes as women's suffrage, and who at the age of 50 began training as a lay analyst.

Old age is the lens rather than the image. "We who are old know that age is more than a disability," she writes. "It is an intense and varied experience, almost beyond our capacity at times, but something to be carried high. If it is a long defeat it is also a victory, meaningful for the initiates of time, if not for those who have come less far."

There is no unseemliness here. The author is not trying to prove that life at 80 can be just as vigorous and insightful as life at 20. But age is a "matrix," at "variance with the times," which enables a view of life all but inaccessible to those who are in the midst of things. "Now that I have withdrawn from the active world I am more alert to it than ever before."

It is in essence perspective which she offers: "Old people have so little personal life that the impact of the impersonal is sharp. Some of us feel like sounding boards, observing, reading; the outside events startle us and we ask in alarm, 'is this good or bad? To where will it lead? What effect will it have on people, just people? How different will they become?'"

Ironically, it is not the past which is celebrated but the future. This I think is the great value of the notebooks. And there is a quality missing from so much writing today: a quiet humor and irony. " . . . And when I play that grim, comforting game of noting how wrong everyone else is, my book is silent, and I listen to the stillness, and I learn."

Continuing, "I am getting fine and supple from the mistakes I've made but I wish a note book could laugh. Old and alone one lives at such a high moral level. One is surrounded by eternal verities, noble austerities to scale on every side and frightening depths of insight. It is inhuman. I long to laugh. I want to be enjoyed, but an hour's talk and I am exhausted."

The sarcasm is subtle and self-directed in much of this, but there is enough for other targets. "What a time of fact finding is this. Research into everything, committees of experts formed to solve each problem that arises." She leaves room to doubt that the computer will accomplish the miracle of solving our problems.

For all our appetite for detail, "Something very different seems the taste of the age, liking for the blurred, the unlabelled, amounting to a preference for sameness, inclusion, oneness. To include and condone is modern, while to differentiate is old fashioned. This seems to hold socially, morally.

Is it a claim that the less good is not exactly the same as the good, yet it has its rights, and must be protected as though it contained a new value? Perhaps it does. New values are coming to birth and the suspension of judgments may be wise. Or are we all so confused that we remain amorphous, hoping a new pattern will form itself without our help?"

It is a truism that awareness disappears with age. Here we see that the verb is wrong. A new sort of sentience emerges. "My eighties are passionate," she writes. "Old people are not protected from life by engagements, or pleasures, or duties; we are open to our own sentience." Solitude has its liveliness. And so does companionship. "When I am with other people I try to find them, or try to make a point in myself from which to make a bridge to them, or I walk on the egg-shells of affection trying not to hurt or misjudge. All this is very tiring, but love at any age takes everything you've got."

Her fealty and faith is to the "ascension of man," a heartening adherence in one who has lived through what many have called the worst of times. It is worth witnessing.

July 18, 1968

TRANSFORMATIONS

"We can readily see the influence of things on history, but it is more difficult to discern the transformation wrought by ideas."

—R. K.

Isaiah Berlin

Vico and Herder:
Two Studies in the History of Ideas

We can readily see the influence of things on history but it is more difficult to discern the transformation wrought by ideas. On first glance the reverse seems true: the history of science, or of politics, or of economics, invites us to track the major contributors; the survey courses result as neat, patterned, connected.

But is this linear, chronological model convincing for intellectual history enough to explain its complexity? For ideas have an odd and curious set of lives; they appear to be born only to be discovered as reborn: they almost always have *Doppelgängers*, antitheses which parallel in shadows the predominant views of the age; they seem to disappear or dissipate under the bullying of predominant views, but they never really do.

Isaiah Berlin's essays on two 18th-century thinkers, Giambattista Vico, a minor academic of Naples, crippled, poor, beset by Job-like suffering, whose work *The New Science* pioneered most of the new fields of study blossoming these days, and Johann Herder, the East Prussian pastor, also out of tune with his own century, are a satisfying intellectual feast.

The two men, though very different in education and temperament, have certain elements in common. They did their work in cultural backwaters, Vico in the Kingdom of the Two Sicilys, Herder in East Prussia, places remote from the centers of an age of intense intellectual and scientific activity.

This isolation, of course, is not complete, but the distance from centers of vogue and fashion seems to favor an independence of mind and indeed a certain creativity among individuals. Both men sought to embrace the entire province of knowledge of their time. Vico, the teacher of jurisprudence and rhetoric, had a touch of "library paranoia," which describes those elderly men zealously at work composing universal systems. If he died obscure (a handful of Neapolitan scholars kept his name alive but it was not until

Jules Michelet, the French historian, discovered and interpreted him that Vico's influence began), his recognition had an irony he would have understood. For his real originality, his innovations in mathematics, aesthetics, his virtual invention of new fields— social knowledge, social anthropology, comparative philology, linguistics, ethnology, jurisprudence, literature, "in effect the history of civilization in its broadest sense"—are again being appreciated. Vico's cyclical view of history, which is given most attention, is virtually his least important concept.

Herder, too, tried to take in science and art, metaphysics and theology, epistemology and ethics, social life, history, anthropology, psychology. He regarded the frontiers between the human sciences as pedantic and artificial, and felt that more was lost between the tidy categories than would be gained by specialization. Pigeon holes were pedantic and artificial devices, irksome hindrances to self-understanding by human beings in all their illimitable variety and spiritual power.

Both thinkers had their publicists and here too Berlin touches upon some fascinating notions in the history of ideas. They are often passed by distortion, modification, even conscious or unconscious misrepresentation. This is not necessarily a moral or ethical problem but really one of communication and even a kind of creativity. What Locke meant in his *Second Treatice*, says Berlin, may and undoubtedly would be modified by what one of the Founding Fathers reading him in Virginia supposed him to mean.

But this transmission or contagion of ideas is secondary to the study; indeed, even the biographical elements are slighted. In each case, Berlin has gone back to the works of the men to seek out, insofar as it is possible, the influential ideas which are novel, important and interesting in themselves. The result is an adventure in the company of a guide unlike most we are accustomed to in these explorations: Berlin approaches these matters with civility and humility, writes with elegance and flair.

So we accompany him. We are warned that the life of ideas is not as tame or remote from ordinary life. Vico and Herder tend to overstate their central thesis. "Such exaggeration is neither unusual nor necessarily to be deplored." The moderation of an Aristotle or a Locke is the exception rather than the rule. Herder wrote with a rhapsodic intensity "not conducive to clear reflection or expression." Vico leaps ahead of himself, his writing in evident contrast to the mundane demands of his life.

Now we begin to see the ideas which represent both manner and matter. Vico: that the nature of man is not static and unalterable; that there is no central kernel or essence which remains identical through change; that man continually transforms his world and himself; that those who make or create something can understand it as mere observers cannot; that there are two worlds which men can know, the external—observed, described, classified—the world created by them which can be known from the inside. This is the dualism of Vico, the division between the natural sciences and the humanities, between observation and self-understanding.

Vico saw society as multicultured, having a common style in arts, language, institutions, but as something vital and flowing, understood only by employing imagination in tandem with facts. That to understand any culture, all the creations of man—laws, institutions, religions, rituals, works of art, language, song, rules of conduct, wisdom—one must be able to enter the minds of the people, primitive, remote in time or foreign. That was the key Vico's *The New Science* sought to provide. So the new aesthetics, the new social sciences, needed to be understood not in terms of timeless principles and standards valid for all men everywhere but by a correct grasp of the purpose and the symbols and language belonging uniquely to their time and place. From this emerges the whole cluster of new comparative disciplines.

From Herder, Berlin draws three concepts which the Prussian philosopher either originated or infused with new life. He calls them: Populism, the notion that humans, in order to exercise their faculties fully, need to belong to identifiable groups, each with outlook, language, traditions, style, common history. To understand each other, they must have *einfuhlen*, empathy; Expressionism, the doctrine that human activity in general and art in particular expresses the entire personality of the individual or group, that all the works of humans are, above all, voices speaking, not objects detached from their makers, that all human expression is some sense artistic and that self-expression is the essence of humanity; Pluralism, the belief not merely in the multiplicity but in the necessary existence of many different ideals and standards, as against the classical notions of an ideal man and an ideal society.

That Vico and Herder are now being rediscovered can come as no great surprise. That an attempt to understand them and what they said should be made on their own terms is essential. For we are beginning to have doubts of monistic theories, we need to question the claim that a single explanatory system suffices, we need to challenge the notion that art and science, politics and philosophy, history and experience must be kept separate from each other.

There are no panaceas in these pages, but there is an attempt to restore and therefore to allow us a chance at understanding what these men expressed and to recognize, perhaps, roots of our own thought and action. It is said that Herder was called a magician and was a model for Goethe's *Faust*. Considering the disparate effects of his ideas, Berlin says, "Those who thought of him as endowed with special powers . . . did him no injustice." And beneath the appearance of Vico, forced to be obsequious to patrons, denied the first-class professorship he sought, was a thinker who helped transform the world of ideas, the notion that "what we call the nature of things is their history and that the nature of things is nothing other than their birth in certain times and in certain guises . . ."

The controversy goes on between the line of ideas which began with the Greeks and culminated in the Enlightenment of the 18th century, went on into the pure sciences, and the line which Vico and Herder drew, more complex, more romantic, less satisfying perhaps to an age unconsciously yearning for certainties but one which promises variety, identity and even a skepticism of its own. Of Berlin's book, I will borrow the words he uses about Vico's writing: "Few intellectual pleasures are comparable to the discovery of a thinker of the first water."

Vico has been rediscovered by many scientists and humanists seeking common ground between the disciplines. Herder, tarred by nationalist exploitation (almost totally undeserved, another example of manipulation by publicists), is perhaps less known.

This study should help. For both men perceived (Herder even more clearly) that reason and imagination, logic and intuition were to each other not as distant and antagonistic poles but more like the Yang and Yin, blending into each other to form a whole.

May 9, 1976

LEWIS MUMFORD

The Myth of the Machine: The Pentagon of Power

> *All things may be reduced to fire and fire to all things, just as goods*
> *may be turned into gold and gold into goods.*
> *—Heraclitus*

Man of the Machine Age arrogantly assumes he is above myth and mysticism. But the central theme of Lewis Mumford's *The Myth of the Machine: The Pentagon of Power* is that technology has provided its own new theology.

It is complete with miracles, saints and Edens. It worships technology and invention, seeks an earthly power, posits man on the model of the machine. Progress is held to be synonymous with change.

As a prophet in this age, Lewis Mumford is without peer. Ecology, the new rise of humanism, adversary science are just now catching up with the warnings he gave years ago. "Utopias," the Russian philosopher Berdaey said, "appear to be much more capable of realization than they did in the past. And we find ourselves faced by a much more distressing problem: How can we prevent their final realization . . . how can we return to a non-Utopian society, less 'perfect,' and more free?"

But Utopias die hard, if, indeed, their attraction for men ever dies. Over the portals of the World's Fair at Chicago in 1933, the fair which was to mark "a century of progress," was emblazoned the Utopian theme: "Science explores: Technology executes: Man conforms."

The Utopia became a nightmare. The Myth of the Machine, that change is a value and an automatic producer of values, has been accompanied by the dehumanization of man, by savage wars and revolution, by violence and psychological damage, by pollution and the threat of ultimate cataclysm.

What seemed a breakthrough by such heroes of science as Kepler and Galileo, Mumford sees as a denial of self and soul, of the nature of man as part of the natural order.

Almost a century ago, William James gave another warning. He was not an enemy of science—far from it. But he knew that history had its lessons and that man's need to believe was far from assuaged by the depersonalized technology which was at the base of the myth of the machine:

"There is nothing in the spirit and principles of science that need hinder science from dealing successfully with a world in which personal forces are the starting point of new effects. The only form of thing we directly encounter, the only experience we directly have, is our own personal life.

" . . . This systematic on science's part of the personality as a condition of events, this rigorous belief that in its own essential and innermost nature our world is a strictly impersonal world, may conceivably, as the whirligig of time goes round, prove to be the very defect that our descendants will be most surprised at in our boasted science, the omission that to their eyes will most tend to make it perspectiveless and short."

That time has come, says Mumford. His privacy invaded, his dignity subverted, his strength overcome by machines, his natural habitat pulluted, he finds himself reduced to a number in a computer. Technology has by its own inertia gone beyond man's competence to control. The servant has become the master.

What has this done to man? Mumford penetrates the way we live now to explain. It has produced infantilism and premature senility, at one end behavior is rebellious, rejecting, irresponsible; at the other men feel their efforts and their identity impotent. Action becomes mindless, flight, through drugs and distractions, compulsive. There is violence and alienation.

But he is not a pessimist. He sees the sign of a transformation, of alternatives. "Though no immediate and complete escape from the ongoing power system is possible, least of all through mass violence, the changes that will restore autonomy and initiative to the human person all lie within the power of each individual soul, once it is roused.

"Nothing could be more damaging to the myth of the machine, and to the dehumanized social order it has brought into existence, than a steady withdrawal of interest, a slowing down of tempo, a stoppage of senseless routines and mindless acts."

If, as Mumford says, technology has become a religion, with all its constituents—faith, incarnation, miracles, worship and ritual—we are witnessing its apocalypse and purgatory.

The mega-machine, fed by its power sources, has brought us to a climactic act of the drama. Air and water are polluted, rubble, slag and waste are mountain high, man has become an alienated integer, political and social systems are now subject to the very instrumentality which was promised to serve the better life.

Its theology is apparent: Mumford calls it the Pentagon of Power: political absolutism, energy, productivity, profit and publicity. None of these are in themselves evil. But precisely because they are placed in the service of myth of the machine, that change is automatically progress, that man himself is viewed as and treated as a machine, that man has become isolated from himself and from that totality of his environment we call nature.

"Mere power and mere knowledge exalt human nature but do not bless it," Bacon said. "We must gather from the whole store of things such as make most for the uses of life."

Mumford reminds us of this truth. And he does not underestimate the prodigious nature of the task of restoring man to the center of his own culture. What we are going through now is as profound a cycle in human issues as any since the birth of Christianity or the Renaissance.

"An age like our own, whose subjectivity trusts only one channel, that through science and technology, is ill-prepared to face the stark realities of life. Even those who still cling to the ancient heritage of religion and art, rich and nourishing though that still is, have become so acclimated to the dehumanized assumptions of technology that only a scattering of faithful souls have dared to challenge even its grossest perversions," he writes.

It is an unfair simplification to regard Mumford as an enemy of technology and new Luddite who would break up the machines. What he seeks is a restoration of other forms of awareness, the most important of which is the subjective.

"To hold that man's subjective impulses and fantasies must be given as much weight as formative influences in culture, indeed as prime movers, as either the impressions made on his senses by the physical world or by the varied tools and machines he has contrived in order to modify that world may seem to many, even today, a somewhat daring hypothesis. In our one-sided picture of the universe, man himself has become the displaced person.

"In reacting against the uncontrolled subjectivism of earlier world pictures, our Western culture has gone to the other extreme . . . But this subjective error has now been overcorrected and has in turn produced a notion that is equally false; namely that the organization of physical and corporeal activities can prosper in a mindless world."

I have dwelt on the conclusions, but the value of the book is in its detail as well as its manifestos. To understand the direction of our art, our fads and fashions, to penetrate such problems as violence and campus unrest, of welfare and crime, or urban life and alienation, Mumford explores not only the history of the last four centuries but the realities of our own period.

"If the key to the past few centuries has been *Mechanization Takes Command*, the theme of the present book may be summed up in Col. John Glenn's words on returning from orbit to earth: 'Let Man Take Over.' "

There is evidence that it is happening. And this comes from the nature of man himself. The measure of a human individual cannot be in the absolutism of computers.

It is, after all, only a part of man's life and his cosmos. And that is the point. The machine for all its accomplishments cannot become a divinity without revealing its essential mindlessness.

March 14 & 15, 1971

Jacques Barzun

Science: The Glorious Entertainment

> *"The new science is for the public a Delphic mystery; it keeps the western intellect troubled but unenlightened, except for the practitioners themselves. Here we touch upon the grim deficiency of the scientific culture, which is also the first general conclusion to be drawn from our historical review: the fundamental lack in our mental and spiritual lives does not come from the trifling division between scientists and humanists, or between scientists and the whole of the laity; it comes from the fact that science and the results of science are not with us an object of contemplation."*
>
> *–Jacques Barzun*

The cultural sovereignty of science and its multiplying effects have long engaged the attention of Jacques Barzun, who is through background and perception, wit and style, one of the few thinkers capable of the neglected function of criticizing science. . . .

In this work, we see a practical manifestation of Barzun's belief in the capacity of the educated intellect to comprehend the amplitude of the world of man. It is thus, as Barzun explains, a continuation of that unique work by Alfred North Whitehead, *Science and the Modern World*, into the new stage of the scientific culture. And the word culture is not used to mean solely an artifact of the social sciences, "an object considered as if it existed by itself," a determinant acting on man, but in the older sense as well, the sense of cultivation, the enlightenment and refinement of taste, the development of intellectual and æsthetic values, conversance with the arts, humanities and the broad and singular aspects of experience.

Thus in this book you will find the very opposite of specialization, you will be exposed to an astonishing (and unapologetic) diversity of subjects: philosophy, religion, history, literature, language, education, and you will find unlikely connections made. The aim is a spur to reasoning; the goal of criticism, at least the internal action of thought "to make two thoughts grow where only one grew before."

At the core is the notion that there is one culture, not two, and that anyone, including the so-called layman, "who has taken the trouble to inform himself and to think," can and should grapple with these questions. Whether in the end you concur with nothing, or part, or all of what Barzun writes, is not important. Exposure to the way his mind works, the way he writes, is important. This experience is rare nowadays: a writer who uses words with regard for their meaning.

One reads this book, not for the indulgence of intellectual masochism. One reads it to witness the kind of activity through which man, self-cornered, defeated, intimidated by size, number, mass, may yet assert his "right to be, as far as he can, a natural and moral philosopher." He can forgo the streamlined "single vision," deny the "passion for unity," investigate all the ways of knowing, to ask the why as well as the proximate how; to ask, What is going on?

This is precisely what Barzun does. He begins by rejecting the idea that there are "two cultures." There is one indivisible culture and that is scientific, because its defining characteristics come from science. And modern science is "the body of rules, instruments, theorems, observations and conceptions with the aid of which man manipulates physical nature in order to grasp its workings." He goes on: "A scientific culture is a type of contemporary society through which the ideas and products of science have filtered—unevenly, incompletely, with results good and bad, but so marked that they qualify the whole unmistakably."

Lest his free discussion be misinterpreted as hostility, Barzun writes: "I affirm without irony or reservation that modern science is one of the most stupendous and unexpected triumphs of the human mind, just as modern machinery is a collection of breathtaking artifacts often too complacently received by a heedless, ignorant public."

Almost immediately, he makes two important points: first, that science and technology have distinct histories, are still different in nature and purpose. The union of the two accounts for the paradox in a scientific culture which worships "the Power" of science because its "truth" and "worth" is demonstrated in machinery and gadgets. Thus the strange situation of a society which knows very little about science, yet places very nearly absolute faith in its capacity to explain everything, to embrace a cosmology.

The scientific revolution is thus a social one and not an intellectual one. The balance Whitehead saw in science of "passionate interest in detailed facts with equal devotion to abstract generalization" as part of "the tradition which infects cultivated thought," somehow disappeared. The equilibrium went. And man was torn between the sense of his increasing control over nature and his increasing helplessness in the wake of automation, potential destruction, robotization.

Into the void of 19th-century belief came the cult of scientism, no less unifying and pervasive than the medieval theological culture. "Just as few men were then theologians so few among us are scientists. Just as the language of theology ended by permeating common thought, so with us the language of science. The ultimate appeal was then to the certitudes or sanctions of theology, as with us to the certitudes or sanctions of science. The highest concern of the culture was to support, to perfect and to disseminate theological truth and practice, as with us to support, perfect and disseminate scientific truth and practice."

The failure to understand and contemplate the meaning, purpose and moral worth of the scientific culture is not solely due to the accelerating complexity of science, its specialism. Science won its battle by the beginning of the 20th century and only too well. They turned to the great challenges of the method. And only a few intellectuals—Huxley, James, Bergson—and a small handful of scientists gave their attentions to the problems raised by Techne and Science. Novelist Andre Beaunier's warning—"Science, admirable science, cannot alone manage the life of persons and societies."

Rather, the victory was so complete that the traditional disciplines of the humanities hastened to get into the act, with the growth of the "social" and the "behavioral sciences." Art, which has become a kind of cult, could only rage against machine and reinforce the *angst*, the alienation, the exile, to which the new society in its bankruptcy of values, its mindless violence, its statistical violence, seemed to drive its writers, artists, musicians. Education fought a rear-guard action to preserve the liberal arts, settled into the most efficient and effective vocational training and life adjustment.

The First World War, says Barzun, broke the continuity of western culture. And only now are we beginning to establish a linkage with that past.

Skeptical, penetrating, concerned, and perhaps most important, capable of that lucid perspective of the comic (the almost forgotten view in the scientific culture), Barzun examines abstract art and the "game," "the entertainment" of science, the fetish of creativity, the "chemical life," the preoccupation with sex, the demolition of sense in painting and fiction, the hollowness of literature, the loss of contact with nature, architecture as "machinery," the cheapening of language.

Barzun writes:

"No one can tell nowadays, whether being conscious or unconscious is considered the better excuse, the better reason, for any act. And in this indecision, possibly, we touch on one of the worst torments inflicted by modernity. Every influence plays upon us to increase our awareness. Self-consciousness is the recommended state of mind; for we think it will save us from error. The stronger the mind, the deeper will introspection plunge to guard against the sin of not seeing itself as it really is. Irony is in readiness, to mortify and forestall contempt from without. But having reached this point, all prescriptions stop. No one seems to know how to make flesh and wisdom out of the augmented contents of consciousness. We stay put, spoiled for spontaneity and never tempted to finer uses, storing up fresh knowledge and suspicion about ourselves and the world without changing either."

It is the lived life we have lost. This realization is surely returning, no less among scientists than among poets or among lay people.

Whether science by itself can give enough to sustain a culture, a cultivation, a taste, a finesse, is open to doubt. We no longer fear other modes of knowing. The lessons of history, the rediscovery of tradition are no longer confined to expression in pseudo-scientific language, careful apologetics.

Barzun offers no philosophy, only the example of a philosopher at work. What will restore man to the high ground of perception, bring public hope "is the passage back from *zoon* to *bios*. Man alone has a biography, and he but shares a zoology."

He suggests a Berkeleyan image: "Earth was not earth before her sons appeared."

April 5, 1964

BEN H. BAGDIKIAN

The Information Machines:
Their Impact on Men and the Media

The communications explosion has thrown up so much dust that pensive and penetrating studies of what has happened and what will happen in the dissemination of information are hard to find. More accessible is a flood of speculation and dire prophecy, uncontrollable hostility and facile vaudeville turns. In some surprising places, in education and government, the response has most often been head in the sand.

There is no easy answer to the questions raised by the revolution in communications. One reason is simply that it is too new; we have too little hard information about it. Another is that it requires, in addition to the detail of research by many disciplines—psychology, political science, history, sociology, linguistics, among others—a broad, synthesizing, humane view. . . .

Unlike many commentators, Bagdikian does not succumb to the worship of technology. The machine is an instrumentality;

man gives it its moral and social tone. This cannot be overemphasized. "Societies in the past had to cope with the radical effects of the telegraph, penny press, telephone and radio, all of which redesigned the nervous system of politics. The coming generation of computers and electronic channels represents that kind of change, but with a larger leap in potential communications power than has ever happened before. . . . The new communications will permit the accumulation of a critical mass of human attention and impulse that up to now has been inconceivable.

"The ultimate effect of these new techniques will, like nuclear fission, depend not only on any inherent evil or virtue in the physical process itself, but on the morality of men who use it and the comprehension of its power by those most affected by it. Like nuclear weapons, it will test the ultimate humanism of civilization."

Where most prognosticators tend to speak with authority, the sources of which may be questioned, Bagdikian is impressively cautious. Certainly, he does not assume that mechanical advance is automatically progress. His approach is rational and humanistic; it is better to know than to guess; better to move with forethought than to move with ignorance.

With such an approach, history and human experience must be given some weight. Methods of research and its product need to be evaluated. Extrapolation of future possibilities must take into account accident and unlooked-for side effects.

Insights into what may occur in the future can be deepened by what has happened in the past. The tempo of dissemination of the news in Washington's day has relevance on the question examined in the chapter, "How Good Is Fast?" The congressional response to the sky-jacking of a Boeing 707 on Aug. 3, 1961, mistakenly reported as the act of Castroite Cubans, illuminates the question of whether instant yes-no responses on private television receivers of the future (in order to get an immediate public opinion poll) is beneficial or dangerous.

The examination of corporate ownership or the background of editors does as much to explain the realities of news selection and dissemination as the study of the effect of national television on the Civil Rights Movement in the South. The speed with which people read will have as much effect on future communication technology as the speed with which electronic channels can send information.

Perhaps the most important part of the book is the care and penetration which comes from questioning the myths which have grown up around the new communications technology. For example: "There are reasons to believe that the new methods of communication will make thought control by authorities harder, not easier. In almost every country where there has been a degree of industrialization and occupational sophistication, there has grown a significant degree of skepticism about official dogma. In countries like the Soviet Union and its Eastern European satellites this skepticism has been fed by communications channels the authorities have been unable to control."

All sorts of surprising information emerge here. "The spasms of change in American society in the mid-1960s are attributable in large part to new methods of communication." But the surprise comes not from the change but the often unintended source of it. The demagoguery of Sen. Joseph McCarthy was strangely enhanced by so-called newspaper objectivity—"the withholding of explicit personal values in a news account"—"The senator had a five-year career of wild charges of communism among the highest officials in the United States government, and though he seldom documented his charges, and often lied or distorted, newspapers continued to report him without dispute in news stories . . ."

Ironically, it was the development of television news which enabled the viewer to see public events directly, which did more to bankrupt McCarthy politically and to deepen the reportage of events in newspapers than any other single factor.

The impact of new media is often felt in fallout rather than conscious intent. "The rebellion of American blacks against the racial caste system, though rooted in deep social and economic trends, was profoundly influenced by a novel medium of communications whose newness was important . . . The mobilization of Negro rejection of their 300-year status, and the comprehension of this by the white majority, is attributable in significant part to the failure of traditional social controls over news media that used to be typical of the American South. . . .

"Television changed this. In the mid- and late 1950s, millions of Deep South blacks received direct and unfiltered racial news for the first time."

In 1956, the Lousiana legislature weighed a bill that would have made it a felony to transmit or receive any television program that portrayed Negroes and whites together in a sympathetic setting. "At the time, the main concern was with an entertainment show, the Arthur Godfrey program, which featured a black singer, and with the Brooklyn Dodgers baseball team, which had a black star, Jackie Robinson. But Louisiana had to abandon the attempt as technically unfeasible."

There has been a tendency to think of audiences for the mass media as homogeneous mass units. But the analysis of audience shows, as one researcher concludes, that " 'the' television audience is a fanciful entity—that the audience is, in fact, many audiences, each of them stratified by age, sex and ethnic differences, by personality needs, by degrees of urbanity and sophistication, and above all else by social-class membership."

Not less significant is the nature of the newspaper audience, shown to be better educated, more sophisticated, generally more affluent, demanding much more depth in newspaper coverage and in the range of its interests in politics, literature and the arts.

Not the least of the myths demolished is McLuhan's notion that print is dying. The evidence is to the contrary. "Whatever other cultural change this generation has seen, and whatever the growth of electronic media, the ability to read and the power to reason abstractly have never been higher. During the rise of television, more children were educated in the print-oriented intellectual process than ever before."

Bagdikian does not deny that new methods of communication create new cultures—that is the main thrust of his book. But he warns against the notion that disruption is unique in history, peculiar to the new changes. He quotes Jack Goody and Ian Watt:

"A great many individuals found . . . so many inconsistencies in the beliefs and categories of understanding handed down to them that they were impelled to much more conscious, comparative and critical attitudes to the accepted word picture, and notably to the notion of God, the universe, and the past."

He goes on to comment: "This fits the assertion of believers in the uniqueness of the impact of television and other multimedia techniques to produce race riots, student rebellions, and the 'generation gap.' But the quoted passage is not about television. It describes the introduction of formal written words by abstract alphabets 2,500 years ago, with new ideas and insights overturning the ancient values that had previously been preserved by a strictly oral tradition.

"Print is neither dead nor dying. It is being forced to make a place in the family of communication for a new way of transferring information and emotion . . . The new medium is disrupting and even revolutionary, but it leaves the alphabet and document still indispensable to the efficient use of eye and brain and to the demands of human rationality."

News remains and will remain "an intellectual artifact fashioned under a code of professional ethics and received as a cultural experience."

There are dangers. But on balance, the new communications revolution can be part of the human adventure and indispensable to a free society. The flow of ideas and information in competitive media, whatever their form, directed to people educated in the pragmatic and philosophic basis of a free society, increased by the professionalization of journalists, diversity and openness, can prevent the nightmare world predicted by the prophets.

"Electrons have no morals. They serve free men and dictators with equal fervor. Their use in transmitting human ideas depends on those who design the machines and control their use, and in the United States this ultimately will depend on the general public."

This book makes an impressive step in the direction of informing and educating that public. In the midst of that revolution in communications, the measure of whether man is the master or the servant of the machines will come from our willingness to study the process, to examine its effects, to elevate the professional skill and obligation of the communicators, and to recognize that the perception of reality of any culture is a function of quality of its communication. There are few activities more essential.

March 21, 1971

DONALD F. THEALL

The Medium is the Rear View Mirror

One can worship Marshall McLuhan or reject him as a devil, but it is impossible to ignore him. He is a condition of our time, not simply because he is a man whose idea has come (or been dragged in by promotion) but because he is eloquent, erudite and seemingly ubiquitous.

He is, says Donald F. Theall, "a medium and quite possibly a medium who is the message."

Theall's study, necessarily conditional because McLuhan is still active, full of surprises, as sensitive to the quakes and quivers of our culture as any seismograph we have, is the most sensible and penetrating assessment I have yet read. It is a tribute to Canadian graduate education (McLuhan was the director of Theall's Ph.D. dissertation) that the author can approach his mentor critically without falling into the trap of adulation or resentment.

To call McLuhan a pop philosopher is to define only part of the man. He is a popularizer, celebrity-hungry, a maverick among English professors. But he is also learned, witty, vivid, poetic, a master of metaphor and, in Theall's view, nothing so much as a 20th-century Addison, inventing a new medium (the *essai concret*), striving to bring the 20th century into an awareness of itself.

McLuhan is himself the product of linear logic, visual emphases and strong commitments to print. His drive into the electric age with its retribalized culture, its audio-tactile orientation, its rites, is in a machine which has a large rear-view mirror. And part of the purpose of Theall's study is to tell us where McLuhan has been: as a scholar of Renaissance literature, as a Roman Catholic, as a disguised poet. McLuhan's greatest contribution in the end may be the result of an imagination generally lacking among academics.

This willingness to surge forward, this sprightliness, this effort to "read" (in the broadest sense of that word) the world in which he now lives, brings forth his surprises. The aphorism is not unlike the eye-catching ad; the TV commercial is epigrammatic. If his notions of sociology are not as deeply formed as his appreciation of literature, in Bacon and Eliot, Pound and Joyce, Wyndham Lewis and Thomas Aquinas, they are with it.

McLuhan, says Theall, is important, not so much in terms of whether and when he is right or wrong, but because he confronts "so directly the most pressing images of violence, unrest, fear and tension of our time." We can no more ignore him than we can any other prophetic artist.

"His weakness," says Theall, is "in deceptively being all things to all men, a priest in jester's clothing." In this, he is more like Erasmus than any other figure of the past. His is the method of paradox, touching serious matters in the guise of absurdity or satire.

But there are flaws. The power of technology romantically becomes a mystical way to salvation. And in this mysticism, what McLuhan, perhaps like many of us, has lost is a view of the individual consciousness of man, his resistance to his environment, or as Theall puts it, his "ability to use his intellect to intuitively reach beyond the world he has created."

Through pun, McLuhan can show us the breakdown of language, can suggest technology as an accidental product of man's probing which in turn alters him. But for all his genius at exposing the breakdown and the apparent change, he is less aware of another process which is what Joyce calls assimilation.

Experience may be fragmented but it is precisely the nature of individual man that recombines the pieces into new insights.

Theall suggests that McLuhan never does. There is no comprehensible theory of social structure. Perhaps that is the result of the medium he has chosen. The aphorist, particularly the one devoted to shock, can supply the nerve, but not the sinew and bone. He may shock us, he may amuse, he may suggest that we pay attention to what is happening, but he cannot give us the drama, the philosophy, the totality. His form is Haiku, economical, even pithy, but incomplete.

His great flaw, then, is not so much as an observer but in the limit of his medium, and hence, his message. Mass man is more real to him than that diverse and difficult character, the individual.

"There is no bridge in McLuhan," says Theall, "between the

account of the human person, his inner life, his multi-sensuousness and creativity and the outer world that is presumably merely an extension of his central nervous system, an extension which he does not control but which controls him."

March 19, 1971

DAVID DAICHES

A Study of Literature: For Readers and Critics

"The fact is that literacy itself is a means and not an end, and it can be put to uses which may be good, bad or indifferent. A book may be read for a great variety of reasons. But the reason for which a book is read determines the way it is read and to some extent the degree of illumination it is possible to get from it."

Originally published in 1948, the Daiches essay was just as important then as it is today, but the intellectual climate in which it was received was perhaps unready for this kind of approach. For Daiches eschewed both extremes in popular and academic criticism: he concerned himself with questions deriving from the *why* of imaginative literature rather than the *how*. In doing so, he was returning to an older, more discerning kind of inquiry at a time when the drift was away from that kind of intellectual pursuit.

Today, I think the response will be more welcoming. For we are beginning to see that mass education, and particularly higher education more accessible to more people than at any previous time in history, is not necessarily producing what Daiches calls "true literacy," which is, at least in part, the capacity to understand deeply, to assess, to experience the "very special kind of intellectual pleasure," which can come from imaginative literature.

It is not what Daiches says, but the way in which this essay illustrates the critical mind at work, not only the tentative answers he gives (for this has always been a complicated and knotty subject) but the kind of questions he asks. Indeed, his method is to question the obvious, and since there is never enough questioning of the obvious, the results are invariably challenging and interesting.

He is not the first critic to recognize the fundamental changes which have taken place in modern times, due not only to the increase in literacy, but the tremendous increase in the flow and variety of communication. But the very least that can be said for him is that he is not awed or cowed by this fact. And a good part of his answer is taken up with defining the difference between literary and non-literary values in the flood of books. For then, "We can come to a stage at which we may see that *value depends on real and not on apparent function.*"

This is an important point and one which enables him to discuss the nature and function of poetry and fiction in terms which enable us to utilize the historical theories and concerns of criticism in an age when it may be asked, as some have asked, "Is literary criticism still possible?"

The answer is given by the book itself. And it is yes. For Daiches knows that though we cannot legislate taste, we can encourage the kind and quality of reading in which common sense, intelligence and values play an essential role. This is, he argues, not so much a matter of intelligence as it is a transaction between the reader and the "possibility" of the work: "We receive but what we give, / And in our life alone does Nature live."

In this connection, he makes an important point about "true literacy." It is the passiveness, the intellectual atrophy, the uncritical awe of culture and of words which may define the "semi-literate" rather than the number of years he has attended school, the position he holds in the community, or his chronological age. "The semi-literacy of the atrophied mind that can read only passively is bound to grow progressively farther away from adequate literacy since such a mind is only further atrophied by further reading. We have, in fact, to deal with three stages—illiteracy, semi-literacy, and true literacy—and as soon as we face the facts we realize that the first and the third have more in common than either has with the second."

This is not a simple romanticizing of what might be called instinctive, common sense response, but a deep penetration of what is going on today. . . .

There is a heartening confidence expressed both explicitly and implicitly in the capacity of the individual human being to make his own judgments, to inform and perfect his own mind, which is in the best tradition of humanism. That is why Daiches is less interested in constructing a system of criticism than in introducing and explaining the varied and traditional modes of criticism.

"The more important a subject is, the less dogmatically it can be discussed: there is no single 'right' theory of literature any more than there is a single 'right' analysis of *Hamlet*," Daiches writes. But this is no reason to assume that values do not exist. They do. And it is precisely "when popular values about the nature and value of literature are as confused as they are today," that the critic's obligation and the reader's obligation to exercise value judgments and reflect on them are most important.

Near the end, he writes, "The trouble with an age which has a rich cultural heritage behind it is that it tends to take complacently for granted those values which in former ages were the subject of passionate debate. Even those who have no real interest in or understanding of literature are willing to assume that there is something in it, that somewhere there are its appointed guardians who look after it and know what they are doing and why they are doing it. There are, of course, no such appointed guardians."

There are those who confuse the transaction of literature and life, assuming that it is a one-way matter, that in some magical way if the writing of the unpleasant stops, life will suddenly turn pleasant. The relationship of life and literature is no simple matter as the common-sense reader must realize. In this book, we are given some measure of its complexity and its challenge.

December 13, 1964

JACQUES BARZUN

Of Human Freedom

It has become a commonplace of history to call every period an "age of transition." And one does not have to argue against the phrase to recognize that the manifestations of politics and culture are in a constant process of change. That is the nature of time and experience.

The questions raised and the insights offered in this thoughtful book cut through the topical to the continuing issues of individual freedom and the system most effective in protecting that freedom.

There is little revision in this book—some distracting topical matter has been removed, a passage shortened here and there, a few explanatory notes added. The substance remains because the problems remain. Democracy is still under attack, not only from the older enemies but from new and sometimes surprising foes as well.

Barzun has no simple answers, certainly not the convenient fiction of either/or. If freedom in democracy is to mean anything at all, its goal must remain "a diversified and vigilant culture, . . . at once the source and the product of successful democracy." The enemies of a free democratic culture have argued in the past and argue now that it is inefficient, it levels down to mediocrity, and "by turning everyone's mind to sham politics, it enables the unscrupulous to fill their pockets." These enemies argue from fear, urging us "to give up democracy before it sinks and to adopt some system of force which will provide the two needful things of a New Feudal Age—food and protection."

In this brilliant and incisive book, Barzun not only defends a free democratic culture, but gives it its most articulate definition. Definition and examination were needed 25 years ago; they are urgently needed today. And that is why Barzun's book survives and even gains in importance.

One consistent mistake, Barzun argues, is to separate the free democratic political system from its larger context of free democratic culture. The latter infuses the former with worth and quality. The forms of politics can become empty of real meaning when intellectual laziness, retreat from reason, distrust of the intellect take over. Every generation every man must enter the search for understanding as though it had just begun.

It is characteristic of the attack on democracy whether it comes from the left or the right, and even when it uses as subterfuge the slogans and catch-phrases of freedom, that it cannot abide variety.

"Freedom, or Free Democracy, is something very different and much more difficult to achieve. It is a balance between popular will and individual rights. It is a civilized society that tries to establish diversity in unity through the guarantee of civil liberties," Barzun writes.

"It wants stability and peace, but recognizing the dynamic character of society it finds it must safeguard criticism as sacred and insure the free expression of thought as an intellectual privilege granted equally to all."

What Barzun means by free democracy is, as *Webster's New International Dictionary* says, synonymous with the modern republic of the United States. I mention this because it has become the mode to argue ferociously about the words democracy and republic as though they remained static and frozen in the meanings they had in ancient times. Arguing backward from the terms, republic and democracy, is an exercise in futility.

Whether you call our form of government republican or democratic, the informing element of the description must be in terms of specifics.

Republic, or free democracy, means a "free popular government in which there are no classes having any exclusive political privileges and in which the electorate includes at least the great body of adult inhabitants (universal suffrage in most republics) under constitutional restrictions."

If this is the political context, there is another and this is what Barzun calls a free democratic culture, "an atmosphere and an attitude . . . the deliberate cultivation of an intellectual passion in people with intellects and feelings." Yet, this is the most difficult part of free democracy. It is almost too easy to let the forms decay; they can only be kept alive while men are committed to those qualities of mind and taste, critical acumen and tolerance of diversity which give it life.

"The human mind at its best . . . seeks to distinguish sense native to the human mind; but being difficult to establish in a world full of conflicting minds, it generates the institutions of political democracy. Democracy is thus the result and not the cause of our deep-seated desire for diversity, freedom and tolerance. It follows—and this is the two-fold thesis of this book that culture must be free if men's bodies are to be free; and culture perished if we think and act like absolutists. Tyranny, like its opposite, Charity, begins at home, but unlike it, alas, does not stay there."

When this book was written in 1939 its devastating analysis of the dangers of Communism caused Barzun to be called a conservative. Read today, these dangers still appear but they also apply to the absolutism of the right. Barzun hasn't changed his view; it is a measure of the depth and penetration of his understanding of the dangers to free democracy which make this book one of enduring importance. Democracy has a place for the absolutes.

"The man who has at last got hold of *the* truth can live among the infidels if his intelligence is as strong as his faith. Let him take out his conviction in superiority and pity . . .

"Let us face with open eyes a pluralistic world in which there are no universal churches, no single remedy for all diseases, no one way to teach or write or sing, no magic diet that will make everyone healthy and happy, no world poets and no chosen races cut to one pattern or virtue but only the wretched and wonderfully diversified human race which can live and build and leave cultural traces of its passage in a world that was apparently not fashioned for the purpose.

"It is far easier to blueprint designs for an absolutist utopia. Uniformity has the appeal of panacea. But in differences is to be found freedom, a culture actively kneaded by critics and creators, . . . affords more air to breathe freely, more room to move in, more variety to encourage further variety." He goes on: "The danger is that wild, unreconciled despair, coming after exorbitant hope, will inspire the creed of action for its own sake." No more important words have ever been written about the perils to a free culture.

November 6, 1964

ALEXANDER SOLZHENITSYN

For the Good of the Cause

> . . . For a country to have a great writer is like having another
> government. That's why no regime has ever loved great writers, only
> minor ones.
>
> –Alexander Solzhenitsyn

The award of the 1970 Nobel Prize for Literature to Alexander
Solzhenitsyn was an embarrassment to the Soviet government. In
some respects it was a reprise of the award to Boris Pasternak in
1958. Pasternak at first accepted but severe pressure forced him to
withdraw. Ironically, but understandably, the Soviet regime
raised no objection when in 1965 the Nobel award went to Mikhail
Sholokhov.

Alexander Solzhenitsyn accepted the award, resisting as he has
for the past years both threats and blandishments. The prize, in a
very real sense, was an antidote to his reduction in his own
country to the status of a nonperson, a validation of his existence,
his identity and his talent as a major writer.

Some notion of his experience and the literary situation in
Soviet Russia is to be found in the republication of Solzhenitsyn's
For the Good of the Cause, translated by David Floyd and Max
Hayward. David Floyd's introduction and appendix containing
the principal reviews of the novelette on its publication in Russia
in 1963 give us a clear picture of the predicament of a writer in that
country. . . .

Solzhenitsyn would neither submit to censorship nor cease
fighting to bring his works to Russian readers. Of his courage and
integrity there is no doubt. But what emerges in the pages of this
new edition of *For the Good of the Cause* is no simple parable of good
and evil. It is, of course, easy to find the villains: those officials
who have pursued and persecuted him, their toadies who have
dutifully carried out the attempt to extinguish him.

Yet, as Solzhenitsyn himself has tried, in *For the Good of the
Cause*, and other works, to show his characters reacting according

to their individual characters, the account of his ordeal is not
without its restoration of individual identity to those involved.
For the men and women who supported him, who tried to carry
out the function of criticism as a seeking of the truth of experience,
emerge in these pages credibly as do the individual students and
teachers who resist the omnipotent and unfeeling bureaucrats in
Solzhenitsyn's story.

In literature as in life, Solzhenitsyn's purpose has been to
restore a sense of the humane, of the individual human being.
"But don't forget," Lidia, a teacher in the school which has losts its
new building because of some decision made by a powerful
bureaucrat, "books are a record of the people of our time, people
like you and me, and about all the great things we accomplished."

For the principal and the teachers, as for the author who por-
trays them so effectively, the students are living, feeling human
beings, complete as they are with conscience, a sense of right and
wrong. These youngsters are recognizable even to us 10,000 miles
away for they are like our own students.

Long promised a new building, they and their teachers refuse to
wait for the planners to get off the dime. They work voluntarily to
make it a reality. At the last minute, there is a decision to give the
building to a research institute. The local party secretary, one of
the "little Stalins" Solzhenitsyn sought to indict, a man named
Knorozov, will not even hear their objections, their call for simple
justice. For him, people don't count. "You can just tell them this is
a State institute and the whys and wherefores of the matter are
none of our business."

Reading the story, we may wonder what all the fuss is about.
Solzhenitsyn's *A Day in the Life of Ivan Denisovich*, would seem a
much more serious indictment of the brutality and injustice of the
system. But *Ivan Denisovich* momentarily suited the policy of
Khrushchev during the icon-breaking thaw. *For the Good of the
Cause* did not deal with history; it dealt with the then-present
moment, revealing with consummate skill the existence of those
officials who survived to symbolize the persistence of an inhuman
attitude.

The story was virtually the last by Solzhenitsyn to be published
in the Soviet Union. His *Cancer Ward* and *The First Circle*, pub-

lished in translation in the West, were circulated through Samizdat, an underground network which passed typewritten copies clandestinely to Russian readers.

Solzhenitsyn suffered every deprivation. His manuscripts and archives were confiscated. A rumor campaign smeared him. He was not allowed to publish so much as an answer to the charges. He was thrown out of the Writers Union. "In this way my work has been finally smothered, gagged and slandered," Solzhenitsyn has written. "I am quite sure, of course, that I shall carry out my task as a writer no matter what happens, and even more successfully and with less controversy from the grave than in my lifetime. No one can prevent the truth from spreading, and to advance it I am ready to accept even death. But perhaps so many lessons will teach us in the end not to stop a writer's pen during his lifetime. Not once has that enhanced our history."

That there are others dedicated to a sense of justice and willing to risk themselves in its behalf is shown in the appendix of reviews and in Floyd's introduction. For his efforts in behalf of Solzhenitsyn and other writers, the critic and editor Alexander Tvardovsky deserves the highest praise. It was he who first published *Ivan Denisovich*, and consistently probed the barriers to literary expression. Those friends of Solzhenitsyn who helped to support him when he was denied the right to make his living as a writer should be recognized. The cellist Rostropovich provided him with a place to live and work. Such writers as Dmitri Granin did not hesitate to speak out in his behalf.

If Solzhenitsyn is a symbol and an eloquent voice in behalf of freedom, he speaks not only for himself but for those who refuse the automatic rationalization that any suppression of humanity can be justified by the good of the cause.

January 31, 1971

JOHN WAIN

A House for the Truth

The most difficult concept to hold on to is the notion that man changes imperceptibly while his environment appears to change with great speed and profound modification. If there is any distortion of perception brought about by the communications revolution it lies in this aspect: that there is no longer any time to reflect, to examine and ponder the past, to balance the longer view of history with the insistent immediacy of news.

Of course, this itself is an illusion. There is an ecology of man, a biosphere of spirit and intellect. We react adrenally to the latest outrage of violence brought into our living rooms by television, but there is rarely any action to resolve the urge to do something. In its place comes numbness or callousness, or occasionally the wish to retreat, or sometimes the feeling of alienation and uselessness. We become addicts of news, longing for something else, but drawn again to the shock machine of headlines and television news film.

In this new world—not wholly novel but not wholly like anything before (which may be the only comforting idea in sight)— many strange things happen: the loss or shift of attention from the locality, the neighborhood, the region. The rise of travel as a symptom of flight, rather than of cheap fares and advertising, is one aspect. Another possible reaction is the odyssey into nostalgia. For still others it is fad and fashion, the desire to be with it, whatever *it* may be at the moment.

This is no simple phenomenon although there is a pronounced and completely understandable yearning for simple answers. John Wain, the British novelist and critic, points up a surprising component of the situation in the eiplog to his latest collection of essays, *A House for the Truth*, when he talks about the "increasingly puritan society" in which we live.

The use of this term will surprise those who associate puritanism with purity "in its specifically sexual sense of chastity." Nobody, he says, could look at our society and "say that chastity was near the top in any dominant scale of values." But the puritanism of which he speaks is made up of much more than this. " . . . As historically understood, [it] signifies the all-or-nothing attitude, the horror of compromise, the impulse to simplify . . . [the belief] that only one issue can override all the others—which will, inevitably, happen from time to time—but that it ought to do so, that this is a moral imperative."

What has happened in our time, says Wain, is an alliance between this puritanism and sensationalism, "that other arch-simplifier." Wain's concern is with art and pseudo-art, but the implications will not cease at the frontier of imaginative expression.

"It is the puritan who does try to police it, forbid it, to channel it into a purpose that suits his emotional needs, who must—to be blunt—be rejected out of hand as a nuisance, a fractious child interfering with grown-up people. He is a simplifier, and art can have no truck with simplification. It cannot simply preach liberation or revolution, inasmuch as these are two-dimensional things, belonging to a world of imperatives, and art is rich with the multidimensional richness of life. It has a memory, and revolution has no memory. It includes negatives and counter stresses, and liberation cannot afford these. It glows with color and puritanism is black and white like a newspaper headline."

Others have pointed out that clinch between the puritan and the pornographer. But Wain, precisely because he takes the meaning of the terms to deeper levels, is able to show its extraordinary effects. "In our time, the pseudo-artist is generally both a puritan and a sensation-monger. To be sensational is to attract attention, and it is the duty of the puritan, the man with a simplifying mission, to attract attention if he can. Hence the cult of the extreme statement. It is as if our age has grown deaf to any language except that of the superlative. Slender talents, competing with one another in staking out the ultimate boundaries of whatever they are trying to express, occupy the forefront of attention."

Explicitness is the result of a puritan insistence. The fiercely moral puritan and the fiercely amoral puritan give us the either/or of the day. Yet, art is often in the middle territory, the territory of individualism and imagination, which contains both past and present, which may reflect contemporary life but which echoes the continuing surprise and paradox of the inquiring mind, "the complex, wide-ranging and subtly tinged interchange between present and past."

It is precisely the imaginative, unpredictable, individual mind which the puritan finds "unbiddable." He speaks of all puritanism, whether of the right or left, the explicit or prohibited, something Hawthorne, who knew puritanism at first hand, dealt with over and over again from the *Maypole of Merrymount* to *The Scarlet Letter*.

I have concentrated on this one essay though there are many more, preferring to give the flavor of a man who has tried in his writings about art and literature to help build "a solid habitat" for continuing truths, in the tradition defined by Raymond Chandler when he wrote that a great critic attempts to build "a house for the truth."

March 12, 1973

ALEC CRAIGS

Suppressed Books: A History of the Conception of Literary Obscenity

Alec Craig's *Suppressed Books: A History of the Conception of Literary Obscenity* is so sensible a piece of work that one is slightly fearful of its fate in an arena where opponents seem hardly capable of communicating with each other.

Certainly, the volume will alienate those who take extreme positions. These extremists on both sides tend to see the problem in the dubious light of oversimplified rules. Craig recognizes this:

"I am well aware that the suggestions . . . for the form of a law of obscene publication will satisfy no one, but come under fire from both sides in the conflict between liberal and authoritarian ideas. On the one hand it will be condemned as a series of weak-kneed concessions to ignorance and reaction and a bolstering-up of a medieval conception which is slowly dying in the light of progress. The other side will regard it as a reckless sacrifice of public morality and social stability for the dubious advantages of intellectual speculation, education, and freedom of artistic creation."

Before we go on to a discussion of Craig's proposals, let me point out that they come at the end of a work which is notable for its scholarship, its understanding of the philosophical and moral implications of freedom of expression, an enlightening and refreshing determination to elevate the dialogue on obscenity to a point at which some understanding of terms and precedents may be employed.

Craig, a noted British critic, makes no secret of where he stands. He is opposed to censorship, clearly shows that the history of suppression is a baleful and unhealthy effort whose victories were Pyrrhic in the moral areas, almost inevitably damaging to literature and the arts, to free scientific inquiry, and on occasion to political and social freedom.

Yet, he does not allow his position to obscure an understanding of the impulse of society, through law, and of individuals, for whatever reasons, to "protect" the community against moral subversion. He recognizes that "the motivation for sex censorship goes very deep into human psychology, having its roots in man's ambivalent attitude toward sex." The danger is that under the guise of morality, a great deal of damage may be done. It is in the end a matter of equities. The free community on the one hand is obligated in the deepest sense to protect freedom of thought and artistic creation. It is also obligated to protect the furtherance of the good life.

Are the two ends incompatible?

The answer implicit in Craig's study is that they are not. "Moral integrity and clear thinking should enable modern communities to resolve the tensions created by these opposing attitudes without

hurt to the spread of truth, the increase of beauty and the furtherance of the good life."

In the recent trend in America, dating from the Woolsey decision on *Ulysses* and culminating in rulings of the U.S. Supreme
Court from the Roth case on, Craig believes this country has come
closest to embodying in law the principle that the community
must proceed with the greatest of caution in handling matters
involving free expression. (Incidentally, in the appendices he
provides the full texts of the Woolsey opinion, the Roth opinion
and the opinion written by Judge Bryan in the *Lady Chatterley's
Lover* case.)

The opinion in the Roth case stated that the First Amendment
did not apply to obscene utterances (properly tracing the legal
origin of obscenity as a form of libel which Craig clarifies in his
careful history of the development of obscenity law) but went on
to say:

"All ideas having even the slightest redeeming social
importance—unorthodox ideas, controversial ideas, even ideas
hateful to the prevailing climate of opinion—have the full protection of the guarantees . . ." Therefore obscenity, the court went
on, is to be judged as material "utterly without redeeming social
importance."

The Roth case satisfied neither of the extreme positions (which
in itself appears a fairly good test of common sense). But it made
explicit: "The fundamental freedoms of speech and press have
contributed greatly to the development and well-being of our free
society and are indispensable to its continued growth. Ceaseless
vigilance is the watchword to prevent their erosion by Congress or
by the states."

Craig's major contribution, it seems to me, is to make available,
with a minimum of passion, factual information on the law, the
development of customs and usages, so that the intelligent citizen
can approach this traditionally murky problem with a maximum
preparation. In this sense, it can be described as an indispensable
work. Morris Ernst, who has written the introduction to the
American edition, says it "tells a more persuasive story even than
the great exhortation of Milton's *Areopagitica*. Certainly, it brings

the spirit of Milton's great work up to date.

If law, as the central artifact of society in meeting the problem, is important, no less important is Craig's assessment of the other methods by which a community exerts its pressure. Law is, after all, administered by men in a community of men. It does not automatically follow that the cases alone will indicate that ephemeral meterorology, the climate of opinion.

The threat of pressure by police or public is very often enough to secure the ends of censorship. There is evidence enough of this both in past and present, in both England and America. Self-appointed guardians of the public weal, however well-intentioned, are likely to be driven to dangerous excess. Robert Burns (himself a victim of considerable censorship and suppression) described them in one poem as the "unco' guid." One English writer voices a fundamental objection to such societies:

"It is hardly possible that a society for the suppression of vice can ever be kept within bounds of good sense and moderation . . . Beginning with the best intentions in the world, such societies must, in all probability, degenerate into a receptacle for every species of tittle-tattle, impertinence and malice. Men whose trade is rat-catching love to catch rats; the bug destroyer seizes on the bug with delight; and the suppressor is gratified by finding his vice."

Craig examines these effects, taking the crucial cases and the central figures, relating them to the general impact on society. One is not only driven to question the motives of such people as Bowdler and Comstock, but to marvel at the extent to which their ends are utilized to justify their means.

He is concerned with the maximum protection of books, of libraries and of mature readers. Thus he makes the distinction between an "obscene book" and an obscene publication, the latter involving the distribution of hard-core pornography under circumstances which are either a public nuisance or a crime, i.e., contributing to the delinquency of a minor. But he makes clear that care should be taken to "see that laws enacted with the ostensible purpose of protecting juveniles do not in fact restrict the range of adult reading."

He calls for a closer examination of the arguments regarding the relationship between reading and conduct. The notion that there is a direct causal effect between the two "would ultimately rob," he writes, "the world of its literature because almost every great book, including the Bible, must have been the cause of . . . misdoing at some time or other. Certainly in the past people have found encouragement in the Bible for witch burning and slave trading."

Most important of all is Craig's faith in the taste and good sense of the average man. Such trust is uncommon in these times. Those who arrogate to themselves the notion of moral superiority, whatever side of the fence they are on, have lost such faith.

Yet, I think at the core of a free society is the essential idea that the individual is responsible in judgment and taste, capable of judgments, worthy of freedom. It is the vigilance of such men which is in the end essential to give any law its meaning. . . .

September 1, 1963

HENRY MILLER

Tropic of Capricorn

Henry James spoke of two basic responses in literature: the emotion of recognition and the emotion of surprise. A third could be added: the emotion of outrage.

It is the third which is the clue to the difficult reception of certain of the works of Henry Miller. And it is likely to be the case in the first American publication of his autobiographical novel, *Tropic of Capricorn*.

The outrage is stirred not so much by the sexual passages (these are merely the excuse for the prosecution). I am not suggesting that they do not offend certain people. They do, indeed. And these people have the privilege of not reading Miller's books. They have the right to speak out against his books. The deeper, and more urgent question is, whether they have the right to impose their restrictions on the free choice of others.

The sexual passages do not go beyond in either content or language, works which are available in publication today. Why then the outrage against Miller?

I think it stems from his assault in other areas: the subjects of religion, of national goals, of the nature of our ideals, of materialism. He challenges; he steps on toes; he is irrepressible in his attack. These are the sins he commits and there are those who seek to punish him because he outrages them.

But this sense of outrage (it is interesting to note how many of the "experts" who testified against the *Tropic of Cancer* touched on these matters in their testimony), no matter how provoking Miller may be to our mores, this, under the law, does not make his books obscene. He is even more provacative, for example, to the Russians whose critics have written diatribes ageinst him in the official party journals which are uncomfortably like the attacks on him in this country.

I go into these matters because I must. *Tropic of Cancer* was held to be obscene by a Los Angeles jury. A San Diego jury cleared the book. There is currently an appeal under way in the Los Angeles case. *Tropic of Capricorn* may not even be generally obtainable in Los Angeles since Grove Press will not guarantee the costs of any possible litigation for booksellers. In short, the bookseller is on his own and a few courageous ones may stock the book. But, in this field, a successful prosecution has a much broader effect on the climate of opinion than the single book involved.

Thus, before I go into the critical merits or defects of *Tropic of Capricorn*, I must say that in my opinion it is not obscene under the present law in the state of California. The legal test, in the words of the statute: " . . . to the average person, applying contemporary standards, the predominant appeal of the matter, taken as a whole, is to prurient interest, a shameful or morbid interest in nudity, sex or excretion, which goes substantially beyond customary limits of candor in description or representation of such matters and is matter utterly without redeeming social importance."

This novel, taken as a whole, has redeeming social importance. It is the statement of one man on his own life and its meaning, an effort to understand who he is, where he is, where he has been and where he is going. "Truth," Miller writes, "lies in this knowledge of the end which is ruthless and remorseless. We can know the truth and accept it, or we can refuse the knowledge of it and neither die nor be born again. In this manner it is possible to live forever, a negative life as solid and complete, or as dispersed and fragmentary as the atom. And if we pursue this road far enough, even this atomic eternity can yield to nothingness and the universe itself fall apart."

In short, he does not urge on us his truth. He does not even say that we cannot live without truth. But he suggests that if we are to seek our own truths we must accept the ruthlessness and remorselessness of the quest. No matter if he outrages us, no matter if we stand against everything he stands for, perhaps in that assault, our truth will emerge. In this argument itself, I find the socially redeeming importance of the novel. There are things about it, ideas expressed, which are repugnant to me personally.

There are other things in it with which I agree. But even where I believe Miller is wrong or mad, I sense in myself that response, that challenge which justifies the work's existence. Does he anger me? Good. Does he turn the world upside down? Fine. It compels me to look at the world and see it right side up. Does he outrage us? If he does, it is, in the end, the healthiest response.

That is why I will take him over the mealy-mouthed hypocrites who trade on sex, and tease with sex, and skate along with an essentially dishonest and unwholesome attitude toward sex. Miller's concern with sex is only part of the commitment toward the "core of a totality which is inexhaustible." The truth which goads and mocks him is the artist's truth, the vision, the shape of the world as seen through the lens of his experience, the mirror of his consciousness.

In a society which rails against conformity, fears the pressure which is making an integer of man, Miller's novel is of the utmost consequence. Perhaps that is why he is under attack. We will accept a little non-conformity: we are offended by anyone who says as he says, pursuing the logic of his position, "I dissent from the current view of things, as regards murder, as regards religion, as regards society, as regards our well-being." (These and the following quotes are taken from *The Erotic in Literature* by David Loth). His own life, he says, "has been a good life, a rich life, a merry life, despite the ups and downs, despite the barriers and obstacles (many of his own making), despite the handicaps imposed by stupid codes and conventions."

Thus, willy-nilly, Miller has become a symbol. His books have become issues. He puts us on trial. Socrates-like he asks the embarrassing and trenchant questions about our own liberty and freedom. Do his books offend us? The libraries are filled with books which offend somebody or other.

Are we so frightened, so uncertain of what we believe in, that we cannot contain within a free society a work of this sort? I think not.

One of the "experts" in the *Cancer* trial, Leon Uris, said of Miller: "I don't think this man is a writer. I don't think this is a book." Uris notwithstanding, Henry Miller is a writer. *Cancer* is a book. *Capricorn* is an even better book. It is ringing, eloquent, poetic, filled with the spirit of comedy and tragedy. Its engagement with life is total and, in consequence, there may be portions of it which make you uncomfortable. But there is certainly nothing in it which goes beyond the bounds of books published and accessible in libraries and supermarkets.

There is nothing of hypocrisy about it, no false righteousness, none of the smirking euphemisms about sex which we are willing to accept in such trash as *Sex and the Single Girl*. Here is all of a man, in the context of his times, fighting for a kind of honesty and understanding which we may differ with but which we must in the end respect. It is a more mature book than *Cancer*, although the years which it covers are those before Miller's French experiences. It is of more importance to us because the setting is America. And one can assess part of the forces which created Miller and made of him the writer he is. *Capricorn* is, to me, without question one of the 10 most important American novels of the 20th century.

Is there a meaning to it? This was the question which gnawed at the experts. Try this, if you are a seeker after meanings:

"Thought and action are one, because swimming you are in it and of it, and it is everything you desire it to be, no more, no less. Every stroke counts for eternity. The heating system and the cooling system is one system and *Cancer* is separated from *Capricorn* only by an imaginary line."

September 23, 1962

FRANK BARRON

Creativity and Psychological Health

Dr. Frank Barron and his colleagues at the Institute of Personality Research and Assessment, UC Berkeley, have been engaged in a 10-year study of the creative personality. From time to time preliminary reports have appeared. Occasionally the subjects have spoken about the experience; one, Kenneth Rexroth, the poet and critic, blared forth with an antagonistic article which was largely a cry against trespassers.

For my part, I felt a gathering and instinctive punitive urge. I sharpened my small armory of critical weapons and lay in wait in the shadows of the path I knew Dr. Barron must inevitably take. This imaginative projection was, I know now, a creative response, or at least part of one. I built up a fantasy about what Dr. Barron was going to say and prepared myself to demolish it—the Rexroth syndrome. As Dr. Barron writes: "There is something in the human mind that does not like things as they are, something that will make up its own little world in whatever way seems to that individual piece of mind to be an improvement." I would add to things as they are, the phrase, "or as they seem to be."

I was dead wrong. Not only does Dr. Barron disarm all my prepared positions, but he goes on to demonstrate a humility, a depth of understanding, an ability to write and a fund of knowledge and wise speculation which makes his book *Creativity and Psychological Health* one of the most important works in its field I have ever read.

And it turns out that he is the first to put the statistical evidence, the test results, the indices of reliability in their proper context. They are clues to understanding creativity. They do not capture the essences of creativy. " . . . The picture is not simple, even in unthinking psychometric terms," he says. Interpreting one set of results, "In brief, if one is to take these test results seriously, the writers appear to be sicker and healthier psychologically than people in general. Or, to put it another way, they are much more

212 / ROBERT KIRSCH

troubled psychologically, but they also have far greater resources with which to deal with their troubles."

He avoids, as far as possible, the jargon of psychological journals. The language is clear and lucid, honest, and even occasionally, emotional and metaphysical. He is not afraid to step on toes. Most of all the irritating timidity and caution or the haranguing hostility (which often disguises the same qualities) is not present. He tells you who he is, what he has done—and why. He introduces the insights of the past in literature and philosophy; he raises the ethical and cosmological questions which cannot be overlooked in any understanding of creativity. In short, he has given us a work which is both readable and illuminating, informative and challenging.

For his concern is not only the creative process but all of its implications. Many of those who have written on creativity in recent years have tended to regard it as a kind of new religion, a shrine at which conforming man may for a moment indulge his fantasies of freedom. But creativity cannot be artificially separated from the human condition. It is a force, which like others, can be, and has been, used for good or evil. The more we know about how it works and why it works and what it may signify, the more it may tell us about ourselves, our ways, our arts and sciences, our education, our philosophies.

The book must be read in this light. Its organization is based on a succession of crucial questions, the answers (if that is not too strong a word) to which are part of the design of the whole. What is freedom? What is mental health? How do we know the world? What is the meaning of life? How do we assess others? How do we assess ourselves? What is belief? What is intelligence? What is independence? What is the relationship between the conscious and unconscious world?

Recognize the questions? Of course; they are, most of them, as old as thinking man.

Reading the book will not make you creative. There are no formulas, no helpful hints, no self-improvement charts. But it may impel in you, differently in each individual, something tending toward that "vitalizing transaction . . . ephemeral, as frail as love or blessedness," which may assist understanding, which may be the first step. There is a certain amount of contagion in the creative engagement.

At the core of creativity is awareness, perception, both of self and of the world. But this is only a beginning. To broaden consciousness can help to enliven imagination. But there must be an identity, an ego strong enough and secure enough to endure the momentary chaos of fantasy and imagination, courageous enough to let the real world go for a moment and flexible enough to return to that world with the fruits of the voyage. There must be the willingness to take risks, the core strength to endure the possibility of foolishness. There must be playfulness and vitality. The lived and imagined life in contrast to Fromm's "unlived life."

"What has emerged most clearly from my own research on creativity," Dr. Barron writes, "is the fact that the creative person is able to find in the developmentally more primitive and less reasonably structured aspects of his own mental functioning the possibility of new insight, even though at first this may be only intuitively and dimly grasped.

"He is willing to pay heed to vague feelings and intimations which on the grounds of good sense are put aside hastily by most of us. Characteristically, the creative individual refuses to be content with the most easily perceptual schemata or perceptual constancies, even such obviously adaptive ones as the discrimination between what is inside the self versus what is outside the self . . ."

We find here the clue to the tendency to connect creativity with neurosis or even psychosis. The all-important difference is that the creative individual is not imprisoned by this state. He not only can return. He does return.

"In paranoia, for instance, the fundamental ego-failure is the chronic inability to distinguish between subject and object, between inner and outer sources of experience, so that introjection and projection appear as characteristic mechanisms. In the creative person, this distinction may indeed have been attained with great difficulty and may have been won out of childhood circumstances that are ordinarily pathogenic, but once attained it is then maintained with unusual confidence. Thus the creative genius may be at once naive and knowledgeable, being at home equally to primitive symbolism and to rigorous logic. He is both more primitive and more cultured, more destructive and more constructive, occasionally crazier and yet adamantly saner than the average person."

One final point: the mysteries of talent aside, it is precisely the average person who can get most from this study. For, the lessons inferred from the creative personality are not designed to produce creative geniuses but to give all of us some access to the creative life. In the ordinary course, we approach the problem from a completely different stance.

We take courses in creative writing, or interpretive dancing, or life painting, assuming that this will make us creative.

I think it wiser to start from the other direction. For indispensable to the creative act is the individual identity. We ought to find that first.

September 29, 1963

LEON SURMELIAN

Techniques of Fiction Writing: Measures and Madness

Creative writing is one of those inexact terms, deplored by the purists, abused by the zealots. I have long sought another expression but I must keep coming back to it. For murky as it may be, it is useful: a you-know-what-I-mean phrase.

What we ought to keep in mind is that there are levels of creativity in writing, in expository prose as in poetry or fiction. All writing is rendering; and the rendering itself may be a creative, imaginative process whether you are composing a history of Reconstruction, a case study in psychology, a Petrarchan sonnet, or a business letter. Something in your mind, or something in the world, is transmuted into words: the goal is precision and perhaps grace. That is the first level.

When the writer imagines, or projects or provides something which emerges from his own psyche rather than directly from a tangible model, we come to the second level of creativity, the one closest to the intended meaning. The modifier then refers to a process within the writing: taking experience and ideas and selecting, rearranging, restating so that something new, original, deeper emerges.

In this sense the creative writer is one whose awareness and perception provides in rich measure what Aristotle calls *matter*. That is what we today would call content. There is, of course, another side, that which Aristotle called *manner*, this is style or form. The question is: can creative writing, matter and manner, be taught? Manner can and has been through the years. Matter, to be redundant, is another matter. Perhaps, it can be learned, by imitation, by inspiration, by the inculcation of attitude.

In any case, a great many teachers have tried. One who has had a considerable success is Leon Surmelian, novelist, translator, professor of English at Cal State L.A., and director of the prestigious Pacific Coast Writers Conference. You can see why in his new book, *Techniques of Fiction Writing: Measure and Madness*, with an introduction by Mark Schorer.

"The true writer," he says, "has a touch of madness in his make-up. He is an ecstatic, the real enthusiast. He is inspired, we say. Such a writer does not always know what he is saying. He has a special sensitivity to language and is drunk with words. But he is scarcely a passive medium for the gods, as Plato suggested. In literature madness uncontrolled is madness, madness controlled is genius. Technique means control and measure. Madness cannot be taught, measure may be. This book deals with measure."

For that is the quality which lends itself to rational handling. But it is the awareness that there is another component, that it is the total being of the writer which is involved, that gives the book its special value.

I like the honesty. Too many writers on writing sell too hard, suggest that *matter* can be imparted. But let us face it. Everyone may possess in experience the makings of fiction. But everyone does not, patently, have the means to transmute that experience into story, play or poem.

"When we say creative writing cannot be taught, we mean that one cannot learn how to write it from books and articles if one does not have the sensory equipment of the born writer, his unifying inner vision, his knack for mimesis, his rage for words."

Can something be learned from books? Yes. A notion of craft and process. "The purpose of this book is to make the apprentice-ship of the writer a bit easier, if possible." It is addressed to the writer with imaginative and expressive gifts and is intended to be an introductory poetics of fiction. It may also prove to be of interest to the general reader and the student of literature who wants to have an understanding of modern fiction from the inside, from the writer's point of view."

I cannot overemphasize the importance of this last sentence. Looking at literature from the writer's point of view is not the only way of appreciating or assessing the work. But it is, unfortu-nately, the most neglected aspect. The point may be argued but I am convinced that most academic criticism is weakened precisely because of a lack of direct understanding of the varied ways writers work, of the disparity between intent and accomplish-ment. Logic and deduction are useful in criticism but they may be overdone. The ultimate critical fallacy is to assume the rational laws of composition always operate. Sometimes they do. But sometimes they don't and some very silly errors can creep in unless one realizes the groping, the essential approximation which is at the base of the creative process.

If Surmelian's concentration is on measure, on scene and sum-mary, dialog and description, setting and plot, characterization and theme, he is not merely interested in definition. Constantly, he informs technique through tracing its origins in experience and human response. It is Schorer who calls attention to this strength in the book: "How the creative literary impulse manages to get itself expressed." He quotes Marianne Moore's sage aphorism: "Ecstacy affords the occasion, and expediency determines the form."

That is the secret. Form is never separate. It grows out of the matter and serves it. If experience is the raw material of fiction, read properly it is also the mentor of patterns. One sees the beginning, middle and ending of plot in the flow of the seasons or of the birth-to-death cycle of life or even of a single day. Drama has its origins in contention: man against man, or against his condition. Dialog springs from communication; description from observation itself. Characterization is a merging of self-knowledge and the perception of others.

In the disorder of life, the writer must learn the secret of its order, or at least the imposed illusion of order. He "begins with the disorder of life and reduces it to some order before he can re-create it in words. He imitates then the rearrangement of life and not life itself, which is too vast, too chaotic. Life cannot be rendered in all its infinite complexity, and a picture of it, in fiction, as we all know, is a selected image," Surmelian writes and we gather the echo of Aristotle in his words.

Reality, that most elusive of qualities, is seen here in far broader terms than mere realism. If this were the only lesson of the crowded book, it would be enough. For what we know of the broad sweep of fiction in the thousands of years it has functioned, is that reality may be evoked by means beyond the photographic and the tape-recorded. This is the true magic of fiction. Mimesis is not the mere imitation of life—but in Surmelian's felicitous definition, the "revealing imitation of life." . . .

March 3, 1968

CATHERINE DRINKER BOWEN

Biography: The Craft and the Calling

Can writing be taught? Catherine Drinker Bowen believes it can. Not talent, of course: "Talent can only be discovered, prodded, encouraged or shamed to action. But where technique is concerned surely it is teachable in any art."

In *Biography: The Craft and the Calling* Miss Bowen has a go at it. The result does not settle the question above but it does provide entry into the process and problems of writing biography. Using illustrations from her own experience in the research for and composition of seven biographies and from the work of such eminent biographers as Garret Mattingly, David Cecil, Hilda Prescott, Elizabeth Jenkins among others, she has written a book which will enthrall lay readers as well as aspiring writers.

Perhaps the most interesting theme which runs through the book is the relationship between the composition of fiction and the art of narrative history. This is usually slighted because of the modern historian's pretensions to objectivity and a "scientific" stance. Older historiographers recognized that the art of writing history had to borrow some of the approaches to the writing of fiction.

This is not to suggest that the biographer has the license to change or distort facts and events. Yet, in matters of characterization, mood and setting, theme, dialog, the challenges are often similar. Selection and emphasis are certainly as much a part of the creative process as imagination.

The biographer, of course, adds research, responsible and meticulous, to his obligation. If research is indispensable, it is not in itself a guarantee of a fine biography, or else every doctoral dissertation would be a quality performance. The difference lies in the capacity to render with grace and the penumbra of experience, a sense of life and period.

Despite her attention to technique, the mystery of talent constantly haunts these pages. This has little to do with form. Good writing transcends function. We may accept that the difference between the novelist and the biographer is that the novelist invents his plot and the biographer finds it in history. But the great novelist shares with the great biographer that system of awareness, insight and perception, that dual angle of vision (the ability to present the surface of events as well as to hint at and evoke their meaning), which is at the heart of talent.

Everywhere this is hinted at in these pages and occasionally made quite explicit. Maurois, for example, believes that the biographer "has greater difficulty than the novelist in composition.

"But he has one compensation: to be compelled to take over the form of a work ready-made is almost always a source of power to the artist. It is painful; it makes his task more difficult; but at the same time it is from this struggle between the mind and the matter that resists it that a masterpiece is born."

Too often in defense, mediocre writers will speak of this quality of mind as popularization. But in the last analysis, popularization is of the same order of process as self-consciously academic writing. Both are written primarily with the audience in view, in a word, outer-directed. The real test it seems to me is not in writing as an instrument but in what it is the writer has to say. And this is inevitably fashioned by that bundle of qualities we call personality and character: spirit, conscience, compassion, empathy, understanding, a view of the world.

Thus, when Miss Bowen points out that it is difficult if not impossible to inject "humor or humanity" after a manuscript is written, she is really saying that these must "grow from the narrative as it progresses, springing hot and hearty from the writer's own bias and involvement as he sits and thinks about his subject."

To some degree this may be learned through practice and experience. Not solely practice in writing but even more in perception. "There is no sense pretending that technique will take the place of talent." One can talk of plot as a technique. To the novelist who told Miss Bowen that a biographer's plot was to hand before he begins to write, she asked what was plot, exactly?

"Birth, education, marriage, career, death."

"Surely," she writes, "the novelist was mistaken, and his five neat sequential nouns indicated a chronology rather than a plot." For plot involves both causality and theme, some network of crossroads and skein of interaction which makes the story come alive.

Miss Bowen can write lucidly about the creative process, admits that it "is easier to tell someone how than to do it oneself." Take for example what she calls "floundering" or "thinking, brooding, dreaming."

"Floundering about is endemic to writers, a phase we all go through at the outset of a work. Psychiatrists say this initial block is intrinsic to the creative process, a forcing of the writer deeper into himself . . . I have heard it said that most authors sit down at their typewriters too soon." Good advice. Yet, this reliance on the total self, for that is what it is, may produce nothing but further floundering. All good writing is at one point a projective test, and the aspiring writer must be prepared to find that for all the tricks and devices taught, he may still have nothing to say. And, as we shall see, Miss Bowen is aware of this.

This is not to question the utility of the book. It is a thoughtful, honest and searching examination of the process. There are certain things which cannot fail to be useful to the apprentice writer whether he works in biography or any other genre: the mode through which form emerges as a reflection of the material, the shape of the work, the opening scene, the summing-up, the biographer's relationship with his hero, research, the sense of the past.

I am inclined however to believe that the book is far more important to the reader. This is not merely in terms of the specific chapter, "What the Reader Must Know," but in taking the reader behind the scenes of biographical writing. To know the fashioning of an art is an exciting experience. To know how and why one biography pulsates with the sense of life and another does not is to be able to read more deeply.

In the final chapter, Miss Bowen returns to the question of talent. It is, after all, the burden of her theme. "I would not leave the impression of authors sitting for years and cannily fitting one paragraph into another paragraph, putting little boxes into bigger boxes—in short that a good book is written simply by virtue of knowing all the tricks."

Only a superficial reader would get such an impression, for in the detailed account of her own experiences we begin to know the depth of involvement, the complexity of the process.

In the final chapter she has collected certain "confessions of the great and the near great" on questions of talent and genius. It is a worthy ending to an unusually fine work.

December 22, 1968

ORVILLE PRESCOTT, ED.

History as Literature

History, it has been said, is too important to be left to the historians. And, if you need further evidence it might be found in the recent discussions at the American Historical Assn. There, Oscar Handlin complained that history has been allowed to "slip into the hands of propagandists, politicians, dramatists, novelists, journalists and social engineers."

What nonsense! If all the history written by non-professionals, past and present, were subtracted from the body of historical literature, there would be precious little reading left.

I am talking both of scholarship and style, of the craft of history and the art. Handlin's nostalgic reference to a time in the past when the profession was "held together by adherence to common standards and conviction" is pure romanticism. Any group of scholars with common conviction is bound to be a craft union, giving out its seal and hallmark only to those who accept its discipline and views.

I have nothing against professionalism in history or in any other discipline. But when it begins to exclude writers solely on the basis of their vocations or amateur status, it goes too far.

The writing of history ought to be a free arena of participation. Accomplishment or failure, validation of research and scholarship ought to be a function of critical transaction. The right to be called historian should be earned by works rather than certification.

The emphasis here is on history as a writing art. And the selection is not only delicious reading but a guide to further exploration in the reading of history.

Prescott's choices are necessarily subjective. But he is not unaware of the many facets of history. One is certainly scholarship, but "not just scholarship." Handlin, I suspect, would agree with Prescott: "The historian who presents information unadorned by art has done only half his job. The other half is to write well."

It is true that the researcher who has neither the inclination nor

222 / ROBERT KIRSCH

the ability to write well may contribute the raw material to those who can. For this they deserve respect.

But it is equally true that those who possess the art without the craft warrant the title historian, for their work gives delight and often insight.

One thing is certain, though this book contains excerpts from the work of professional historians such as A. L. Rowse, Sir Arthur Bryant, J. Huizinga, the bulk of it is drawn from writers who made their mark or served their apprenticeships in other professions or vocations.

There are, of course, some quibbles as to those excluded. C. V. Wedgwood seems to me to be among the best historians writing today. Josephus and Carlyle might well have been included out of the past. But what is here from Herodotus and Tacitus to J. Christopher Herold and Benjamin P. Thomas is a collection of rare power and grace.

Some might argue that Gibbon has been superceded and that chroniclers such as Bede, Froissart and Gregory of Tours, or such memorists as Philippe de Commines, Diaz, the Earl of Clarendon and Saint Simon are not proper historians, certainly not in the modern sense.

Here we must remember that it is history as literature which is the theme. And Prescott's definition is broad enough to contain them: "Most history . . . is a record and interpretation of the past as seen through the distorting lens of an individual mind. Some prefer "objective" history but one wonders if, as long as it is written by men, professionals or not, that is possible.

February 11, 1971

C. V. WEDGEWOOD

The Sense of the Past: Thirteen Studies in the Theory and Practice of History

Well-written history, as literature, as a form of art (both propositions which are discussed in this book), is entertainment in the oldest sense of the word. " 'Work it out for yourself' is the tacit message of most creative writers to their readers," C. V. Wedgewood writes. "Why then should the historian assume that his readers alone have too little imagination, perception and responsive power to take the challenge? I cannot feel that it is the function of the historian to do all the thinking for the public. If history is educational—and I have a vested interest in believing it's so—it must be an education in thinking not merely remembering."

For Miss Wedgwood, history is both science and art, creative in the sense that data must be rendered in approximation of the truths of the past. "All literature arises from human experience and therefore all literature arises in the ultimate resort from historical material. The discipline and technique to which the historian submits his material is different from that of the imaginative writer. But the nature of his material is the same and the historian, in so far as he stands or wishes to stand within the bounds of literature, has the same task as that of the creative artist. He is not to judge and prophesy and create systems, but within the limits allowed to him, to illuminate the human soul."

In her own work she exemplifies these functions, allowing the "reader to make the imaginative leap from our own epoch to an earlier one," illuminating the why of history as well as the how, tracing through such varied and disparate figures as Machiavelli, Gibbon, Scott, and Henry James, showing how the lens of the present distorts the sense of the past. This is indeed the trap of history: "The historian who fails to make allowance for these deep changes in ways of human thought is unlikely to develop an illuminating sense of the past."

This is where art inevitably enters. For the historian's task is, in addition to seeking out the evidence of the past, to provide a context of moral and value judgments, to provide insights into the nature of human experience.

"This is the first paradox. The things which we believe to be right, the things which we believe to be true, vary widely from age to age and the same holds good for the past times which are the historian's province. If we make no allowance for these variations we become rigid and stultified, lacking in human imagination, unable to bring full understanding either to the present or to the past, accepting received ideas and traditional prejudices instead of judging for ourselves. If we make too much allowance for the changing of standards and the shifting of opinions we begin to lose all sense of moral stability. Historical thinking has always fluctuated between these two dangers, the danger of having no perspective at all, and the danger of having one only; the danger of having no principles at all and the danger of having principles that are too rigid."

Those who have read Miss Wedgwood's works know well how she handles this tension. "The good historian, whatever his theme, must be an artist. Without art there may be accumulations of statements, there may be calendars or chronicles but there is no history . . . History in any intelligible form is art."

The proof may be found in the last six essays: the irony of King Charles I's last *masque;* the tragic blindness of the monarch to the forces which erupted in the Civil War; the emergence of the common man in history during the 17th century; the life and death of Capt. Hind the highwayman, who could have saved his life if he, as the gentleman he claimed to be, had ever learned to read.

All of this is the best sort of writing, life-enhancing, thoughtful, erudite, an experience which should not be missed.

March 27, 1967

PAGE SMITH

The Historian and History

"The historian must recognize that history is not a scientific enterprise but a moral one," writes Page Smith in *The Historian and History*. "It is the study of human beings involved in an extraordinary drama, and its dramatic qualities are related to the moral values inherent in all life . . . Judgment is a continual part of the dialogue of the historian—although, if he is true to his muse, he will temper his judgment with understanding and compassion." . . .

Under attack is an approach which now seems bankrupt: the notion of history as a scientific discipline, the by-product of the overwhelming scientism in our education and culture. Indicted along with historicism are the claims which it makes: the claims of objectivity, detachment, the tedious and unimaginative concern with trivia which degenerates in pedantry and sterile specialization.

Dr. Smith, author of the recent biography, *John Adams*, is much more specific in his criticism of the flaws and defects of academic history. . . . It is where he undertakes his specific criticism of American academic history and the system of higher education in which it functions, that his important contributions are made. The final chapter is brilliant, for in it he does what his brilliant teacher, Eugen Rosenstock-Heussy, also did so well: to show his ideas in execution (i.e., the examination of history and the crisis of identity in the present) rather than purely in theory. . . .

Dr. Smith's own sense of history is at the source of the brilliant final chapter. In it he not only criticizes the modern tendency to "escape from history," but he shows this amputation from the past is related to our oversensitivity (which degenerates into sentimentality), to alienation and the erosion of meaning, to the suspension of the sense of time and coherence which has its effect in art and on psyche. Our impatience and our desire for novelty, our worship of self-realization or self-expression, come from the poverty of the historical sense. On the other extreme, there is a more and uncritical worship of a golden past. Neither involves man in a sense of history as an expression of nobility and life style, as a meaningful drama from which we may draw sustenance.

He suggests that this concern with the present is the problem. But here he contradicts an earlier point. A real rather than a spurious concern with the present is almost inevitably connected with a sense of history both existential and symbolic. And we may question his statement that the "individual, per se, is without history; the community is historic."

It is precisely through the individual that much of history is made, and, more importantly, is given its meaning. That central point is implicit and often explicit in both volumes. The chronicler records. Archives contain the raw material of history. Artifacts are evidence. But it is man who is witness, man who is historian.

Authentic history is a form of art. It is through the judgment, the shaping vision, the quest for meaning, always a function of the individual, that the events and contentions, the small truths and the great universals emerge and are made viable. In the end, a sense of history is part of the very nature of man; it may grow dim and narrow, it may be exploited or distorted. Ultimately, it is the quality that endows him with endurance and worth that is indispensable to survival and a structure of values.

June 7, 1964

RUDOLF ARNHEIM

Visual Thinking

"Art works best when it remains unacknowledged. It observes shapes, objects and events by displaying their own nature, can evoke those deeper and simpler powers in which man recognizes himself. It is one of the rewards we earn for thinking by what we see."

Rudolf Arnheim's *Visual Thinking* is both a culmination and a beginning, a culmination of his work in the psychology of art and the beginning of an effort to relate, or perhaps more accurately, re-relate sense and thinking.

This is partially a speculative book. Much work remains to be done to validate his thesis that human beings explore and comprehend by acting and handling rather than by mere (his term) contemplation. It also is limited to the sense of sight which is the one he has studied most intensively. In this attempt to sense and reason, he has crossed many disciplinary lines. But the result is exciting and filled with implications for education.

The effort to split awareness-perception, sensory contact with the environment, from cognition, making the latter a higher, more abstract activity, is an old one. Arnheim's studies in art and visual perception led him inexorably to conclude that artistic activity is a form of reasoning in which perceiving and thinking are indivisibly intertwined. "A person who paints, writes, composes, dances, I felt compelled to say, thinks with his senses. This union of perception and thought turned out to be not merely a specialty of the arts."

This is not an easy book to read, particularly in the first three chapters. But it repays care. For part of the problem which emerges from this separation of image-contact from abstract thinking is evident in man's condition today. Insulated from sensory contact, unable to read in the imagery of experience some meaning, abstract thinking often loses its roots in humanity. Arnheim reminds us of Plato's remark:

"And the soul is like the eye: When resting upon that on which truth and being shine, the soul perceives and understands and is radiant with intelligence; but when turned toward the twilight of becoming and perishing, then she has opinion only and goes blinking about, and is first of one opinion and then of another and seems to have no intelligence."

If the Greeks saw a dichotomy between perception and reason, they did not apply the notion with the rigidity the doctrine assumed in recent centuries. They were aware that the senses could distort, but equally they never forgot that the senses provided the first and final source of wisdom. Aristotle could say, "the soul never thinks without an image."

The separation of art and general education is one aspect of the division. After kindergarten, the major emphasis of our approach is based on the study of words and numbers. If the experience of seeing and handling shapes, inventing their own shapes in clay or in drawing, is given the student, it is usually marginal, rarely associated with thinking and reasoning.

"The neglect of the arts is only the most tangible sympton of the wide-spread unemployment of the senses in every field of academic study," says Arnheim. The arts are neglected because they are seen as perception alone, and perception it is assumed does not involve thought.

Step by step, Arnheim attempts to heal the division, not by emotional appeals to an esthetic but a close examination of the process which links visual imagery and cognition. In this connection, he rests heavily on the work of Piaget and Kohler, showing that perception displays intelligence, selection, discernment, a completion of the incomplete, that shapes are concepts, that the very notion of abstraction is perceptual in origin.

Perhaps most important is that perception takes place in the field of time and motion. Perception thus enables a far more supple mode of thinking, one which encompasses flux, change and metamorphosis. To see the specific and detailed within the norm of an object (a daisy as typical of its kind and yet still individual) gives a dimension of imagery to thinking.

Experience interacts with ideas through imagery. This mediation is obvious in the arts, but no less in the process of abstract thinking. Part of thinking may be in words, but words gain their meaning from perceptual experience. A great deal of the evidence adduced here is taken from studies of children and of the arts. Arnheim shows the relevance to more mature activities. The result is an exciting and challenging work for all interested in thought and imagination.

February 23, 1970

E. M. CIORAN
The Short History of Decay

"The obsession with remedies marks the end of a civilization; the search for salvation that of a philosophy," writes E. M. Cioran, the French writer whose post-existentialist reflections have excited more attention in his country than almost any since Sartre's *Being and Nothingness*.

I don't expect that American readers will take to Cioran's *The Short History of Decay* although to miss reading the book would be a deprivation. Unlike Sartre, Cioran is a vivid and intense aphorist who shapes memorable lines; although these are more likely to anger and upset readers in this country. But I suspect we could do with his shaking up.

The trouble is not so much that he celebrates qualities we, as the new Romans, normally fear: decay, ennui, dilettantism. But that he attacks all the elements we have held dear: progress, perfectibility, idealism, and evangelical optimism, civic obligation.

"What Diogenes was looking for with his lantern was an indifferent man . . ." Cioran writes. "The devil pales beside the man who owns a truth, his truth."

The trouble, he says, is that man is rarely content to let it be. "Idolators by instinct, we convert the objects of our dreams and our interests into the Unconditional . . . Once man loses his faculty of indifference he becomes a potential murderer; once he transforms his idea into a god the consequences are incalculable

. . . In every mystic outburst, the moans of the victims parallel the moans of ecstasy . . . No wavering mind, infected with Hamletism, was ever pernicious . . ."

He is not proof against the "compulsion to preach," even though he is an antiprophet. What Cioran has attempted is an annihilation of self, moving away from the righteous center of perception, off to the side. "We must be thankful to the civilizations which have not taken an overdose of seriousness . . . The age of Alcibiades and the 18th century in France are two sources of consolation . . . These two epochs knew the tedium heedless of everything and permeable to everything."

It is not only the categorical imperative he sees as the seeds of madness; "Reality is a creation of our excesses, of our disproportions and derangements." "Ennui" is the "incurable convalescence."

In language it is the shift from I to we, from me to others. Man, he writes, "is the chatterbox of the universe; he speaks in the name of others; his self loves the plural. And anyone who speaks in the name of others is an impostor. Politicians, reformers and all who rely on a collective context are cheats. There is only the artist whose lie is not a total one, for he invents only himself. Outside of the surrender to the incommunicable, the suspension amid our mute and unconsoled anxieties, life is merely a fracas on an unmapped space, and the universe a geometry of apoplexy."

Even this bare sampling should start the blood pulsing, for there are few concepts and myths dear to man that escape this assault. Cioran seeks nothing more than the ultimate heresy, that existence is a nothingness, salvation an impossible dream, happiness an illusion, love a placebo "to help us endure those cruel and incommensurable Sunday afternoons which torment us for the rest of the week—and for eternity," knowledge a game, wisdom "the last word of an expiring civilization."

The effect is homeopathic. A little outrage may produce a massive antitoxin. Exaggeration and hyperbole can become an earthquake in which only the strongest buildings survive. It is then that we begin to see the values, not merely in style or expression, but in daring to be absurd, Cioran offers us.

The attempt to reduce our existence to its essentials, our issues to their demonic essence, is, despite the heroic attempt to erase man, reaching a final irony. " . . . I invalidate my illusions only to irritate them the more . . . How long must I keep telling myself: 'I loathe this life I idolize'?

"History confirms skepticism; yet it is and lives only by trampling over it; no event rises out of doubt, but all considerations of events lead to it and justify it . . . man is much more vexed by the absence than by the profusion of events; thus history is the bloody product of his rejection of boredom."

Decadence, he concludes, "is merely instinct gone impure under the action of consciousness." Not life but the effort to understand and explain it is the sign of ripe civilizations. One may turn away from its idols, but they set the world in motion. It is ennui which is unbearable; it cannot be raised as a banner.

August 13, 1975

This first edition was designed
and typeset by Mackintosh & Young
in Santa Barbara, California
using the typeface Janson.
Camera work by Santa Barbara Photoengravers;
printed and bound by R. R. Donnelley & Sons
during August 1978.